CuR
510
EM/2
2004

W9-ADL-558

Second Grade

Everyday Mathematics®

Math Masters

DISCARD

Lourdes Library
Gwynedd Mercy College
P. O. Box 901
Gwynedd Valley, PA 19437-0901

DISCARD

**The University of Chicago
School Mathematics Project**

McGraw Hill **Wright Group**

The McGraw-Hill Companies

UCSMP Elementary Materials Component

Max Bell, Director

Authors

Max Bell
Jean Bell
John Bretzlauf*
Amy Dillard*

Robert Hartfield
Andy Isaacs*
James McBride, Director
Kathleen Pitvorec*
Peter Saecker

Technical Art

Diana Barrie*

*Second Edition only

Photo Credits

Phil Martin/Photography, Jack Demuth/Photography,
Cover Credits: Bee/Stephen Dalton/Photo Researchers Inc.,
Photo Collage: Herman Adler Design

Permissions

page 294: Cylindars/cans: Jack Demuth
page 294: Quilt: Gary Conner/PhotoEdit
page 294: Robert Brenner, Empire State Builing/PhotoEdit
page 329: John Lee/*Chicago Tribune*

Contributors

Librada Acosta, Carol Arkin, Robert Balfanz, Sharlean Brooks, Jean Callahan, Ann Coglianese,
Ellen Dairyko, Tresea Felder, James Flanders, Dorothy Freedman, Rita Gronbach, Deborah Arron
Leslie, William D. Pattison, LaDonna Pitts, Danette Riehle, Marie Schilling, Robert Strang,
Sadako Tengan, Therese Wasik, Leeann Wille, Michael Wilson

Wright Group

Copyright © 2004 by Wright Group/McGraw-Hill.

All rights reserved. Permission is granted to reproduce the
material contained herin on the condition that such material be
reproduced only for classroom use; be provided to students,
teachers, or families without charge; and be used solely in
conjunction with *Everyday Mathematics*. Any other reproduction,
for use or sale, is prohibited without the prior written permission
from the publisher.

Send all inquiries to:
Wright Group/McGraw-Hill
P.O. Box 812960
Chicago, IL 60681

Printed in the United States of America.

ISBN 0-07-584467-2

7 8 9 10 11 12 13 QPD 08 07 06 05

The McGraw-Hill Companies

Contents

Teaching Masters

A note at the bottom of most Teaching Master pages indicates when that master is first used. Many masters will be used again during the course of the year.

Home Link Masters

Assessment Masters

Number Lines

1.

2.
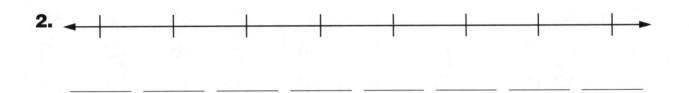

3.

4.
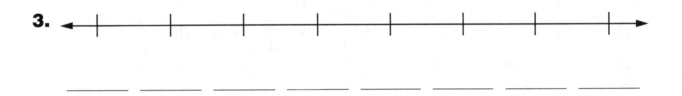

5.
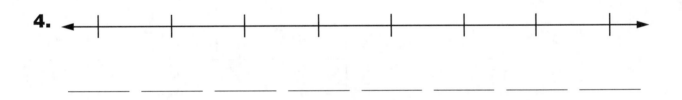

6.
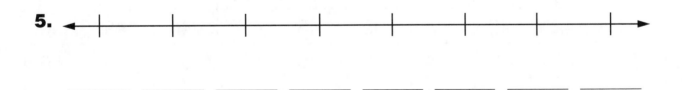

Copyright © SRA/McGraw-Hill

Use with Lesson 1.1.

1

Number Grid

									0
1	2	3	4	5	6	7	8	9	10
11	12	13	14	15	16	17	18	19	20
21	22	23	24	25	26	27	28	29	30
31	32	33	34	35	36	37	38	39	40
41	42	43	44	45	46	47	48	49	50
51	52	53	54	55	56	57	58	59	60
61	62	63	64	65	66	67	68	69	70
71	72	73	74	75	76	77	78	79	80
81	82	83	84	85	86	87	88	89	90
91	92	93	94	95	96	97	98	99	100
101	102	103	104	105	106	107	108	109	110

Copyright © SRA/McGraw-Hill

									0
1	2	3	4	5	6	7	8	9	10
11	12	13	14	15	16	17	18	19	20
21	22	23	24	25	26	27	28	29	30
31	32	33	34	35	36	37	38	39	40
41	42	43	44	45	46	47	48	49	50
51	52	53	54	55	56	57	58	59	60
61	62	63	64	65	66	67	68	69	70
71	72	73	74	75	76	77	78	79	80
81	82	83	84	85	86	87	88	89	90
91	92	93	94	95	96	97	98	99	100
101	102	103	104	105	106	107	108	109	110

Copyright © SRA/McGraw-Hill

Use with Lesson 1.4.

Coin Combinations

Copyright © SRA/McGraw-Hill

D D N

Q N P
P P P

Q D
P P P

Q D D
P P

Q Q N P

Q Q D

Q D D
D D

Q Q Q

Q Q Q
N P P

Q Q Q
D P

Q Q Q
D N P

Q Q Q Q

Money Exchange Game

	One Hundred Dollars **$100**
	Ten Dollars **$10**
	One Dollar **$1**

Copyright © SRA/McGraw-Hill

Use with Lesson 1.6.

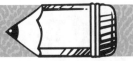

$1 Bills

Copyright © SRA/McGraw-Hill

Use with Lesson 1.6.

5

$10 Bills

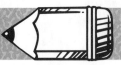

Use with Lesson 1.6.

Copyright © SRA/McGraw-Hill

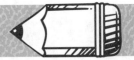

$1, $10, and $100 Bills

Copyright © SRA/McGraw-Hill

$100 Bills

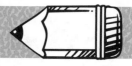

Copyright © SRA/McGraw-Hill

$1,000 Bank Drafts

$1,000   **B A N K   D R A F T** $1,000
100,000 cents

Pay to _____

$1,000   *One Thousand Dollars* $1,000

$1,000   **B A N K   D R A F T** $1,000
100,000 cents

Pay to _____

$1,000   *One Thousand Dollars* $1,000

$1,000   **B A N K   D R A F T** $1,000
100,000 cents

Pay to _____

$1,000   *One Thousand Dollars* $1,000

$1,000   **B A N K   D R A F T** $1,000
100,000 cents

Pay to _____

$1,000   *One Thousand Dollars* $1,000

$1,000   **B A N K   D R A F T** $1,000
100,000 cents

Pay to _____

$1,000   *One Thousand Dollars* $1,000

$1,000   **B A N K   D R A F T** $1,000
100,000 cents

Pay to _____

$1,000   *One Thousand Dollars* $1,000

$1,000   **B A N K   D R A F T** $1,000
100,000 cents

Pay to _____

$1,000   *One Thousand Dollars* $1,000

$1,000   **B A N K   D R A F T** $1,000
100,000 cents

Pay to _____

$1,000   *One Thousand Dollars* $1,000

$1,000   **B A N K   D R A F T** $1,000
100,000 cents

Pay to _____

$1,000   *One Thousand Dollars* $1,000

$1,000   **B A N K   D R A F T** $1,000
100,000 cents

Pay to _____

$1,000   *One Thousand Dollars* $1,000

Copyright © SRA/McGraw-Hill

Money Exchange Game

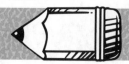

	$100 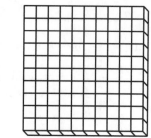
	$10
	$1

Copyright © SRA/McGraw-Hill

Use with Lesson 1.6.

Money Exchange Game: $ and ¢

One Cent 1¢	Ten Cents 10¢	One Dollar $1

Copyright © SRA/McGraw–Hill

Penny Cup Record Sheet

Example

We started with __20__ pennies.

We could see __6__ pennies on top.

We figured there were __14__ pennies inside.

We counted __14__ pennies inside.

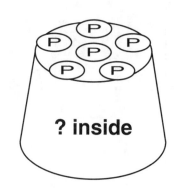

? inside

Round 1

We started with _____ pennies.

We could see _____ pennies on top.

We figured there were _____ pennies inside.

We counted _____ pennies inside.

Round 2

We started with _____ pennies.

We could see _____ pennies on top.

We figured there were _____ pennies inside.

We counted _____ pennies inside.

Round 3

We started with _____ pennies.

We could see _____ pennies on top.

We figured there were _____ pennies inside.

We counted _____ pennies inside.

Round 4

We started with _____ pennies.

We could see _____ pennies on top.

We figured there were _____ pennies inside.

We counted _____ pennies inside.

Copyright © SRA/McGraw-Hill

Beginning Number-Scroll Sheet

0

Copyright © SRA/McGraw–Hill

Continuing Number-Scroll Sheet

Paste/tape to here.

Copyright © SRA/McGraw–Hill

Use with Lesson 1.8.

Number-Grid Cutouts

Copyright © SRA/McGraw-Hill

Number-Grid Pieces

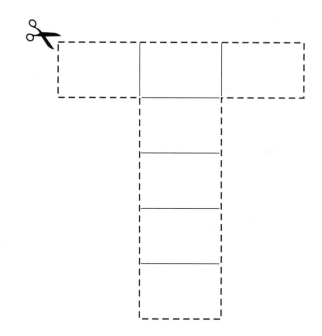

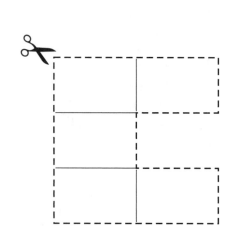

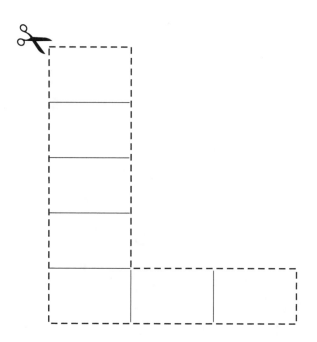

Copyright © SRA/McGraw-Hill

                                           Use with Lesson 1.9.

Number Grid

0	10	20	30	40	50	60	70	80	90	100	110
−1	9	19	29	39	49	59	69	79	89	99	109
−2	8	18	28	38	48	58	68	78	88	98	108
−3	7	17	27	37	47	57	67	77	87	97	107
−4	6	16	26	36	46	56	66	76	86	96	106
−5	5	15	25	35	45	55	65	75	85	95	105
−6	4	14	24	34	44	54	64	74	84	94	104
−7	3	13	23	33	43	53	63	73	83	93	103
−8	2	12	22	32	42	52	62	72	82	92	102
−9	1	11	21	31	41	51	61	71	81	91	101

Copyright © SRA/McGraw-Hill

Counting on the Number Grid

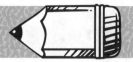

−9	−8	−7	−6	−5	−4	−3	−2	−1	0
1	2	3	4	5	6	7	8	9	10
11	12	13	14	15	16	17	18	19	20
21	22	23	24	25	26	27	28	29	30
31	32	33	34	35	36	37	38	39	40
41	42	43	44	45	46	47	48	49	50
51	52	53	54	55	56	57	58	59	60
61	62	63	64	65	66	67	68	69	70
71	72	73	74	75	76	77	78	79	80
81	82	83	84	85	86	87	88	89	90
91	92	93	94	95	96	97	98	99	100

Count by 6s.

1. First, put your finger on the 0. Move it to the 1 as you count "1." Move it to the 2 as you count "2." Continue counting. When you reach 6, stop. Draw an X through the 6.

2. Put your finger on 6 and repeat the process. Move to 7 as you count "1." Move to 8 as you count "2," and so on. The second X you draw should be through the 12.

3. Continue until you reach the end of the grid.

Count by 4s.

Start again at 0. This time count by 4s. When you stop on a number, draw a circle around it. Look for patterns so that you can predict when you will stop next.

Copyright © SRA/McGraw-Hill

Temperature

Work in a group of 3 or 4 children.

Materials
☐ Class Thermometer Poster

☐ quarter-sheets of paper

Directions

Activity 1

1. Take turns. One person names a temperature. Another person shows that temperature on the Class Thermometer Poster.

2. Everyone in the group checks to see that the temperature is shown correctly.

3. Keep taking turns until each person has named a temperature and has shown a temperature on the Class Thermometer Poster.

Activity 2

1. Take turns showing a temperature on the Class Thermometer Poster. Everyone reads the thermometer and writes that temperature.

2. Everyone in the group compares the temperatures they wrote. Did everyone write the same temperature? Discuss any differences.

Follow-Up

Look at all of the temperatures that you recorded on your quarter-sheets of paper.

• Were some temperatures easier to read than others? Explain.

• Order the temperatures from coldest to hottest.

Copyright © SRA/McGraw-Hill

Base-10 Structures

Work in a group of 3 or 4 children.

Materials   ☐ base-10 blocks (cubes, longs, and flats)

                ☐ quarter-sheets of paper

Directions

1. Each person uses base-10 blocks to make a "building." The picture shows an example.

2. Each block has a value.

The value of the cube is 1.
The value of the long is 10.
The value of the flat is 100.

$$\begin{aligned}
\blacksquare &= 1 \\
| &= 10 \\
\square &= 100
\end{aligned}$$

What number does your building show? Use the symbols in the box above to help you.

3. Draw your building on a quarter-sheet of paper. Write the number with your drawing.

4. Have a friend help you check the number.

5. If there is time, make more buildings. Draw each building and record the number of each building.

Follow-Up

• Look at the numbers shown by your group's buildings.

• Order the numbers from smallest to largest.

Copyright © SRA/McGraw-Hill

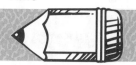

Sorting Dominoes

Work in a group of 3 or 4 children.

Materials   ☐ 1 or 2 sets of double-9 dominoes

☐ number cards 0–18 (from the
Everything Math Deck, if available)

Directions

1. Lay down the number cards in order from 0 through 18.

2. Place each domino above the number card that shows the
sum of the domino dots.

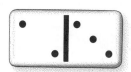

3. List the addition facts shown by the dominoes on a sheet of
paper. Before you begin, decide how your group will record
the facts.

Follow-Up

• Look at the list of addition facts your group made.

• Try to think of a better way to record the facts.

• Talk about why you think the new way is better.

Copyright © SRA/McGraw-Hill

A Number Story

Unit

_____

_____

_____

_____

_____

_____

_____

Copyright © SRA/McGraw-Hill

Use with Lesson 2.1.

Grid Paper

Copyright © SRA/McGraw–Hill

Use with Lesson 2.3.

Facts Table

+,−	0	1	2	3	4	5	6	7	8	9
0	0	1	2	3	4	5	6	7	8	9
1	1	2	3	4	5	6	7	8	9	10
2	2	3	4	5	6	7	8	9	10	11
3	3	4	5	6	7	8	9	10	11	12
4	4	5	6	7	8	9	10	11	12	13
5	5	6	7	8	9	10	11	12	13	14
6	6	7	8	9	10	11	12	13	14	15
7	7	8	9	10	11	12	13	14	15	16
8	8	9	10	11	12	13	14	15	16	17
9	9	10	11	12	13	14	15	16	17	18

Copyright © SRA/McGraw-Hill

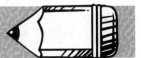

Doubles Facts

Example

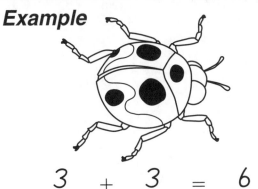

<u> 3 </u> + <u> 3 </u> = <u> 6 </u>

1.

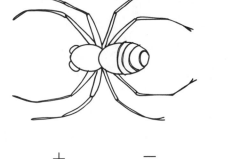

_____ + _____ = _____

2.

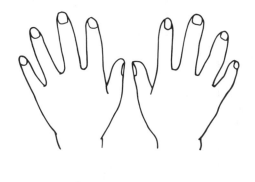

_____ + _____ = _____

3.

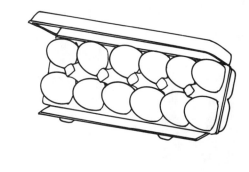

_____ + _____ = _____

4.

January 2001

Sun	Mon	Tues	Wed	Thurs	Fri	Sat
	1	2	3	4	5	6
7	8	9	10	11	12	13
14	15	16	17	18	19	20
21	22	23	24	25	26	27
28	29	30	31			

_____ + _____ = _____

5.

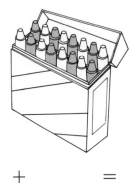

_____ + _____ = _____

6.

_____ + _____ = _____

Copyright © SRA/McGraw-Hill

Use with Lesson 2.3.

Ten-Frame Card

Copyright © SRA/McGraw-Hill

Use with Lesson 2.4.

Egg Nests

Work with a partner.

Materials

- ☐ 1 six-sided die
- ☐ 1 sheet of plain paper
- ☐ 36 counters (for example, pennies, centimeter cubes, or dried beans)
- ☐ 6 quarter-sheets of paper

Directions

Pretend that the quarter-sheets of paper are birds' nests.

Pretend that the pennies, cubes, or beans are eggs.

1. Roll the die twice.

- The first roll tells how many nests to use.
- The second roll tells how many eggs to put in each nest.

2. Work together to set up the nests and eggs for the numbers you rolled. How many eggs are there in all of the nests?

3. Use your sheet of plain paper and draw a picture.

- Show all the nests.
- Show all the eggs in each nest.

4. Start again. Repeat Steps 1–3.

Copyright © SRA/McGraw-Hill

Fact Triangle

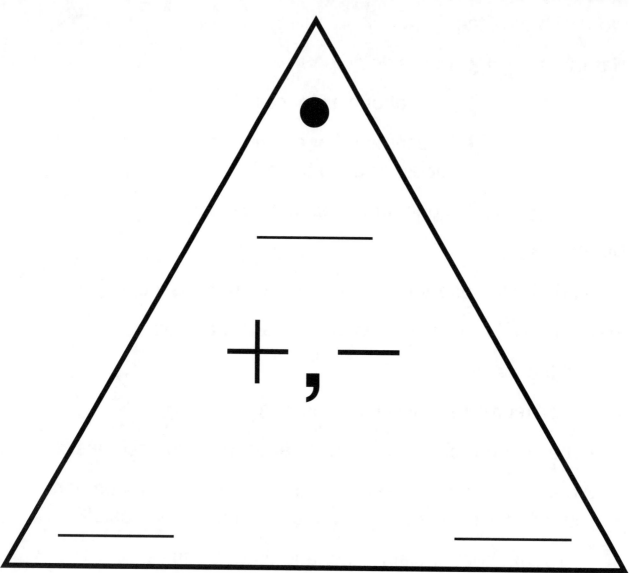

Copyright © SRA/McGraw–Hill

Use with Lesson 2.8.

Frames and Arrows

1.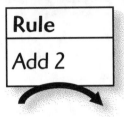

Rule

Add 2

| 5 | | | | |

2.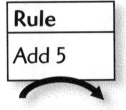

Rule

Add 5

( ) ( ) (20) ( ) ( )

3.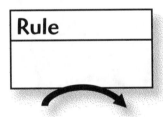

Rule

| 15 | 12 | 9 | 6 | 3 |

4.

Rule

⬡ ⬡ ⬡ 25 ⬡ 35 ⬡

5.

Rule

| | | 10 | | 6 | |

Copyright © SRA/McGraw-Hill

Frames-and-Arrows Problems

1. Rule

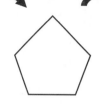   

2. Rule

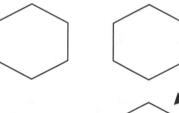 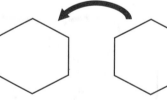

3. Rule

 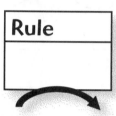 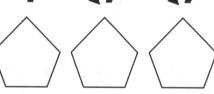 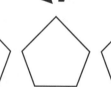 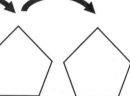

4. Rule

5. Rule

  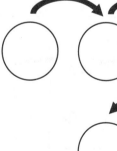 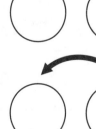    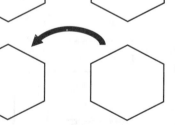

Copyright © SRA/McGraw-Hill

Use with Lesson 2.10.

Function Machine

in	out

Copyright © SRA/McGraw–Hill

Use with Lesson 2.11.

"What's My Rule?"

1. Rule

in	out

2. Rule

in	out

3. Rule

in	out

4. Rule

in	out

5. Rule

in	out

6. Rule

in	out

Copyright © SRA/McGraw-Hill

Use with Lesson 2.11.

"What's My Rule?" Problems

Write the rule for the table. Complete the table.

1.

Rule	

in	out
44	34
26	16
78	
82	
	54

2.

Rule	

in	out
15	7
10	2
13	
12	
17	

3.

Rule	

in	out
18	9
13	4
16	
15	
	5

Complete the table.

Write a rule of your own. Fill in the table.

4.

Rule	
−9	

in	out
37	
83	
71	
62	
	87

5.

Rule	
−8	

in	out
81	
53	
77	
	54
	27

6.

Rule	

in	out

Copyright © SRA/McGraw-Hill

Name   Date   Time

Teacher's Place-Value Mat

hundreds	tens	ones

Copyright © SRA/McGraw-Hill

Use with Lesson 3.1.

Children's Place-Value Mat

□ **ones**	▭ **tens**	▦ **hundreds**

Copyright © SRA/McGraw-Hill

Fruit and Vegetables Stand Poster

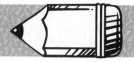

Copyright © SRA/McGraw-Hill

Use with Lesson 3.2.

Spinning for Money

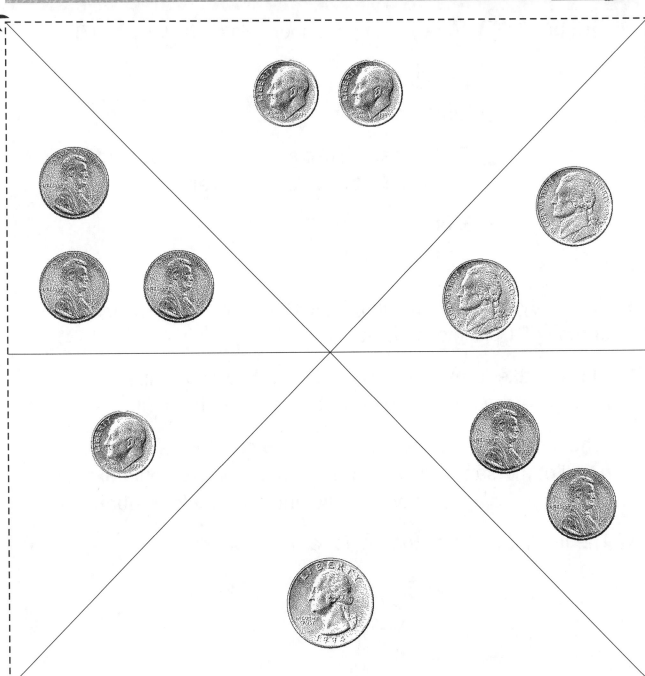

Before beginning the game, cut out this **Money-Game Spinner** on the dashed lines.

Copyright © SRA/McGraw-Hill

Spinning for Money (cont.)

Materials

- ☐ Money-Game Spinner (*Math Masters,* p. 37)
- ☐ pencil
- ☐ large paper clip
- ☐ 7 pennies, 5 nickels, 5 dimes, 4 quarters, and one $1 bill for each player

Players   2, 3, or 4

Directions

1. Each player puts 7 pennies, 5 nickels, 5 dimes, 4 quarters, and one $1 bill into a "bank."

2. Players take turns spinning the Money-Game Spinner and taking the coins shown by the spinner from the bank.

3. Whenever possible, players exchange coins for a single coin or bill of the same value. For example, a player could exchange 5 pennies for a nickel or 2 dimes and 1 nickel for a quarter.

4. The first player to exchange for a $1 bill wins.

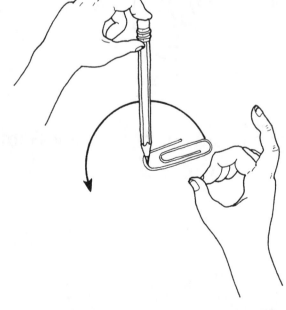

Use a large paper clip and pencil to make a spinner.

Copyright © SRA/McGraw-Hill

Use with Lesson 3.2.

Demonstration Clock

a brad

✂ hour hand

✗

Copyright © SRA/McGraw–Hill

5-Minute Clock

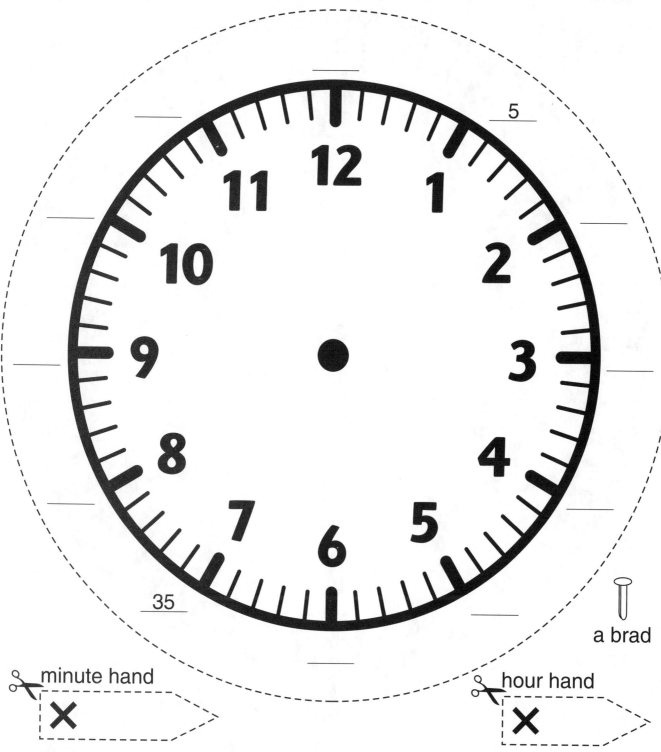

5

35

a brad

minute hand

✂ hour hand

X   X

- Color the hour hand red, and color the minute hand green.

- Cut out the clock face and hands.

- Punch a hole through the center of the clock face and through the Xs on the hands. Fasten the hands to the clock face with a brad.

Use with Lesson 3.3.

Copyright © SRA/McGraw-Hill

Build a Number

Do this activity with a partner.

Materials   ❑ *Math Masters,* p. 35 (Place-Value Mat)

             ❑ base-10 blocks: 9 flats (optional), 9 longs, and 9 cubes

             ❑ number cards 0–9 (from the Everything Math Deck, if available)

1. Mix the cards and stack them facedown.

2. Draw 2 cards.

3. Place the first card in the tens column of your Place-Value Mat. (If the card is a 0, put it back and draw again.) Then put the second card in the ones column.

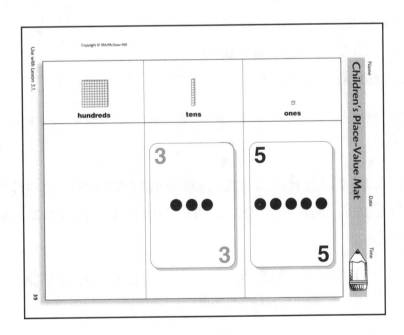

Copyright © SRA/McGraw-Hill

Build a Number (cont.)

4. Build the number.

- Place longs in the tens column to show the tens digit.

- Place cubes in the ones column to show the ones digit.

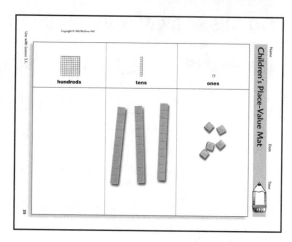

5. Record your work in the table on journal page 61. Draw pictures of the longs and cubes you used.

6. Use the Place-Value Mat and blocks to build the same number in a different way. Draw the longs and cubes you used.

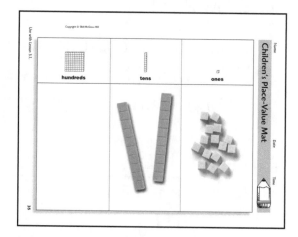

7. Build 3 or 4 more numbers in the same way. Record your numbers and draw pictures to show the two ways you built each number.

Challenge

Draw 3 cards instead of 2. Put 1 card in each column of the Place-Value Mat. Draw flats, longs, and cubes on journal page 61 to show your number.

Build the same number in a different way. Draw the blocks you used.

Use with Lesson 3.4.

Copyright © SRA/McGraw-Hill

A Clock Booklet

Do this activity with a partner.

Materials
☐ at least 2 sheets of plain paper   ☐ scissors

☐ clock-face rubber stamp   ☐ stapler

☐ stamp pad

1. Each partner folds a sheet of paper into 4 parts.

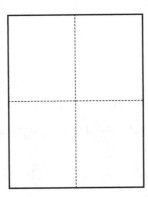

2. Cut each sheet along the folds.

3. Set aside 2 of the small pieces of paper.
You will use them for covers later.

4. Stamp a clock face on each side of the other small pieces.

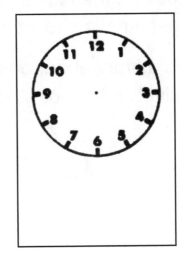

Copyright © SRA/McGraw-Hill

Use with Lesson 3.4.

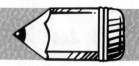

A Clock Booklet (cont.)

5. For each clock face:

    • Think of a time. Help each other draw the hour and minute hands to show that time.

    • Write the time as you would see it on a digital clock.

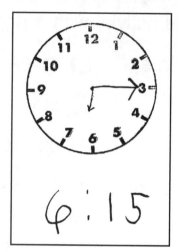

6. Stack the pieces. Put a piece without a clock face on the top. Put the other piece without a clock face at the bottom.

    • Staple the left side of the pieces together to make a book.

    • Write a title and your names on the front cover.

Follow-Up Activities

You and your partner can use your book to do these activities:

• Take turns. One partner covers the digital time on a page. The other partner tells what time is shown on the clock face.

• Work together to make up a story about one or more of the times shown in your booklet. Write your story on another piece of paper.

Copyright © SRA/McGraw-Hill

Geoboard Shapes

Materials per child   ☐ geoboard

                      ☐ rubber bands

Number of children   1, 2, 3, or 4

Do this activity on your own:

1. Make at least 4 shapes, designs, or pictures on your geoboard. Make things like a house, a boat, or a car.

2. Record your favorites on the geoboard dot paper on journal page 62.

Do this activity with a partner:

1. Make an easy shape on a geoboard. Make sure your partner can't see it.

2. Tell—but don't show—your partner how to make the shape.

3. Your partner makes the shape on another geoboard.

4. Compare the two shapes. How are they alike? How are they different? Did you give good directions?

5. Repeat the activity. This time your partner makes the shape first.

Do this activity in a small group:

1. Agree on a shape that everyone will make. Describe the shape in words, but don't draw it.

2. Everyone in your group makes the shape on his or her own geoboard.

3. Compare results. How are your shapes the same? How are they different?

Copyright © SRA/McGraw-Hill

Use with Lesson 3.4.

Geoboard Dot Paper (5 × 5)

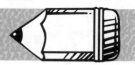

1.

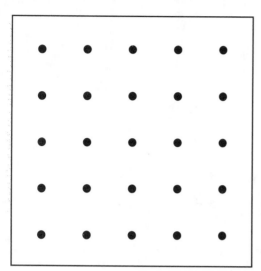

2.

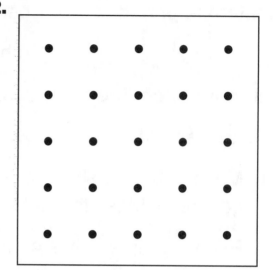

3.

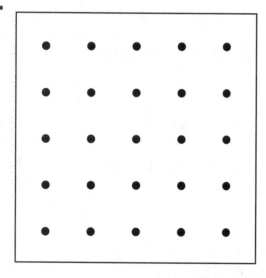

4.

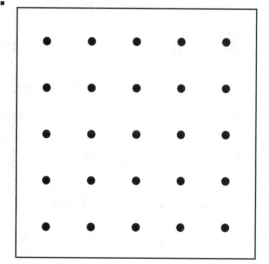

Use with Lesson 3.4.

Copyright © SRA/McGraw-Hill

Geoboard Dot Paper (7 × 7)

1.

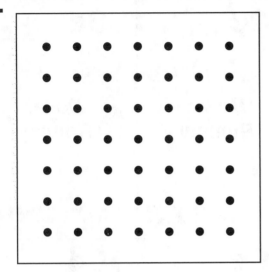

2.

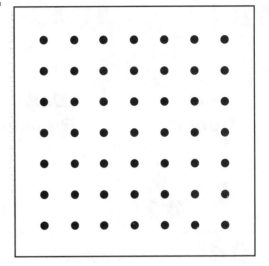

3.

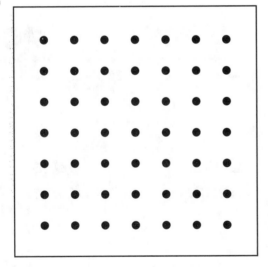

4.

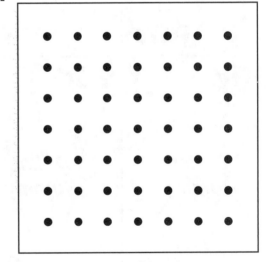

Copyright © SRA/McGraw-Hill

Use with Lesson 3.4.

Dollar Rummy Cards (Regular)

10¢ Dollar Rummy **10¢**	**10¢** Dollar Rummy **10¢**	**20¢** Dollar Rummy **20¢**	**30¢** Dollar Rummy **30¢**
40¢ Dollar Rummy **40¢**	**50¢** Dollar Rummy **50¢**	**50¢** Dollar Rummy **50¢**	**50¢** Dollar Rummy **50¢**
60¢ Dollar Rummy **60¢**	**70¢** Dollar Rummy **70¢**	**80¢** Dollar Rummy **80¢**	**90¢** Dollar Rummy **90¢**

Copyright © SRA/McGraw-Hill

Dollar Rummy Cards (Advanced)

5¢	5¢	5¢	15¢
Dollar Rummy	Dollar Rummy	Dollar Rummy	Dollar Rummy
5¢	5¢	5¢	15¢
25¢	25¢	35¢	45¢
Dollar Rummy	Dollar Rummy	Dollar Rummy	Dollar Rummy
25¢	25¢	35¢	45¢
55¢	65¢	85¢	95¢
Dollar Rummy	Dollar Rummy	Dollar Rummy	Dollar Rummy
55¢	65¢	85¢	95¢

Copyright © SRA/McGraw–Hill

Counting Pockets

Name _____

**Math Message:
Counting Pockets**

1. How many pockets
are in the clothes
you are wearing now?

2. Count the pockets
on your shirt,
on your pants or skirt,
and on anything else
that you are wearing.

3. Complete the diagram.

Total		
Shirt	**Pants or Skirt**	**Other**

4. Write your total number
of pockets very large
on the back of this sheet.

Name _____

**Math Message:
Counting Pockets**

1. How many pockets
are in the clothes
you are wearing now?

2. Count the pockets
on your shirt,
on your pants or skirt,
and on anything else
that you are wearing.

3. Complete the diagram.

Total		
Shirt	**Pants or Skirt**	**Other**

4. Write your total number
of pockets very large
on the back of this sheet.

Copyright © SRA/McGraw-Hill

Pockets Data Table

Pockets	Children	
	Tallies	**Number**
0		
1		
2		
3		
4		
5		
6		
7		
8		
9		
10		
11		
12		
13 or more		

Copyright © SRA/McGraw-Hill

Name   Date   Time

Graphing Pockets Data

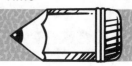

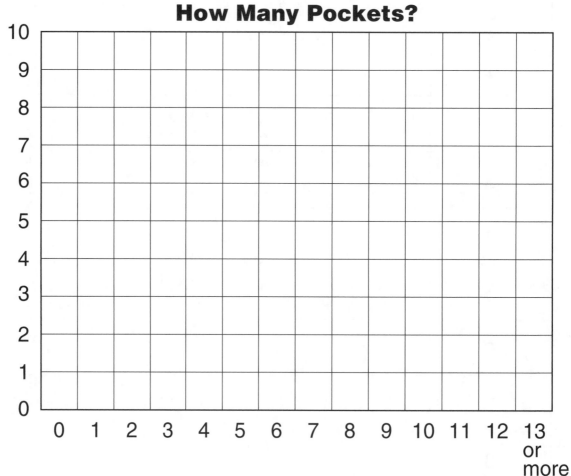

How Many Pockets?

Number of Children

Number of Pockets

Copyright © SRA/McGraw–Hill

Use with Lesson 3.5.

Copyright © SRA/McGraw-Hill

Name   Date   Time

Frames-and-Arrows Diagrams

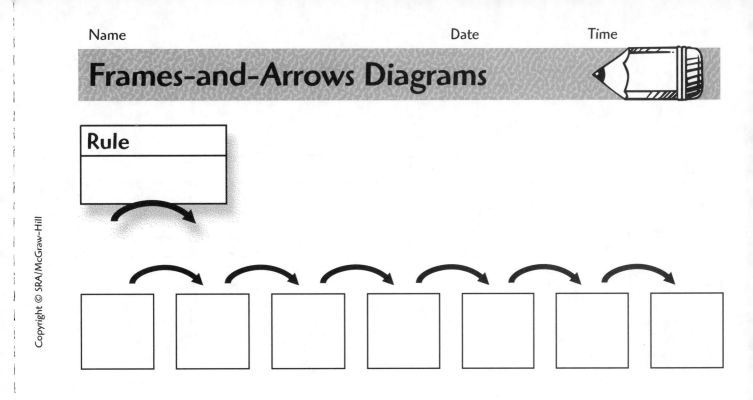

Rule

Use with Lesson 3.6.

✂ -

Copyright © SRA/McGraw-Hill

Name   Date   Time

Frames-and-Arrows Diagrams

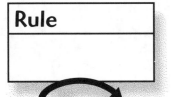

Rule

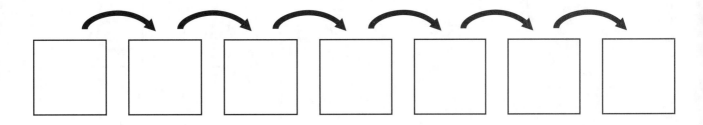

Use with Lesson 3.6.

Two-Rule Frames and Arrows

Example

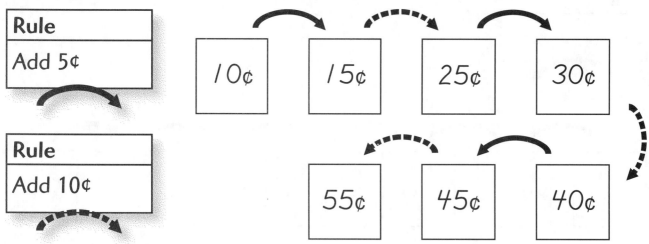

Rule
Add 5¢

Rule
Add 10¢

| 10¢ | 15¢ | 25¢ | 30¢ |

| 55¢ | 45¢ | 40¢ |

1.

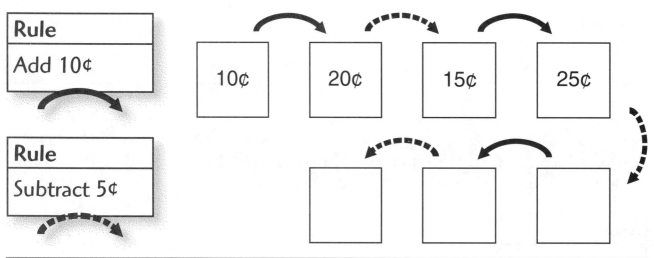

Rule
Add 10¢

Rule
Subtract 5¢

| 10¢ | 20¢ | 15¢ | 25¢ |

2.

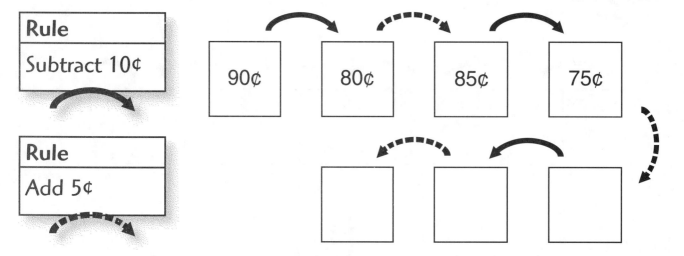

Rule
Subtract 10¢

Rule
Add 5¢

| 90¢ | 80¢ | 85¢ | 75¢ |

Copyright © SRA/McGraw-Hill

Use with Lesson 3.6.

Two-Rule Frames and Arrows (cont.)

3.

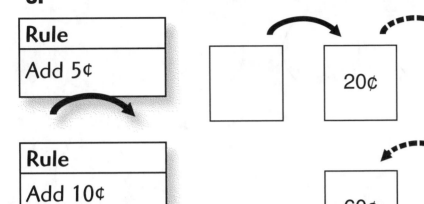

Rule
Add 5¢

Rule
Add 10¢

20¢

60¢

4.

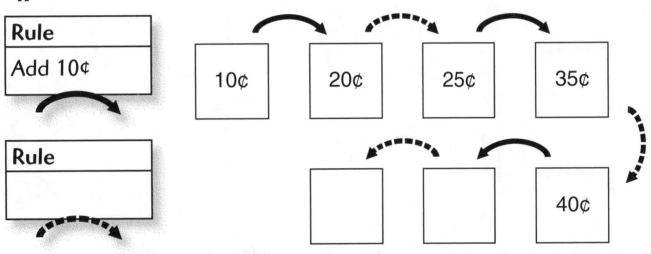

Rule
Add 10¢

Rule

10¢   20¢   25¢   35¢

40¢

5.

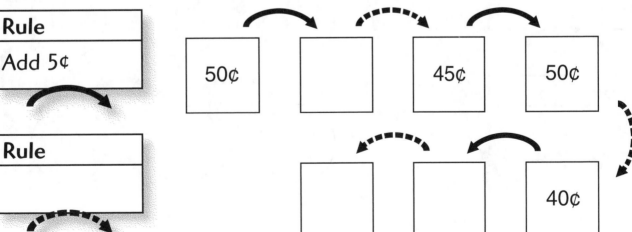

Rule
Add 5¢

Rule

50¢   45¢   50¢

40¢

Copyright © SRA/McGraw-Hill

Two-Rule Frames and Arrows

Rule

Rule

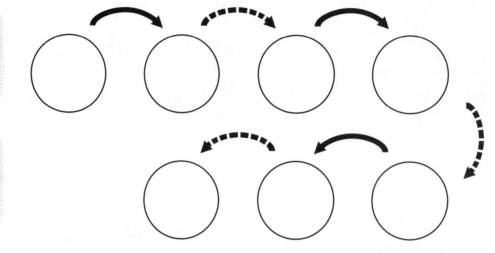

Rule

Rule

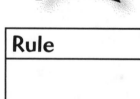

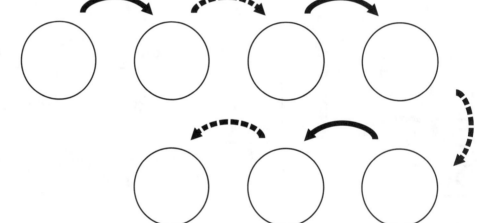

Rule

Rule

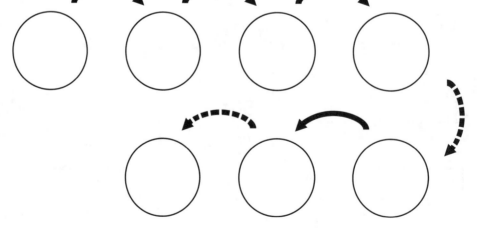

Copyright © SRA/McGraw-Hill

     Use with Lesson 3.6.

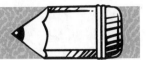

Coin Puzzles

Use the clues to solve the coin puzzles.

Example

Clue 1: I have two coins.

Clue 2: Together they are worth 30¢.

Clue 3: One is not a nickel.

Coin Puzzle: What are the coins? *A quarter and a nickel*

---

1. Clue 1: I have 46¢.

Clue 2: I have 7 coins.

Coin Puzzle: Which coins do I have?

---

2. Clue 1: I have 49¢ in one pocket.

Clue 2: I have 16¢ in another pocket.

Clue 3: When I put all my coins on the table,
          I count 10 pennies.

Clue 4: None of the coins is a nickel.

Coin Puzzle: What are the coins?

---

3. Clue 1: I have 5 coins.

Clue 2: I have a total of 46¢.

Clue 3: Three coins are not nickels.

Coin Puzzle: Which coins do I have?

Copyright © SRA/McGraw-Hill

Milk and Juice Vending Machine

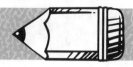

Copyright © SRA/McGraw-Hill

Use with Lesson 3.8.

Change Diagrams

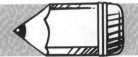

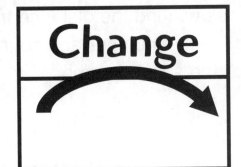

Start	Change	End

Start	Change	End

 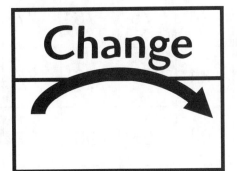

Start	Change	End

Copyright © SRA/McGraw-Hill

Use with Lesson 4.1.

Distances on a Number Grid

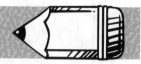

Use the number grid below. Find the distance from the first number to the second. Start at the first number and count the number of spaces moved to reach the second number.

1. 53 and 58 _____

2. 64 and 56 _____

3. 69 and 99 _____

4. 83 and 63 _____

5. 77 and 92 _____

6. 93 and 71 _____

7. 84 and 104 _____

8. 106 and 88 _____

9. 94 and 99 _____

10. 85 and 76 _____

11. 58 and 108 _____

12. 107 and 57 _____

13. 61 and 78 _____

14. 72 and 53 _____

15. 52 and 100 _____

16. 100 and 78 _____

51	52	53	54	55	56	57	58	59	60
61	62	63	64	65	66	67	68	69	70
71	72	73	74	75	76	77	78	79	80
81	82	83	84	85	86	87	88	89	90
91	92	93	94	95	96	97	98	99	100
101	102	103	104	105	106	107	108	109	110

Use with Lesson 4.1.

Copyright © SRA/McGraw-Hill

Parts-and-Total Diagram

Total

Part	Part

Copyright © SRA/McGraw-Hill

Addition Spin Mats

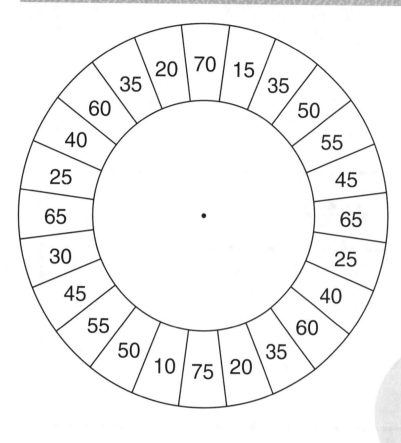

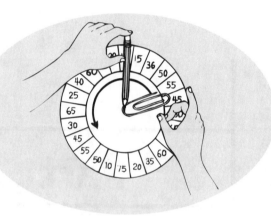

Use a pencil and paper
clip to make a spinner.

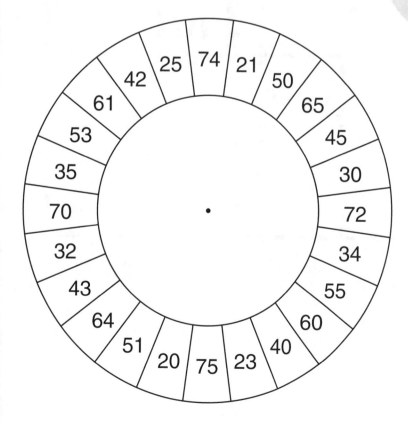

Copyright © SRA/McGraw-Hill

Use with Lesson 4.2.

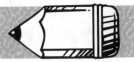

Blank *Addition Spin* Mats

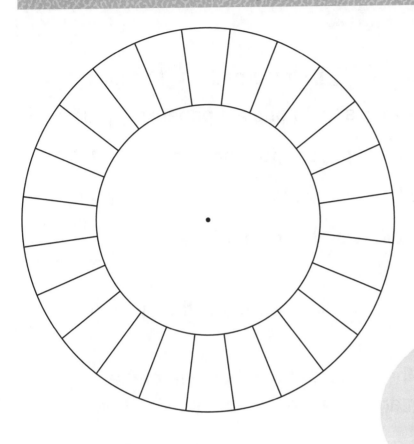

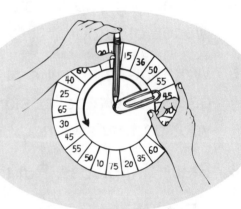

Use a pencil and paper
clip to make a spinner.

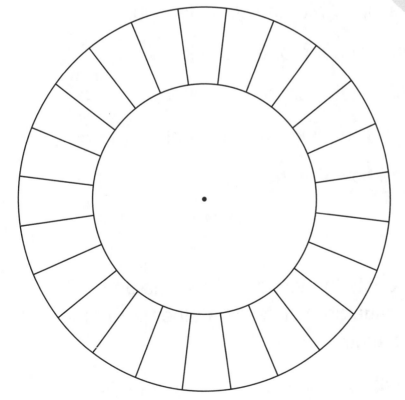

Copyright © SRA/McGraw–Hill

Use with Lesson 4.2.

63

Coin-Stamp Booklets

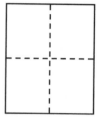

Work with a partner.

Materials   ❑ coin stamps   ❑ stamp pad   ❑ stapler

❑ scissors   ❑ sheets of plain paper   ❑ slate

1. Each partner folds a sheet of paper into 4 parts.

2. Cut the sheet along the folds.

3. Put aside 2 pieces of paper. Use them later for a book cover.

4. Stamp a group of coins on one side of each of the other six pieces of paper.

5. Write the total value of the coins on the other side of the paper. Use a dollar sign and a decimal point: $0.00. Check your partner's work.

6. Stack the pieces. Put the sides with the coins faceup.

• Put 1 blank piece of paper on top of the stack.

• Put the other blank piece at the bottom.

• Staple the pieces together to make a small book.

• Write your names on the cover of the book.

Follow-Up

• Take turns. One partner counts the value of the coins on a page and writes the total value on a slate. The other partner checks that the value is correct.

• Work together. Make up a story about the coins on a page and write it on a piece of paper.

Copyright © SRA/McGraw-Hill

Attribute Sorts

Work in a small group.

Materials   ☐ set of attribute blocks

              ☐ paper for recording

1. Work together to sort the blocks by *color.*

   • One way to do the sorting is to use a different sheet of paper for each color. Label each sheet with a different color.

   • Record how you sorted the blocks. On each sheet, write words or draw pictures to show which blocks belong with that color.

2. Sort the blocks again. Sort them by *size.*

   • Remember to label each sheet with a different size.

   • Record how you sorted the blocks by writing words or drawing pictures.

3. Sort the blocks once more. This time sort them by *shape.*

   • Did you label each sheet with a different shape?

   • Did you make a record of your work?

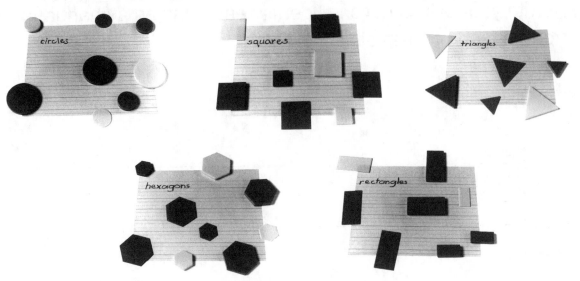

Copyright © SRA/McGraw–Hill

Use with Lesson 4.3.

Change to More or Change to Less?

Decide if each situation is a change-to-more or a change-to-less situation. Circle the answer.

1. *Gained* 15 pounds.   change to more   change to less

2. *Stretched* a rubber band.   change to more   change to less

3. *Grew* 7 inches.   change to more   change to less

4. *Lost* 95 cents.   change to more   change to less

5. Temperature got *warmer*.   change to more   change to less

6. Temperature got *cooler*.   change to more   change to less

7. *Blew up* a balloon.   change to more   change to less

8. *Filled* the gas tank.   change to more   change to less

9. *Earned* a dollar.   change to more   change to less

10. Had my hair *cut*.   change to more   change to less

11. Write your own situations. Identify each one as a change-to-more or a change-to-less situation.

_____

_____

Copyright © SRA/McGraw-Hill

Use with Lesson 4.4.

Shopping Cards

Telephone
$46

Camera
$43

Radio
$38

Tape Recorder
$25

Calculator
$17

Toaster
$29

Iron
$32

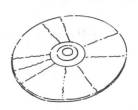

Compact Disc
$14

Copyright © SRA/McGraw-Hill

Use with Lesson 4.6.

"What's My Attribute?"

Work with a small group.

Materials
- ☐ *Math Journal 1*, p. 104
- ☐ Attribute Rule Cards (*Math Masters,* p. 70)
- ☐ scissors
- ☐ 2 sheets of paper
- ☐ 1 set of attribute blocks: triangles, circles, squares (large and small; red, yellow, and blue)
- ☐ red, yellow, and blue crayons

Directions

1. Cut apart the Attribute Rule Cards on *Math Masters,* page 70.

2. Mix the cards. Stack them facedown.

3. Label one sheet of paper "These fit the rule."

4. Label another sheet "These do not fit the rule."

5. Take turns being the "Rule Maker."

6. The Rule Maker takes the top card from the stack.

7. The Rule Maker puts the card faceup for everyone to see.

8. Group members take turns choosing a block.

Copyright © SRA/McGraw-Hill

"What's My Attribute?" (cont.)

9. If the block fits the rule on the card, place it on the paper that says "These fit the rule."

10. If the block does not fit the rule, place it on the paper that says "These do not fit the rule."

11. Repeat Steps 6–10 until everyone has been the Rule Maker.

Follow-Up

• Write one of the rules on journal page 104.

• Draw or describe all of the blocks that fit the rule.

• Draw or describe all of the blocks that do not fit the rule.

Challenge

Make up two rules of your own. Write them on the two blank cards given on *Math Masters,* page 70.

Copyright © SRA/McGraw-Hill

Attribute Rule Cards

small blue shapes	large red shapes	large shapes, but not triangles	circles, but not red
blue and yellow shapes, but not circles	red and yellow small shapes	not triangles or squares	large triangles, but not yellow
large circles, but not red	large circles or squares		

Copyright © SRA/McGraw-Hill

Base-10 Blocks

For each problem, draw a new set of base-10 blocks that uses the fewest possible number of flats, longs, and cubes.

1. ||| ▪▪▪▪▪ ▪▪▪▪▪	
2. ||||| ▪▪▪▪▪ ▪▪▪▪▪	
3. || ▪▪▪ ▪▪▪ ▪▪▪ ▪▪▪	
4. |||| ▪▪▪▪ ▪▪▪▪ ▪▪▪▪ ▪▪▪▪	
5. □ |||||| ||||||	▪▪▪▪▪ ▪▪▪▪	
6. □ ||||| ||||| |||| ▪▪▪▪▪ ▪▪▪▪▪	

Copyright © SRA/McGraw-Hill

Pattern-Block Designs

Materials
- ☐ pattern blocks
- ☐ Pattern-Block Template
- ☐ *Math Masters*, p. 73

Directions

1. Use pattern blocks to cover each shape on *Math Masters*, page 73. Use at least 2 different kinds of pattern blocks to cover each shape. Cover each shape in a different way.

2. Draw the blocks you used for each shape. Use your Pattern-Block Template.

3. Use crayons. Make an X on each shape to match the color of the blocks you used.

Follow-Up

Compare your answers with a partner's.

- How many different ways was the small hexagon covered? Are there more ways?

- How many different ways was the large hexagon covered? Are there more ways?

Copyright © SRA/McGraw-Hill

Use with Lesson 4.9.

Pattern-Block Designs (cont.)

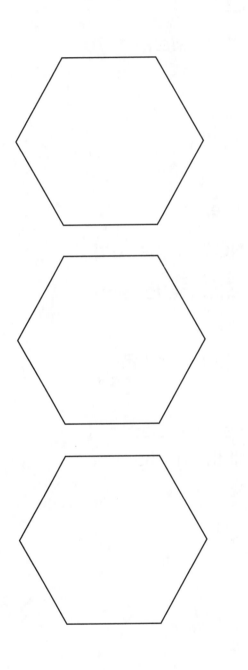

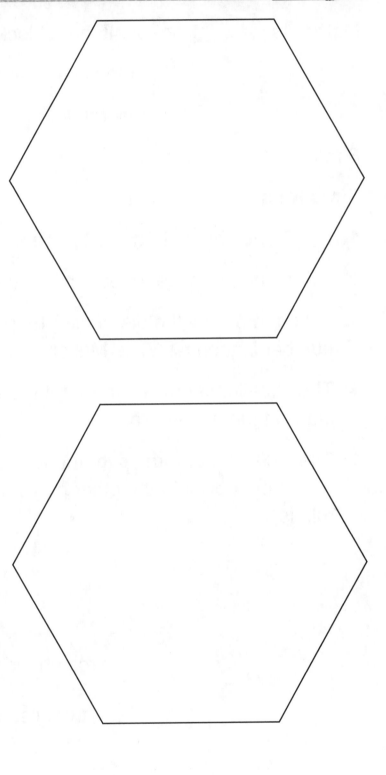

Copyright © SRA/McGraw–Hill

Use with Lesson 4.9.

"What's My Attribute Rule?"

Materials   ❑ set of attribute blocks

❑ Attribute Rule Cards (*Math Masters,* p. 70)

❑ 1 six-sided die

Players   3 or more

Directions

1. Label one sheet of paper: **These fit the rule.**

2. Label another sheet of paper: **These do NOT fit the rule.**

3. Take turns. Roll the die once. The player with the lowest number is the first "Rule Maker."

4. The Rule Maker mixes the Attribute Rule Cards and then stacks them facedown.

5. The Rule Maker turns over the top Attribute Rule Card but does not show it to the other players or tell them what the rule is.

large shapes,
but not
triangles

Sample Attribute Rule Card

Copyright © SRA/McGraw-Hill

"What's My Attribute Rule?" (cont.)

6. The Rule Maker chooses 3 or 4 attribute blocks that fit the rule on the card. The Rule Maker puts them on the sheet labeled "These fit the rule."

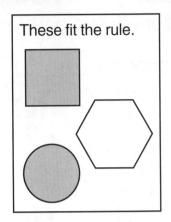
These fit the rule.

7. The Rule Maker chooses 3 or 4 blocks that do NOT fit the rule. The Rule Maker puts them on the sheet labeled "These do NOT fit the rule."

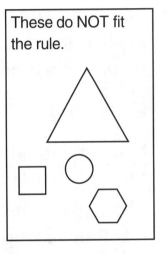
These do NOT fit the rule.

8. The other players are the "Guessers." The Guessers take turns. Each one chooses a block that he or she thinks might fit the rule.

9. The Rule Maker tells each Guesser "yes" or "no." The Guesser puts the block on the correct sheet. The Guesser suggests what the rule might be. The Rule Maker tells the Guesser if his or her rule is correct.

10. The Guessers continue until someone figures out the rule. Then that player becomes the Rule Maker for the next round.

Copyright © SRA/McGraw-Hill

Secret Shapes

Work with a partner.

Materials   ☐ 2 geoboards

                       ☐ rubber bands

Directions

1. One partner makes an easy shape, design, or picture on his or her geoboard. The other partner does not watch.

2. The first partner gives directions to the other partner for making the picture on the geoboard. The directions should be very clear so that the pictures will look alike.

Example

Make a flag on a flagpole.
The flagpole is 4 units long.
The flag is a rectangle.
It is 2 units long and 1 unit high.
The flag is at the top of the flagpole.

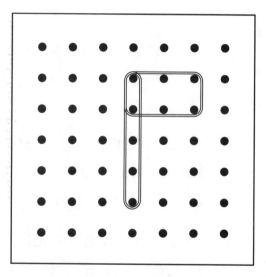

3. Partners compare pictures. How are they alike? How are they different?

4. Partners change roles and do Steps 1–3 again.

Copyright © SRA/McGraw-Hill

Clock Concentration

Materials
- [ ] 10 index cards
- [ ] clock-face stamp
- [ ] stamp pad
- [ ] envelope
- [ ] scissors

Players   4 to 6

Directions

Make a set of *Clock Concentration* cards.

1. Fold each index card in half. Then unfold it.

2. Stamp a clock face on one half of the card. Then draw an hour hand and a minute hand on the face to show a time.

3. Write the matching digital time on the other half. Check one another's work.

4. Cut the card in half.

5. Write **C** on the back of each card with a clock face.

6. Write **T** on the back of each card with a time.

7. Choose a mark your group will use to identify your cards. Make that mark in the same corner on the back of every card.

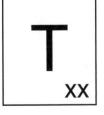

Copyright © SRA/McGraw-Hill

Clock Concentration (cont.)

Play *Clock Concentration.*

1. One player shuffles the cards and places them facedown in an array.

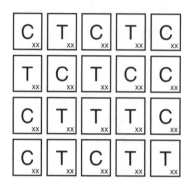

2. Take turns. For each turn, a player turns a **C** card and a **T** card faceup. If the cards match, that player takes both cards and takes another turn.

3. If the cards do not match, put them back in the array facedown. Then the next player takes a turn.

4. Play until the time is up or until all the cards have been taken. The player with the most cards wins.

5. Store your group's cards in an envelope until you play again.

Copyright © SRA/McGraw-Hill

Clock Concentration Cards

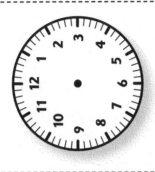

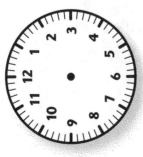

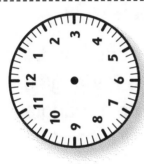

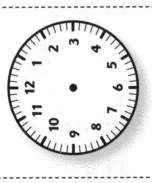

Copyright © SRA/McGraw-Hill

Geoboard Triangles

Work with a partner or a small group.

Materials   ☐ geoboard

☐ rubber bands

☐ geoboard dot paper

☐ paper

Directions

1. How many different-looking triangles can you make on your geoboard? Each partner or person in your group should try to find out.

2. Draw your triangles on geoboard dot paper.

3. Make the largest triangle you can on your geoboard. Use more rubber bands to split the triangle into 2 triangles. Then split it into 3 triangles. Now split it into 4 triangles. Can you make more than 4 triangles? Try.

4. Draw your triangles on geoboard dot paper.

Follow-Up

Look at the triangles that your partnership or group drew.

• How are all the triangles alike? Make a list of the ways.

• How are some of the triangles different? Talk about the ways. Then make a list of the ways you found.

Copyright © SRA/McGraw-Hill

Sharing Equally

Work with a partner.

Materials   ❑ quarter-sheets of paper   ❑ plain paper

                 ❑ 1 regular die or number cube

                 ❑ centimeter cubes, pennies, or dried beans

Directions

1. Think of the quarter-sheets of paper as nests.
   Think of the cubes, pennies, or beans as eggs.

2. Choose a number between 8 and 32.
   Then count out that many "eggs."

3. Roll the die once. The number that lands faceup
   tells how many "nests" (quarter-sheets) to lay out.

4. Work together to share the eggs equally among all the
   nests. When you finish, count the eggs in each nest.
   Make sure each nest has the same number of eggs.

5. Make a record of your work on the sheet of plain paper.

   • Show the number of eggs you started with.

   • Show the nests and the eggs in each nest.

   • Show any eggs that were left over.

6. Choose a different number of eggs. Then follow Steps 1–5 again.

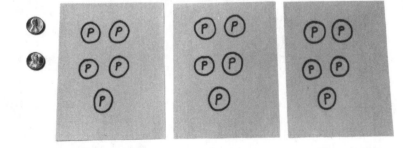

Copyright © SRA/McGraw-Hill

Geoboard Dot Paper (5 × 5)

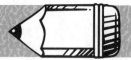

1.

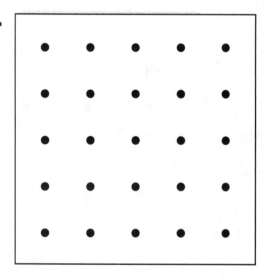

2.

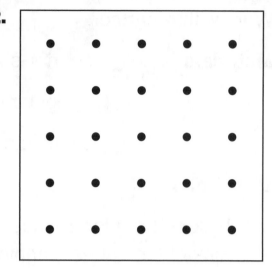

3.

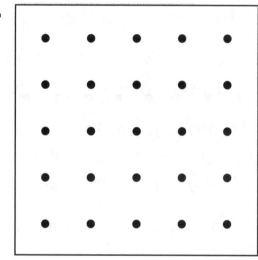

4.

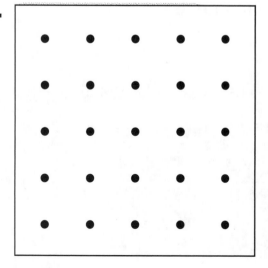

5.

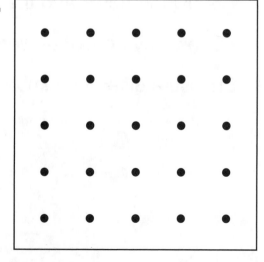

6.

Copyright © SRA/McGraw-Hill

Use with Lesson 5.2.

Geoboard Dot Paper (7 × 7)

1.

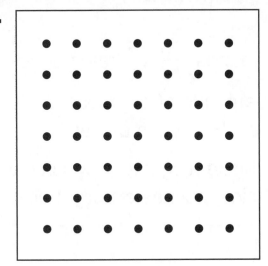

2.

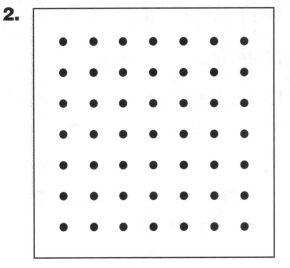

3.

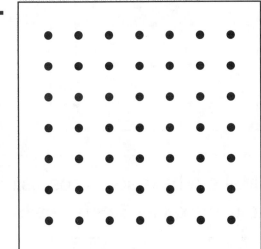

4.

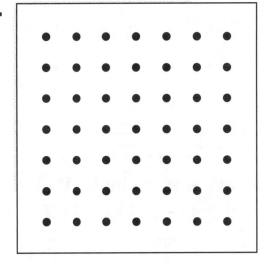

5.

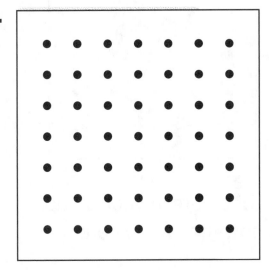

6.

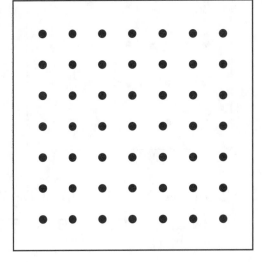

Copyright © SRA/McGraw-Hill

Use with Lesson 5.2.

Geoboard Polygons

Work in a small group.

Materials ☐ geoboard   ☐ rubber bands   ☐ straightedge

Directions: Each person uses the square side of a geoboard to make the following polygons. Copy each polygon below.

1. Make a triangle in which each side touches exactly 3 pins.

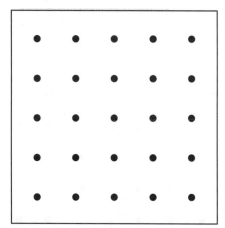

2. Make a square in which each side touches exactly 4 pins.

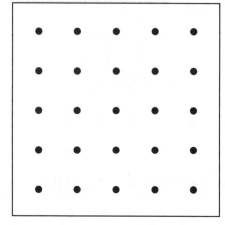

3. Make a pentagon that touches at least 5 pins.

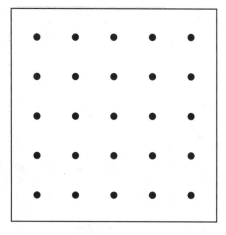

4. Make a hexagon whose sides touch exactly 6 pins in all.

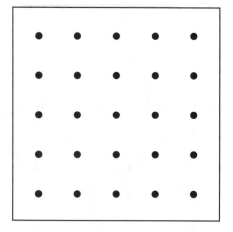

5. Compare your polygons with those of others in your group. Talk about how they are alike and how they are different.

          Copyright © SRA/McGraw-Hill   Use with Lesson 5.3.

Cube Arrays

Work with a partner or a small group.

Materials
- ☐ centimeter grid paper from *Math Masters,* p. 86
- ☐ 2 six-sided dice
- ☐ about 40 centimeter cubes

Directions

Follow these steps to build arrays with centimeter cubes:

1. Pick one member of your group to roll the dice.

2. Use the number that is faceup on one die for the number of rows in the array. Use the number that is faceup on the other die for the number of cubes in each row.

   Example: If you roll this: You can make either array:

3. Work together. Use centimeter cubes to build the array.

4. On grid paper, fill in squares to show your array. Underneath the array, write

   - how many rows are in the array

   - how many cubes are in each row

   - how many cubes there are in all

   5 rows
   3 cubes in each row
   15 cubes in all

5. Take turns rolling the dice. Together, make at least five different arrays. Record each array on grid paper.

Copyright © SRA/McGraw-Hill

Name _____ Date _____ Time _____

Centimeter Grid Paper

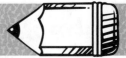

Use with Lesson 5.3.

Copyright © SRA/McGraw-Hill

Make a Dollar

Work together in a small group.

Materials
- ☐ 20 nickels
- ☐ 10 dimes
- ☐ 4 quarters
- ☐ paper and pencil

Directions

1. Use the coins to find as many different ways as you can to make $1.00.

2. Before you begin, THINK about how to do this. *Hint:* First, make a dollar using 3 quarters and some other coins.

3. Plan how you will record the different ways to make $1.00.

4. On a sheet of paper, record the different ways you find to make $1.00. Use Ⓝ, Ⓓ, and Ⓠ to show the coins.

Follow-Up

- How many ways did you find to make $1.00? Check with other groups to see if they thought of any ways that your group didn't find.

- Did you have a plan to find all the combinations? Compare your plan with the plan used by another group.

Copyright © SRA/McGraw-Hill

Making Up Codes

1. Draw the shape for the code.

$B \rightarrow A \rightarrow E \rightarrow F \rightarrow D \rightarrow C$

You should have drawn the letter *G*.

A•   •B

•D

C

E•   •F

2. Make up a code for each of the following capital letters.

   a. The letter *R*

   Code: _____

A•   •B

C•   •D

E•   •F

   b. The letter *S*

   Code: _____

A•   •B

C•   •D

E•   •F

Challenge

3. The letter *Z*

   Code: _____

A•   •B

C•   •D

E•   •F

4. Name the line segments you drew to make the letter *Z*.

Copyright © SRA/McGraw–Hill

                                    Use with Lesson 5.4.

Line Segments

Draw the line segments. Use a straightedge.

$\overline{AB}$ $\overline{BC}$ $\overline{CJ}$ $\overline{JA}$ $\overline{AI}$ $\overline{IJ}$ $\overline{CD}$

$\overline{DE}$ $\overline{EF}$ $\overline{FN}$ $\overline{NM}$ $\overline{MG}$ $\overline{FG}$ $\overline{GH}$

$\overline{HI}$ $\overline{KL}$ $\overline{OP}$ $\overline{PQ}$ $\overline{QR}$ $\overline{RO}$ $\overline{JE}$

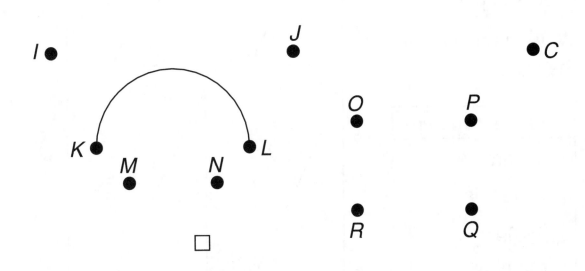

Copyright © SRA/McGraw-Hill

Make Shapes

1. Cut out the triangles and rectangles.

2. Make some of the shapes listed below. Use at least 2 triangles or rectangles to make each new shape. You may have to turn some of the pieces over.

3. Paste the shapes on sheets of paper.

4. Write the names of the shapes.

Shapes to Make
square
rectangle
triangle
rhombus
kite
trapezoid
parallelogram
4-pointed star
any shape you choose

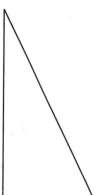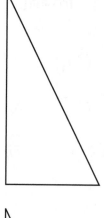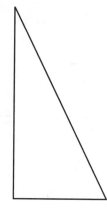
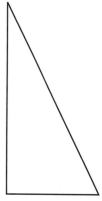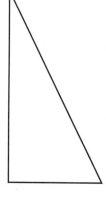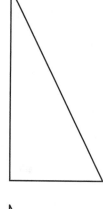
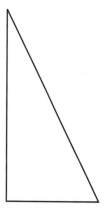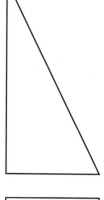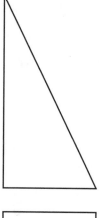

Copyright © SRA/McGraw-Hill

Use with Lesson 5.6.

Make Shapes (cont.)

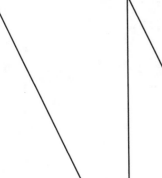
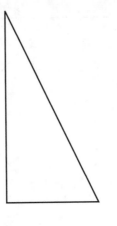
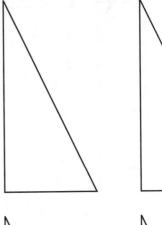

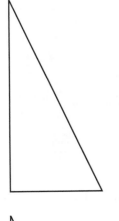
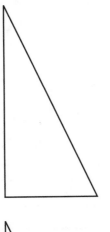
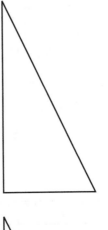
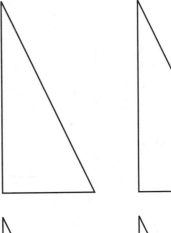
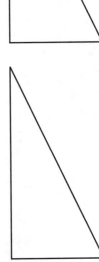

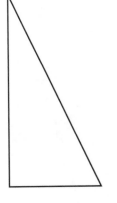
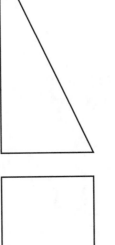
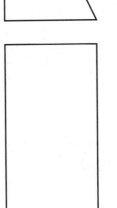

Copyright © SRA/McGraw–Hill

Use with Lesson 5.6.

Tangram Puzzle

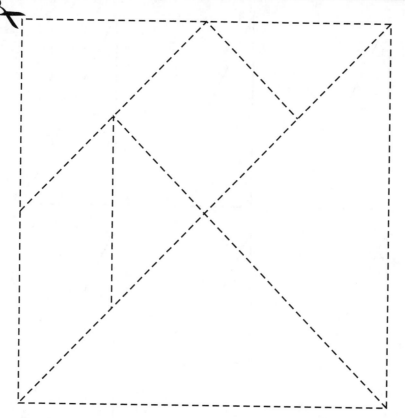

Copyright © SRA/McGraw-Hill

Use with Lesson 5.6.

Touch-and-Match Quadrangles

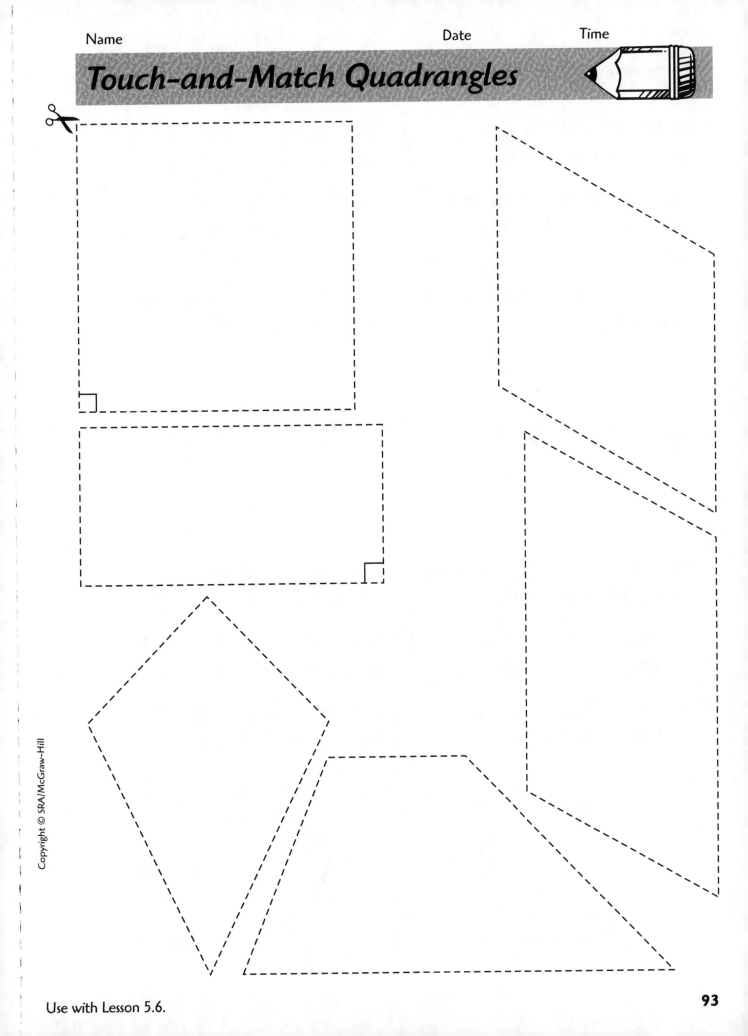

Copyright © SRA/McGraw-Hill

Use with Lesson 5.6.

Pyramid Base Cards

Use straws and twist-ties to build a **triangular pyramid.**

Use short straws for the base. Use long straws for the other edges.

The base of a triangular pyramid is a triangle:

Use straws and twist-ties to build a **rectangular pyramid.**

Use 2 short straws and 2 long straws for the base. Use long straws for the other edges.

The base of a rectangular pyramid is a rectangle:

Use straws and twist-ties to build a **pentagonal pyramid.**

Use short straws for the base. Use long straws for the other edges.

The base of a pentagonal pyramid is a pentagon:

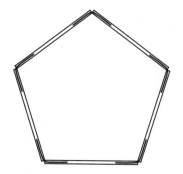

Use straws and twist-ties to build a **hexagonal pyramid.**

Use short straws for the base. Use long straws for the other edges.

The base of a hexagonal pyramid is a hexagon:

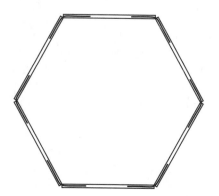

Copyright © SRA/McGraw-Hill

Construct a Decagon

Materials   ☐ *Math Masters,* p. 96

☐ tape or paste   ☐ scissors

Directions

1. Carefully cut out the triangles on *Math Masters,* page 96.

2. Arrange the triangles to make a decagon.

3. Paste or tape your decagon inside the decagon below.

4. Color the triangles inside the decagon. Use at least 2 different colors.

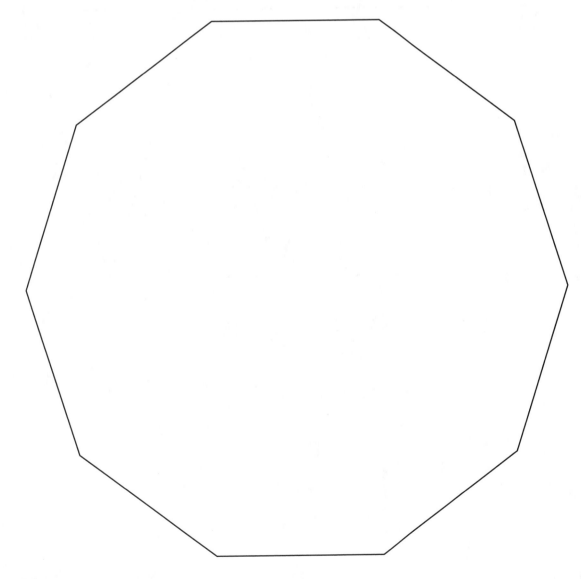

Copyright © SRA/McGraw–Hill

Use with Lesson 5.8.

Construct a Decagon (cont.)

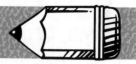

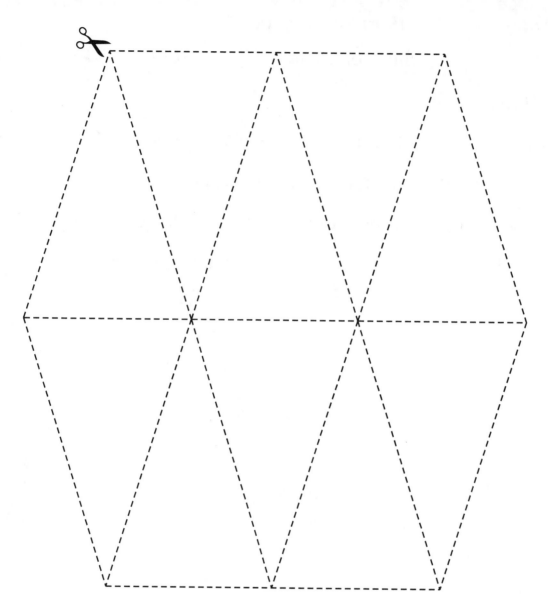

Copyright © SRA/McGraw-Hill

Use with Lesson 5.8.

Make a Square Pyramid

Materials   ☐ scissors

                ☐ glue or tape

Directions

1. Cut on the dashed lines.

2. Fold on the dotted lines.

3. Tape or glue tabs "inside" or "outside."

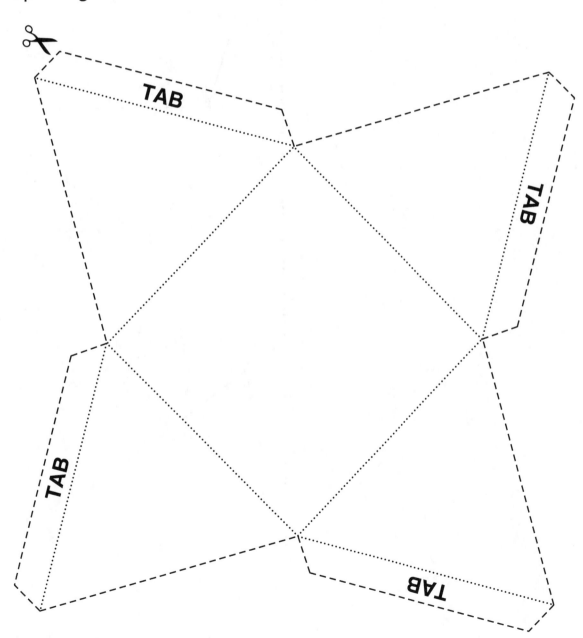

Copyright © SRA/McGraw-Hill

What's Missing?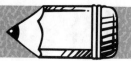

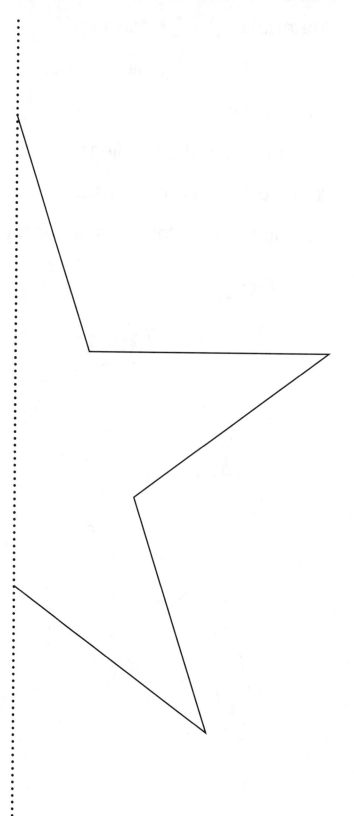

Copyright © SRA/McGraw-Hill

Use with Lesson 5.9.

Lines of Symmetry

Cut out each shape. Find all the lines of symmetry for each shape by folding it in half.

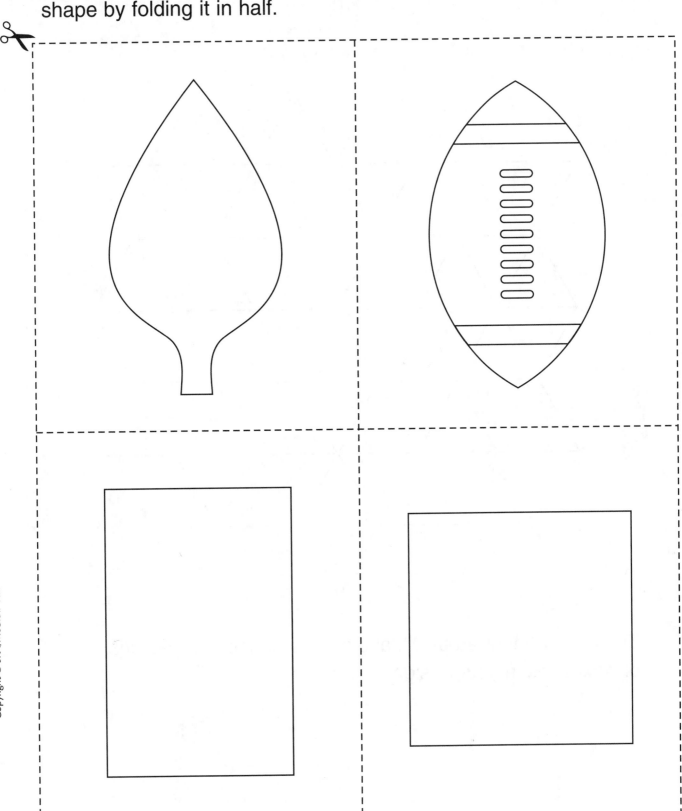

Copyright © SRA/McGraw-Hill

A Geometric Pattern

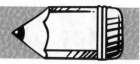

1. Color the pattern. Use 2 or more colors.

2. Trace your finger around triangles, rhombuses, trapezoids, or hexagons in your design.

Copyright © SRA/McGraw–Hill

Three Addends Record Sheet

For each turn:

- Write the 3 numbers.

- Add the numbers.

- Write a number model to show the order in which you added.

1. Numbers: ____, ____, ____

Number model:

____ + ____ + ____ = ____

2. Numbers: ____, ____, ____

Number model:

____ + ____ + ____ = ____

3. Numbers: ____, ____, ____

Number model:

____ = ____ + ____ + ____

4. Numbers: ____, ____, ____

Number model:

____ = ____ + ____ + ____

5. Numbers: ____, ____, ____

Number model:

____ + ____ + ____ = ____

6. Numbers: ____, ____, ____

Number model:

____ + ____ + ____ = ____

7. Numbers: ____, ____, ____

Number model:

____ + ____ + ____ = ____

8. Numbers: ____, ____, ____

Number model:

____ + ____ + ____ = ____

9. Numbers: ____, ____, ____

Number model:

____ = ____ + ____ + ____

10. Numbers: ____, ____, ____

Number model:

____ = ____ + ____ + ____

Copyright © SRA/McGraw-Hill

Use with Lesson 6.1.

Base-10 Flat

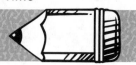

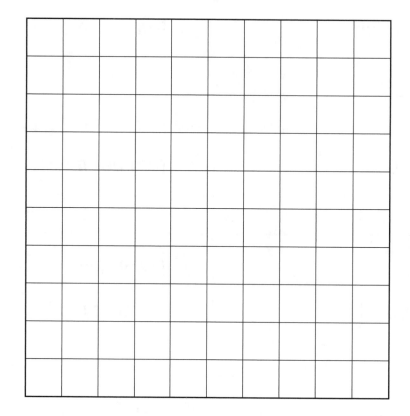

Copyright © SRA/McGraw-Hill

Use with Lesson 6.1.

Comparison Diagram

Quantity

Quantity	Difference

Copyright © SRA/McGraw-Hill

Food Guide Pyramid

**Fats,
Oils,
Sweets**
Use sparingly.

**Dairy
Products**

**Meat,
Poultry,
Fish,
Beans,
Eggs,
Nuts**

2 to 3 servings | 2 to 3 servings

Vegetables

Fruit

3 to 5 servings

2 to 4 servings

Bread, Cereal, Rice, Pasta

6 to 11 servings

Copyright © SRA/McGraw-Hill

Use with Lesson 6.3.

The 4 Basic Food Groups (Samples)

fruit/ vegetables	bread/cereal/ rice/pasta	dairy products	meat/poultry/ fish/ beans/ eggs/nuts
watermelon	pancakes	ice cream	hamburgers
bananas	fried rice	Swiss cheese	omelets
grapes	French toast	yogurt	almonds
pears	cornflakes	chocolate milk	peanut butter
apples	muffins	cream cheese	chicken
broccoli	crackers	milk shakes	fish
corn	spaghetti	frozen yogurt	pork chops
potatoes	bagels		black beans
carrots	English muffins		refried beans
squash	waffles		scrambled eggs
raisins			turkey
strawberries			bacon

Copyright © SRA/McGraw–Hill

What Is Your Favorite Food?

1. Make tally marks to show the number of children who chose a favorite food in each group.

fruit/ vegetables	bread/cereal/ rice/pasta	dairy products	meat/poultry/ fish/beans/ eggs/nuts

2. Make a graph that shows how many children chose a favorite food in each group.

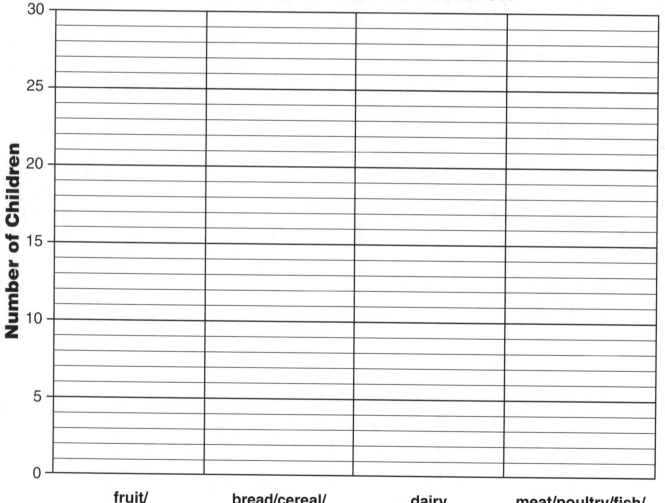

Favorite Foods of Children

Number of Children

30 — 25 — 20 — 15 — 10 — 5 — 0

fruit/ vegetables   bread/cereal/ rice/pasta   dairy products   meat/poultry/fish/ beans/eggs/nuts

Food Groups

Copyright © SRA/McGraw-Hill

Use with Lesson 6.3.

Adults: What's Your Favorite Food?

1. Make tally marks to show the number of adults who chose a favorite food in each group.

fruit/ vegetables	bread/cereal/ rice/pasta	dairy products	meat/poultry/ fish/beans/ eggs/nuts

2. Make a graph that shows how many adults chose a favorite food in each group.

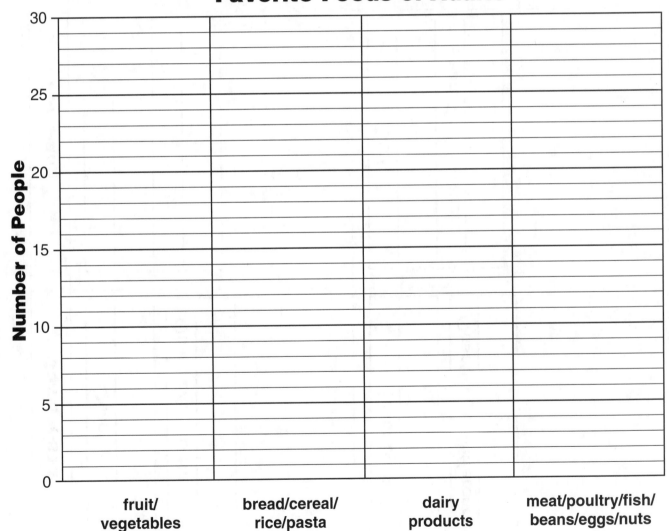

Favorite Foods of Adults

Number of People (y-axis: 0, 5, 10, 15, 20, 25, 30)

fruit/ vegetables   bread/cereal/ rice/pasta   dairy products   meat/poultry/fish/ beans/eggs/nuts

Food Groups

Copyright © SRA/McGraw-Hill

Use with Lesson 6.3.

Diagrams for Number Stories

	Change	Parts-and-Total	Comparison

1.

Start	Change	End

Total	
Part	Part

Quantity	
Quantity	Difference

2.

Start	Change	End

Total	
Part	Part

Quantity	
Quantity	Difference

Copyright © SRA/McGraw-Hill

A Number Story

_____

_____

_____

_____

_____

_____

_____

Answer to my number story: _____

Number model: _____

Copyright © SRA/McGraw–Hill

Geoboard Arrays

Materials
- ❑ geoboard dot paper for each person
- ❑ geoboard for each person
- ❑ rubber band for each person
- ❑ scissors for the group
- ❑ glue or paste for the group (optional)
- ❑ large sheet of paper for the group (optional)

Work by yourself to complete Steps 1–5.

1. Use one rubber band to make a rectangle on your geoboard. The pegs inside the rubber band make an array.

2. Draw your array on the geoboard dot paper.

3. Write about your array at the bottom of the geoboard dot paper. Tell how many rows are in your rectangle, how many dots are in each row, and how many dots in all are in your rectangle.

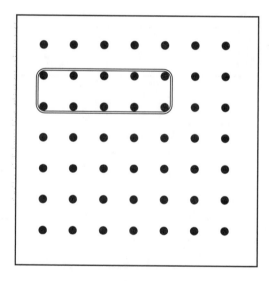

4. Make 3 more arrays—all different. Draw each array on the geoboard dot paper. Write about each array at the bottom of the geoboard dot paper.

There are 2 rows of 5 pegs.
10 pegs are in the array.

5. Cut apart the dot-paper records of your 4 arrays.

Work with your group to complete Step 6.

6. Sort your group's arrays into piles that have the same number of dots. You might want to use the arrays in each pile to make a display about that number.

Copyright © SRA/McGraw-Hill

Use with Lesson 6.7.

Geoboard Arrays (5 × 5)

1.

2.

3.

4.

	How many rows?	How many dots in each row?	How many dots in all?
1.			
2.			
3.			
4.			

Copyright © SRA/McGraw-Hill

Use with Lesson 6.7.

Geoboard Arrays (7 × 7)

1.

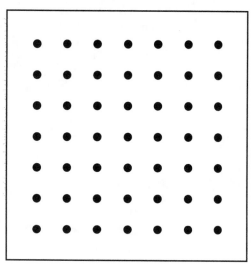

2.

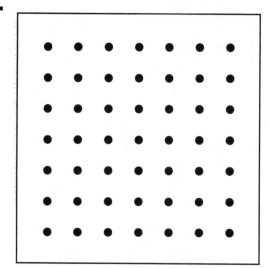

3.

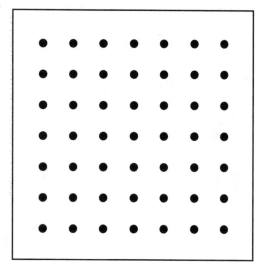

4.

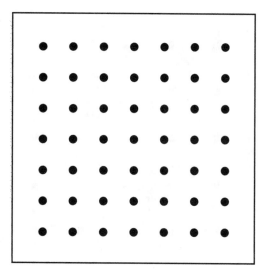

	How many rows?	How many dots in each row?	How many dots in all?
1.			
2.			
3.			
4.			

       Use with Lesson 6.7.

Copyright © SRA/McGraw-Hill

Pattern-Block Symmetry

Materials
- ☐ Pattern-Block Template
- ☐ pattern blocks
- ☐ 2 blank sheets of paper
- ☐ straightedge

1. Fold 2 sheets of paper in half the short way. Then use a straightedge to draw a line along the fold on each sheet.

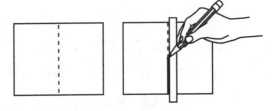

2. Use pattern blocks to make a design that fits up against the line on one sheet of paper.

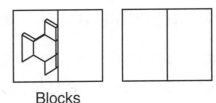

Blocks

3. Draw the mirror image of your design on the second sheet of paper. Use the Pattern-Block Template to draw on the right side of the line. The *mirror image* is how the design would look if it were flipped over the line. Color the shapes to match the blocks.

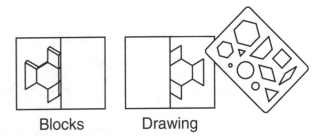

Blocks   Drawing

4. Make the mirror image of the design on the blank side of the second sheet of paper. Use the Pattern-Block Template. Then color the shapes.

Blocks   Drawing

Copyright © SRA/McGraw-Hill

How Many Persons Get *n* Things?

Materials
- ❏ *Math Journal 1,* p. 151 (per person)
- ❏ one container with about 50 pennies or other counters (per group)
- ❏ 1 six-sided die (per group)

Use counters to make up and solve problems like this one:
Your group has been given 32 crayons.
Each person is to get 8 crayons.
How many of you will get 8 crayons?
Are there any crayons left over?

Now make up your own problems. Follow these steps:

1. Each person takes a handful of counters. Put all the counters together in a pile.

   How many counters are in the pile? Count them and record the number on the journal page.

2. Make equal-size groups of counters. One person rolls the die. The number that lands faceup tells how many counters to put in each group.

   Record this number on the journal page.

3. Make as many groups as you can with the counters in the pile.

4. Record on the journal page how many groups you made. If any counters are left over, record that number, too.

5. Put the counters back in the container. Repeat Steps 1–4.

Copyright © SRA/McGraw-Hill

Array Multiplication

Array

○   ○   ○   ○   ○   ○   ○   ○   ○   ○

○   ○   ○   ○   ○   ○   ○   ○   ○   ○

○   ○   ○   ○   ○   ○   ○   ○   ○   ○

○   ○   ○   ○   ○   ○   ○   ○   ○   ○

○   ○   ○   ○   ○   ○   ○   ○   ○   ○

○   ○   ○   ○   ○   ○   ○   ○   ○   ○

○   ○   ○   ○   ○   ○   ○   ○   ○   ○

○   ○   ○   ○   ○   ○   ○   ○   ○   ○

Multiplication Diagram

rows	_____ per row	_____ in all

Number model: _____ × _____ = _____

Copyright © SRA/McGraw–Hill

Array Number Stories

Array

Multiplication Diagram

rows	_____ per row	_____ in all

Number model: _____ × _____ = _____

Array

Multiplication Diagram

rows	_____ per row	_____ in all

Number model: _____ × _____ = _____

Array

Multiplication Diagram

rows	_____ per row	_____ in all

Number model: _____ × _____ = _____

Array

Multiplication Diagram

rows	_____ per row	_____ in all

Number model: _____ × _____ = _____

Use with Lesson 6.9.

Copyright © SRA/McGraw-Hill

Array Bingo Cards

A 2 by 2	**A** 2 by 3	**A** 2 by 4	4 by 4
A 2 by 5	**A** 2 by 6	3 by 5	6 by 3
A 3 by 3	**A** 1 by 7	**A** 4 by 3	3 by 6
5 by 3	**A** 6 by 1	4 by 5	5 by 4

Copyright © SRA/McGraw-Hill

Use with Lesson 6.10.

Array Bingo

Materials   ❑ 2 six-sided dice, 1 twelve-sided die, or an egg-carton number generator

❑ 9 cards labeled "A" cut from
Math Masters, p. 117 for each player

Players   2–5

Directions

1. Each player arranges the 9 cards at random in a 3-by-3 array.

2. Players take turns. When it is your turn:

Generate a number from 1 to 12, using the dice, die, or number generator. This number represents the total number of dots in an array.

Look for the array card with that number of dots.
Turn that card facedown.

3. The first player to have a row, column, or diagonal of facedown cards calls "Bingo!" and wins the game.

Copyright © SRA/McGraw-Hill

Use with Lesson 6.10.

Array Bingo (cont.)

Another Way to Play

Materials

- ☐ 1 twenty-sided die or number cards with one card for each of the numbers 1–20

- ☐ all 16 array cards from *Math Masters,* p. 117 for each player

Each player arranges his or her cards at random in a 4-by-4 array. Players generate numbers using the die or number cards. If you use number cards to generate numbers, do this:

- Shuffle the cards.

- Place them facedown on the table.

- Turn over the top card.

- If all 20 cards are turned over before someone calls "Bingo," reshuffle the deck and use it as before.

Copyright © SRA/McGraw-Hill

Use with Lesson 6.10.

Building Arrays

Materials ❑ pattern blocks ❑ Pattern-Block Template

❑ 1 six-sided die or number cube

❑ *Math Masters,* p. 121

1. Choose one of these blocks.

 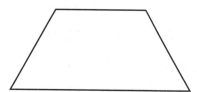 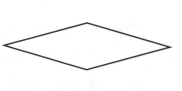 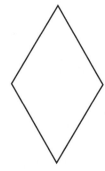

2. Roll the die 2 times.

The first number you roll tells how many rows to make in your array.

The second number you roll tells how many blocks to put in each row of your array.

Example

If you roll a 1 first and then a 5, you might make this:

  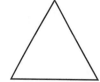 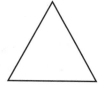

3. Record the arrays you make on *Math Masters,* page 121.

Use the Pattern-Block Template. At the top of the page, draw the first array you made.

Fill in the table for Number 1 at the bottom of the page.

4. Make 4 more arrays. Follow the same steps. If you have room, draw the arrays you make. After you run out of room, fill in the table only.

Copyright © SRA/McGraw-Hill

Use with Lesson 6.10.

Building Arrays (cont.)

Use your Pattern-Block Template. Show one or more of your arrays.

Record the arrays you made.

	How many rows?	How many shapes in each row?	How many shapes in all?
1.			
2.			
3.			
4.			
5.			

Copyright © SRA/McGraw–Hill

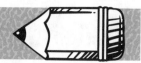

Number Patterns

1. Count by 5s starting with the number 102. Color in the numbers on the grid with a crayon. Can you find a pattern?

									100
101	102	103	104	105	106	107	108	109	110
111	112	113	114	115	116	117	118	119	120
121	122	123	124	125	126	127	128	129	130

2. Pick a number to start with. Pick a number to count by. Mark your counts using a crayon.

									300
301	302	303	304	305	306	307	308	309	310
311	312	313	314	315	316	317	318	319	320
321	322	323	324	325	326	327	328	329	330
331	332	333	334	335	336	337	338	339	340
341	342	343	344	345	346	347	348	349	350
351	352	353	354	355	356	357	358	359	360
361	362	363	364	365	366	367	368	369	370

I counted by _____ starting with the number _____.

I used a _____ crayon to mark the counts.
(color)

Here is the pattern I found: _____

Copyright © SRA/McGraw-Hill

Use with Lesson 7.1.

Addition and Subtraction Facts

1. 3 + 4 = _____   **2.** 1 + 6 = _____   **3.** 8 + 2 = _____

4. 0 + 1 = _____   **5.** 8 + 0 = _____   **6.** 3 + 1 = _____

7. 2 + 7 = _____   **8.** 2 + 4 = _____   **9.** 5 + 4 = _____

---

10. 8 − 3 = _____   **11.** 6 − 3 = _____   **12.** 8 − 6 = _____

13. 5 − 1 = _____   **14.** 7 − 2 = _____   **15.** 9 − 0 = _____

16. 10 − 7 = _____   **17.** 10 − 4 = _____   **18.** 8 − 1 = _____

---

19. 9 + 9 = _____   **20.** 4 + 8 = _____   **21.** 5 + 7 = _____

22. 5 + 8 = _____   **23.** 9 + 3 = _____   **24.** 8 + 3 = _____

25. 7 + 6 = _____   **26.** 8 + 8 = _____   **27.** 2 + 9 = _____

---

28. 15 − 8 = _____   **29.** 14 − 9 = _____   **30.** 14 − 7 = _____

31. 14 − 6 = _____   **32.** 16 − 7 = _____   **33.** 11 − 6 = _____

34. 11 − 4 = _____   **35.** 17 − 8 = _____   **36.** 13 − 9 = _____

Copyright © SRA/McGraw-Hill

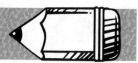

Making Patterns

Make designs by coloring the grids. Use more than one color in each design.

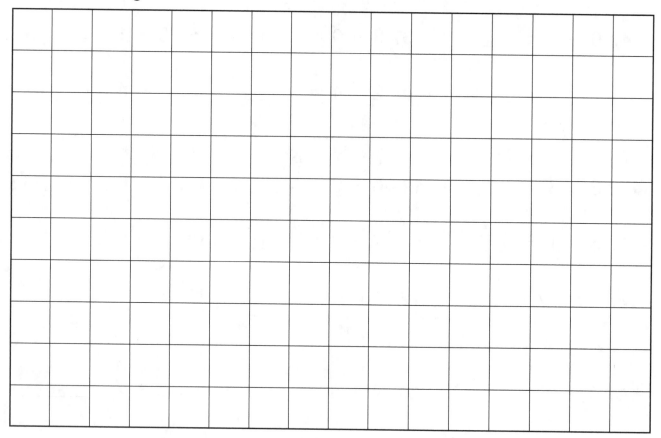

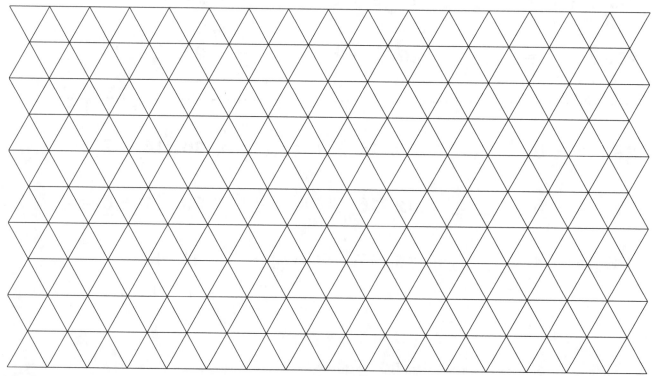

Copyright © SRA/McGraw-Hill

Use with Lesson 7.1.

Square Grids

Copyright © SRA/McGraw-Hill

Use with Lesson 7.1.

Triangular Grids

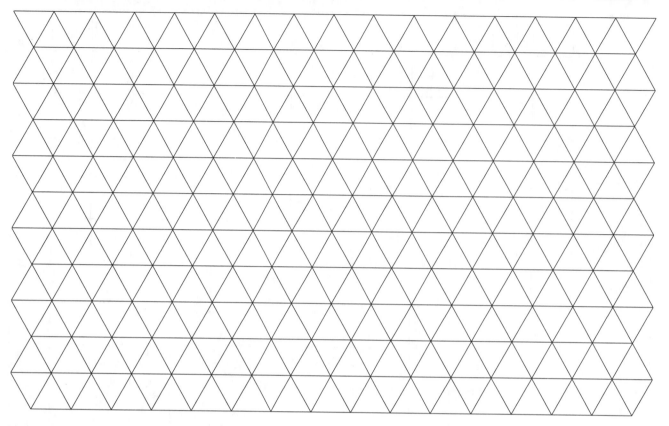

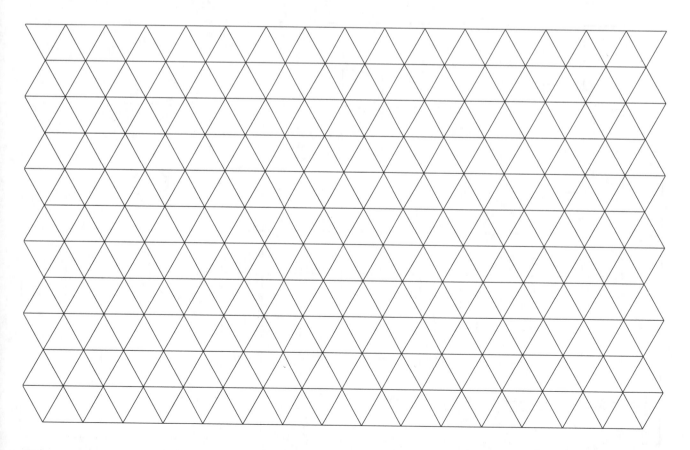

Copyright © SRA/McGraw-Hill

Use with Lesson 7.1.

Attribute Train Game

Work in a small group.

Materials   ☐ set of attribute blocks

Game 1

1. Place the blocks in the center of the table.

2. The first player takes a block and puts it down to start a train.

3. The next player chooses a block that is different from the first block. The second block should be different in *only one* way—in shape, size, or color. The second player adds that block to the train.

4. Players continue taking turns until no more blocks can be played.

small red circle	small red **triangle**	small **yellow** triangle	**large** yellow triangle	large **blue** triangle

Game 2

1. Share the blocks equally among all of the players in the group.

2. The first player begins the train by laying down a block.

3. The next player adds a block that is different in only one way.

4. Players take turns.

5. Any player who does not have a block that is different in only one way loses that turn.

6. Continue until no more blocks can be played.

7. The player with the fewest number of blocks left wins.

Copyright © SRA/McGraw-Hill

Use with Lesson 7.2.

Hit the Target

Round 1

Target Number: _____

Starting Number	Change	Result	Change	Result	Change	Result

Round 2

Target Number: _____

Starting Number	Change	Result	Change	Result	Change	Result

Round 3

Target Number: _____

Starting Number	Change	Result	Change	Result	Change	Result

Round 4

Target Number: _____

Starting Number	Change	Result	Change	Result	Change	Result

Copyright © SRA/McGraw–Hill

Use with Lesson 7.3.

Basketball Addition

	Points Scored			
	Team 1		Team 2	
	1st Half	2nd Half	1st Half	2nd Half
Player 1				
Player 2				
Player 3				
Player 4				
Player 5				
Team Score				

Point Totals	**1st Half**	**2nd Half**	**Final**
Team 1	_____	_____	_____
Team 2	_____	_____	_____

1. Which team won the first half? _____

By how much? _____ points

2. Which team won the second half? _____

By how much? _____ points

3. Which team won the game? _____

By how much? _____ points

Copyright © SRA/McGraw-Hill

Basketball Scoreboard

	Points Scored			
	Team 1		Team 2	
	1st Half	2nd Half	1st Half	2nd Half
Player 1				
Player 2				
Player 3				
Player 4				
Player 5				
Team Score				

Final Score _____   _____

Copyright © SRA/McGraw-Hill

Use with Lesson 7.4.

Measuring Weight with a Bath Scale

1. Place books on a bath scale. Try to make a stack of books that weighs about 5 pounds. Lift the stack of books and feel the weight of that stack.

2. Start again. Make a stack of books that weighs about 10 pounds. Then lift the stack and feel the weight.

3. Start again. Make a stack of books that weighs about 15 pounds. Then lift the stack and feel the weight.

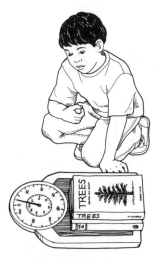

Make a 5-pound stack of books.

Make a 10-pound stack of books.

Make a 15-pound stack of books.

4. Make a stack of books on the floor. Estimate how much your stack weighs. Weigh the stack and see how close your estimate was.

5. Repeat with other stacks of books that are different sizes.

   Are you getting better at estimating weight?

Copyright © SRA/McGraw-Hill

Sharing Money

Work in a small group.

Materials   ❑ $5 bill, $1 bills, quarters, dimes, nickels, pennies

                 ❑ half-sheets of paper

At school, 4 children found an envelope. Inside was a $5 bill. They took the envelope to the principal. A week went by and nobody claimed it. The principal returned the money to the children and said that it now belonged to them.

How would you divide $5 so that each of the children gets the same amount of money?

1. First, think about what you could do.

   • How could you begin?

   • What could you do next?

2. After you have divided the money, count each person's share. Did each one get the same amount?

3. Write a group report or make a drawing. Tell how you divided the $5 equally among the 4 children.

Follow-Up

• Make up your own problems for dividing an amount of money equally among 4 or 5 children.

• Write some of your problems on half-sheets of paper for others to solve.

Copyright © SRA/McGraw-Hill

Use with Lesson 7.6.

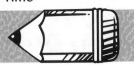

Two-Block Patterns

Work on your own or with a partner.

Materials ☐ Pattern-Block Template

☐ pattern blocks

1. Choose two different pattern-block shapes.

2. Explore. Try to make a pattern using just these two shapes.

- Do not leave any open spaces in your pattern.

- Make the pattern so that it covers about a quarter of a sheet of paper.

- Make the pattern so that you could continue it forever if you had enough blocks.

3. Use your Pattern-Block Template and crayons to record your pattern on a quarter-sheet of paper.

   Example

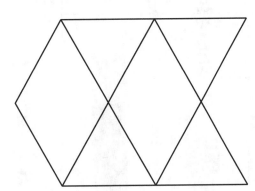

4. If there is time, explore with two other different pattern blocks.

Copyright © SRA/McGraw-Hill

Amazing Leaps

Amazing Leaps

Gray kangaroo	about 44 ft
Human	Running long jump record: 29 ft 4 $\frac{1}{2}$ in. Standing long jump record: 12 ft 2 $\frac{1}{4}$ in.
Goliath frog	about 9 ft
Jumping mouse	about 12 ft
Flea	about 1 ft 1 in.
Tree frog	about 3 ft

Feet: 0　5　10　15　20　25　30　35　40　45　50

Copyright © SRA/McGraw-Hill

Use with Lesson 7.7.

Finding the Median

List the data in order from smallest to largest.

Bob: 48 years old	Amy: 61 years old	Peter: 50 years old	Kathy: 38 years old

_____ years   _____ years   _____ years   _____ years

smallest   **largest**

What is the median? _____

Use with Lesson 7.9.

135

Copyright © SRA/McGraw-Hill

Finding the Median

List the data in order from smallest to largest.

Bob: 48 years old	Amy: 61 years old	Peter: 50 years old	Kathy: 38 years old

_____ years   _____ years   _____ years   _____ years

smallest   **largest**

What is the median? _____

Use with Lesson 7.9.

135

Copyright © SRA/McGraw-Hill

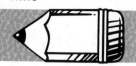

Table of Our Arm Spans

Make a table of the arm spans of your classmates.

Our Arm Spans

Arm Span (inches)	Frequency	
	Tallies	Number
	Total =	

Copyright © SRA/McGraw-Hill

Use with Lesson 7.9.

Bar Graph of Our Arm Spans

Make a bar graph of the arm spans of your classmates.

Our Arm Spans

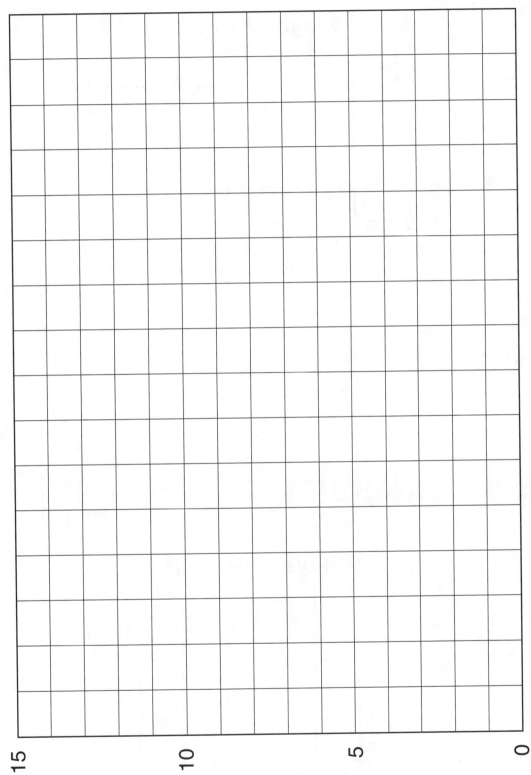

Number of Children

15   10   5   0

Arm Span (inches)

Copyright © SRA/McGraw-Hill

Use with Lesson 7.9.

137

Plotting Data on a Bar Graph

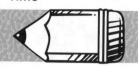

Players' Heights

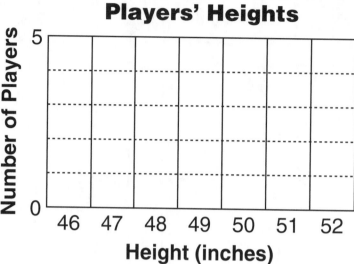

Copyright © SRA/McGraw-Hill

Use with Lesson 7.10.

Plotting Data on a Bar Graph

Players' Heights

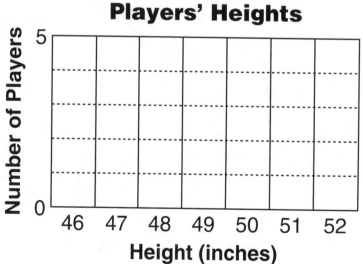

Copyright © SRA/McGraw-Hill

Use with Lesson 7.10.

Equal Parts

Do the following for each problem:

- Make the shape on a geoboard.

- Divide the shape into equal parts.

- Show how you did it on the dot paper.

1. Use 1 rubber band to make the square shown at the right. Then use several rubber bands to divide it into 8 equal parts.

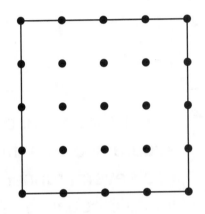

2. Divide the square into 8 equal parts in a different way.

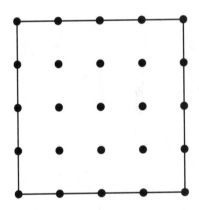

3. Use 1 rubber band to make the shape shown at the right. Then use several rubber bands to divide it into 4 equal parts.

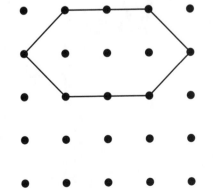

Copyright © SRA/McGraw-Hill

Equal Parts (cont.)

Challenge

4. Try to divide the shape into
6 equal parts.

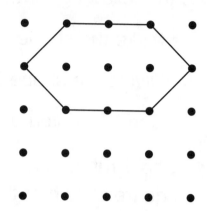

5. Use 1 rubber band to make the
square shown at the right. Then
use several rubber bands to divide
it into 6 equal parts.

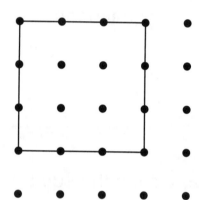

Copyright © SRA/McGraw–Hill

Use with Lesson 8.1.

Pattern-Block Fractions

Work with a partner.

Materials
- ❑ *Math Journal 2*, pp. 191 and 192
- ❑ pattern blocks
- ❑ straightedge or Pattern-Block Template

Study the example at the top of journal page 191. Cover the ⬠ with △s.

You need 3 triangles, so a △ is $\frac{1}{3}$ of a ⬠.

1. Do Problem 1 on journal page 191.

   Cover the larger shape with hexagon blocks.

   The number of hexagons helps you find the fraction to write as the answer.

   Use your straightedge or Pattern-Block Template to divide the larger shape into hexagons.

2. Do the rest of the problems on journal pages 191 and 192 in the same way.

3. Get together with other partners in the class. Check one another's work.

   Each smaller shape on page 191 is $\frac{1}{3}$ of the larger shape.

   Are the smaller shapes all the same size? _____

   Each smaller shape on page 192 is $\frac{1}{4}$ of the larger shape.

   Are the smaller shapes all the same size? _____

Copyright © SRA/McGraw-Hill

Use in Lesson 8.2.

Geoboard Fences

Work in a small group.

Materials   ❑ *Math Journal 2*, p. 193   ❑ geoboard

❑ 4 rubber bands   ❑ straightedge

Each group member does Steps 1–6:

1. Make a rectangle on a geoboard. Use 1 rubber band. Think of the rubber band as a fence.

2. Draw your rectangle (fence) on geoboard 1 on journal page 193.

3. Count the number of pegs inside your rectangle (fence). Include the pegs that touch the rubber band.

4. Fill in the table at the bottom of the journal page. Include

   • the number of pegs inside the fence.

   • the number of rows of pegs inside the fence.

   • the number of pegs in each row.

5. Make 3 more rectangles (fences) on your geoboard. Draw each rectangle (fence) on the journal page.

6. Fill in the table for your other three fences.

Follow-Up

Compare your table to those of the other members of your group.

Do any members of your group have the same total number of pegs inside a fence (but with a different number of rows)? What else is different? Can you tell why this happened?

Copyright © SRA/McGraw-Hill

Use in Lesson 8.2.

Volumes of Base-10 Structures

Work in a group.

Materials
- ☐ base-10 blocks: cubes, longs, flats; a big cube (thousands), if available
- ☐ slate for each person

1. Two group members use the blocks to build a structure. They should work quickly so that others can have a turn later.

2. Each small cube has a volume of 1 cubic centimeter.

Each group member writes an estimate of the total number of cubes (cubic centimeters) in the structure on her or his slate.

3. Together, count the cubes as the builders take the structure apart.

The total number of cubes equals the **volume** of the structure in **cubic centimeters.**

Record the result like this:

"This structure has a volume of _____ cubic centimeters."

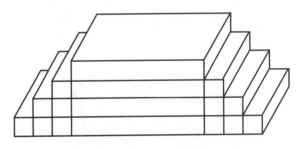

This structure has a volume of 520 cubic centimeters.

4. Compare the actual number of cubes to the estimates of the group members.

5. Change builders. Repeat Steps 1–4. Continue until everyone has had a turn. As you build the structures, think of ways to improve your estimates.

6. Write a group report about your estimates and the actual volumes of the structures.

Copyright © SRA/McGraw-Hill

Fraction Circles

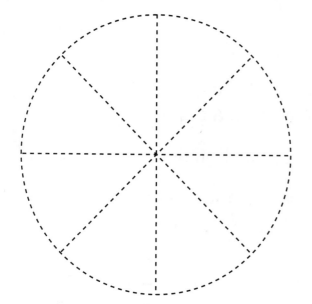

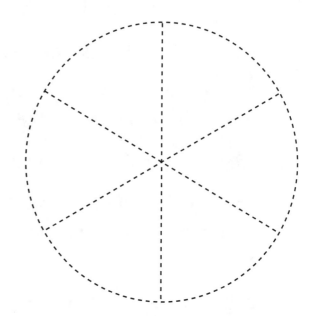

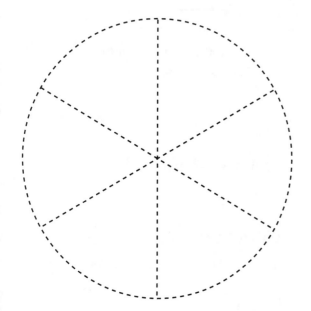

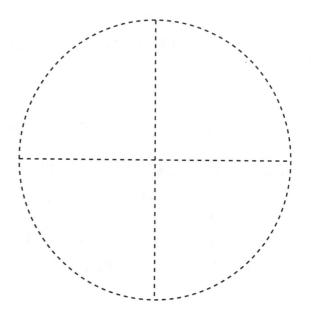

Copyright © SRA/McGraw–Hill

Use with Lesson 8.4.

A Foot and a Decimeter

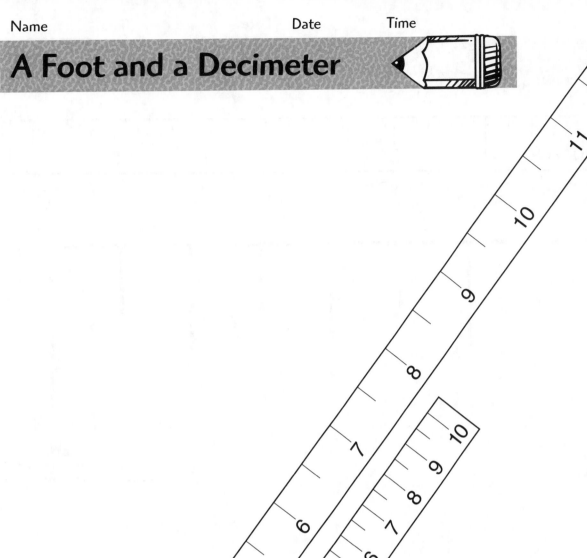

Copyright © SRA/McGraw-Hill

Use with Lesson 9.2.

An Inch

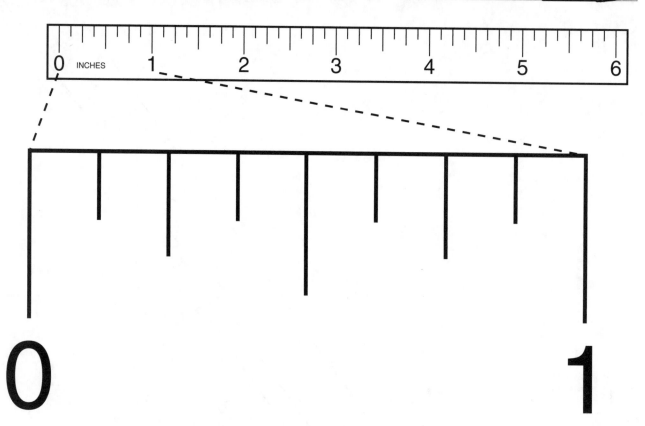

Copyright © SRA/McGraw-Hill

Use with Lesson 9.3.

Name   Date   Time

A Centimeter

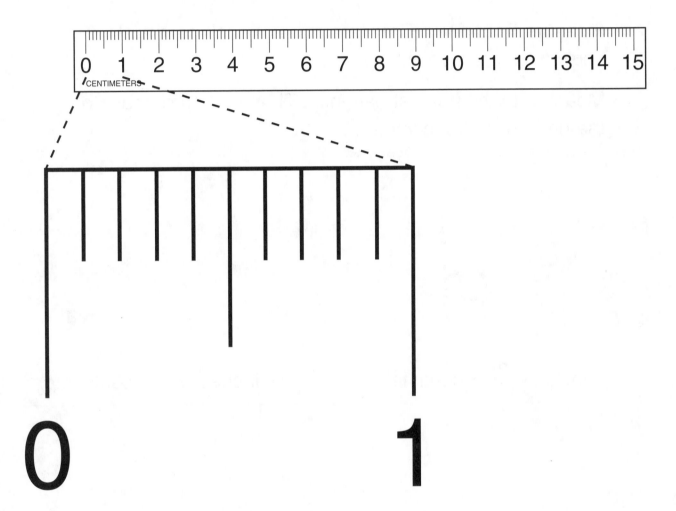

Copyright © SRA/McGraw-Hill

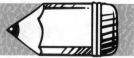

Measures around the Classroom

Materials   ☐ tape measure

Directions

- Measure five things. Draw a picture of each item and show which part you measured.

- Measure to the nearest half-inch. Then measure again to the nearest half-centimeter.

Example 	**1.**
__14__ inches __35½__ centimeters	_____ inches _____ centimeters
2.	**3.**
_____ inches _____ centimeters	_____ inches _____ centimeters
4.	**5.**
_____ inches _____ centimeters	_____ inches _____ centimeters

Copyright © SRA/McGraw-Hill

Metric Units of Linear Measure

Work with 1 or 2 people.

Materials   ☐ tape measures

☐ metersticks

☐ string or ribbon from your teacher

Directions

1. Check your measuring tools. Look for these units:

• 1 meter (100 centimeters)

• decimeters (10 centimeters each)

If the units are hard to see, mark them with a crayon.

2. Measure the string or ribbon you get from your teacher. Measure it 3 times.

Use meters the first time you measure. Use decimeters the next time. Use centimeters the last time.

_____ meters

_____ decimeters

_____ centimeters

Copyright © SRA/McGraw–Hill

Metric Units (cont.)

3. Choose a different item to measure. *For example:*

- the width of a door, the classroom, or a window

- the length of someone's arm or leg

- the length and width of a rug, a table, or the hall

Measure the item 3 times. Use meters the first time you measure, decimeters the next time, and centimeters the last time.

_____ meters

_____ decimeters

_____ centimeters

4. Talk about the measurements in Problems 2 and 3. Can anyone see any patterns among the 3 measurements? Is the measure in centimeters about 10 times the measure in decimeters? About 100 times the measure in meters?

5. Name some things that would best be measured in …

a. meters _____

b. centimeters _____

c. decimeters _____

Copyright © SRA/McGraw-Hill

Thumb and Wrist Measurements

Name _____

Work with a partner.

Measure, to the nearest centimeter, the distance around:

your thumb   **your wrist**

_____   _____
centimeters   centimeters

Name _____

Work with a partner.

Measure, to the nearest centimeter, the distance around:

your thumb   **your wrist**

_____   _____
centimeters   centimeters

Name _____

Work with a partner.

Measure, to the nearest centimeter, the distance around:

your thumb   **your wrist**

_____   _____
centimeters   centimeters

Name _____

Work with a partner.

Measure, to the nearest centimeter, the distance around:

your thumb   **your wrist**

_____   _____
centimeters   centimeters

Copyright © SRA/McGraw-Hill

Measuring Perimeter in Paces

Your teacher will put two lines of tape on the floor that are 18 feet apart.

1. Start with your toes on one line. Count the number of paces you take to reach the other line. Each time your foot hits the floor counts as 1 pace.

Number of paces: _____

2. Use this table to find out how long your pace is.

Number of Steps Taken	Length of Your Pace Is About ...
15 or more	1 foot
11 to 14	$1\frac{1}{2}$ feet
8 to 10	2 feet
7	$2\frac{1}{2}$ feet
6	3 feet

The length of my pace is about _____ feet.

Use with Lesson 9.4.

Copyright © SRA/McGraw-Hill

Measuring Perimeter in Paces (cont.)

3. Mr. Dean's garden is square.
Each side is 30 feet long.

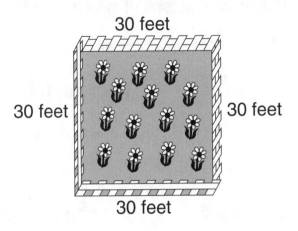

30 feet

30 feet   30 feet

30 feet

a. How many paces would
you take to walk along
one side of the garden?

_____ paces

b. How many paces would
you take to walk around
the whole garden?

_____ paces

c. The perimeter of the garden is _____ feet.

d. The perimeter of the garden is _____ of my paces.

Copyright © SRA/McGraw–Hill

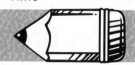

Which Cylinder Holds More?

Work with a small group.

Materials
- ❏ *Math Journal 2,* p. 228
- ❏ rulers; masking tape; macaroni
- ❏ pieces of cardboard
- ❏ 2 sheets of $8\frac{1}{2}$" × 11" construction paper
- ❏ 2 same-size sheets of construction paper (not $8\frac{1}{2}$" × 11")

Directions

1. Draw a line 1 inch from a long edge on one construction paper rectangle.

   - Roll the rectangle into a long cylinder and tape the paper along the line.

   - Then tape the cylinder to a piece of cardboard.

2. Draw a line 1 inch from a short edge on the other rectangle.

   - Roll the rectangle into a short cylinder and tape the paper along the line.

   - Then tape the cylinder to a piece of cardboard.

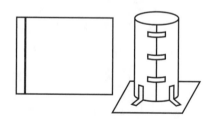

Copyright © SRA/McGraw-Hill

Which Cylinder Holds More? (cont.)

3. Talk about these questions with your group.

- Suppose that you fill both containers with macaroni. Will one of the cylinders hold more macaroni than the other?

- If so, which one? Why? Record your prediction on journal page 228.

4. Find out. Fill the tall cylinder with macaroni.

Then carefully pour the macaroni from the tall cylinder into the short cylinder.

Record what happened on journal page 228.

5. Make another pair of cylinders. Use two paper rectangles that are the same size. The rectangles should be a different size from the ones you used in Steps 1 and 2. Repeat Steps 1–4.

Follow-Up

Plan how to make two cylinders that will hold about the same amount of macaroni. Try your plan. Record the results.

Copyright © SRA/McGraw-Hill

Measuring Area

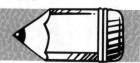

Work in a small group.

Materials

- ☐ centimeter grid paper

- ☐ inch grid paper

- ☐ Everything Math Deck, if available

- ☐ for tracing: slate, Pattern-Block Template, crayon box, and other objects

- ☐ *Math Journal 2*, p. 228

Directions

1. Place the deck of cards on the centimeter grid paper.

   Trace around the deck. The tracing shows the border of the deck.

2. Count the squares that cover the space inside the border.

   - If more than half of a square is inside the border, count the whole square.

   - If less than half of a square is inside the border, do not count the square at all.

3. The amount of space inside the border is called the **area.**

   The number of squares you counted is a measurement of the area in **square centimeters.**

Copyright © SRA/McGraw-Hill

Use with Lesson 9.7.

Measuring Area (cont.)

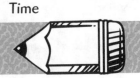

4. Repeat Steps 1 and 2 using inch grid paper.

5. Find the area of four or five more objects.

You might trace things like …

- a Pattern-Block Template

- pattern blocks

- a crayon box

- objects from the Measures All Around Museum

6. Record the areas you measured on journal page 228.

Follow-Up

Work together as a group. Explain why your results are estimates and not exact measurements. How are the units used to measure area different from those used to measure perimeter?

Copyright © SRA/McGraw-Hill

Inch Grid Paper

Copyright © SRA/McGraw–Hill

Use with Lesson 9.7.

Build a Wall

Materials ☐ pattern blocks

☐ Pattern-Block Template

☐ sheet of paper

☐ crayons or coloring pencils

Directions

1. Make a wall with pattern blocks. Make your wall as high as you can. Here is one idea:

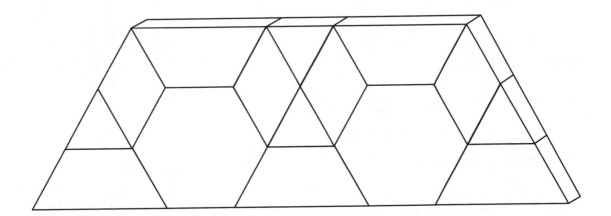

2. Draw your wall on your paper. Use your Pattern-Block Template.

3. Color the shapes to match the blocks.

Follow-Up

Look at the walls made by other children in your class.

How many different pattern-block shapes were used in each wall?

Were all of the shapes used? Which were not used? Why not?

Copyright © SRA/McGraw-Hill

Use with Lesson 9.7.

Measuring Capacity

Materials
- ❑ half-gallon container
- ❑ tape
- ❑ measuring cup
- ❑ water

1. Make a measuring container.

- Attach a piece of tape from the bottom to the top of an empty half-gallon container.

- Fill a measuring cup with a half-cup of water.

- Pour the water into the container. Do all of your pouring on a tray to catch the drips.

- Mark the tape to show how high the water is inside the container.

- Write $\frac{1}{2}$ **c** next to the mark.

- Pour another half-cup of water into the container.

- Mark the tape and write **1 c** next to the mark.

- Continue. Mark the tape $1\frac{1}{2}$ **c** to show 3 half-cups, **2 c** for 4 half-cups, and so on. Fill the container.

- Pour the water back into the pitcher.

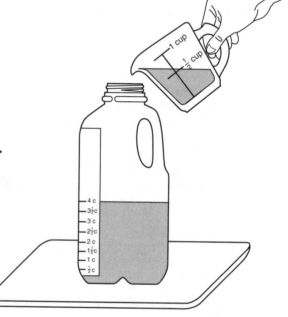

Copyright © SRA/McGraw-Hill

Use with Lesson 9.9.

Measuring Capacity (cont.)

2. In the first column of the table below, write the names or draw pictures of several containers in the Measures All Around Museum. In the second column, estimate the capacity of each container.

Container (description or picture)	Estimated Capacity	Measured Capacity
	_____ C	_____ C
	_____ C	_____ C
	_____ C	_____ C
	_____ C	_____ C

3. Measure the capacity of each container.

- Fill the container with water.

- Pour the water into your measuring container.

- See how high the water is on the tape. Write the number of the nearest mark in the third column above.

- Pour the water back into the pitcher.

Copyright © SRA/McGraw–Hill

Use with Lesson 9.9.

Fish Poster

Fish A
1 lb
12 in.

Fish B
3 lb
14 in.

Fish C
4 lb
18 in.

Fish D
5 lb
24 in.

Fish E
6 lb
24 in.

Fish F
8 lb
30 in.

Fish G
10 lb
30 in.

Fish H
14 lb
30 in.

Fish I
15 lb
30 in.

Fish J
24 lb
36 in.

Fish K
35 lb
42 in.

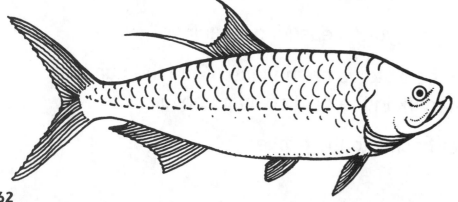

Fish L
100 lb
72 in.

Copyright © SRA/McGraw-Hill

Use with Lesson 9.11.

Good Buys Poster

Fruit/Vegetables Group

Seedless Grapes
99¢ lb

Carrots
1-lb bag
3/$1.00

Plums
69¢ lb

Oranges
$1.49 lb

Bananas
59¢ lb

Watermelons
$2.99 ea.

Celery
59¢ lb

Meat Group

U.S.D.A. Choice Fresh
Ground Beef
$1.99 lb

Peanut Butter
18-oz jar
$1.29

Chunk Light
Tuna
6.5 oz
69¢

Lunch Meat
1-lb package
$1.39

Milk Group

Gallon
Milk
$2.39

American
Cheese
8 oz
$1.49

6-pack
Yogurt
$2.09

Grain Group

Wheat Bread
16 oz
99¢

Potato Chips
8 oz
89¢

Pork & Beans
16 oz
2/89¢

Saltines
1 lb
69¢

Hamburger
Buns
16 oz
69¢

Miscellaneous Items

Mayonnaise
32 oz
$1.99

Catsup
32 oz
$1.09

Grape Jelly
2-lb jar
$1.69

Copyright © SRA/McGraw-Hill

Name-Collection Boxes

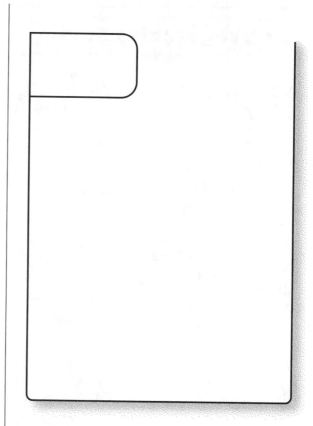

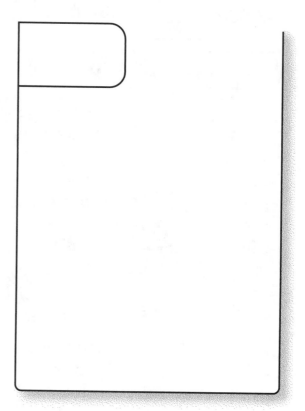

Copyright © SRA/McGraw–Hill

Use with Lesson 10.1.

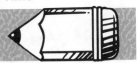

Many-Name Scramble

Cut out the names of ![dollar bill], ![dime], and ![penny] from *Math Masters,*

page 166. Then paste them in the proper columns below.

![one dollar bill]	![dime]	![penny]

Copyright © SRA/McGraw–Hill

Use with Lesson 10.2.

Many-Name Scramble (cont.)

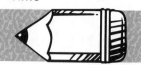

$1.00	$\frac{1}{100}$ of a dollar
$0.01	100 pennies
a dollar	10 dimes
one-tenth of a dollar	$\frac{1}{10}$ of a dollar
10¢	one-hundredth of a dollar
a dime	1¢
$0.10	a penny

Copyright © SRA/McGraw-Hill

Use with Lesson 10.2.

10 × 5 Grid

Paste/tape to here to create a 10 × 10 grid.

Copyright © SRA/McGraw-Hill

Use with Lesson 10.2.

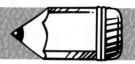

Pick-a-Coin Record Tables

If you wish, cut apart the 3 tables.

	Ⓟ	Ⓝ	Ⓓ	Ⓠ	$1	Total
1st turn						$____ . ____
2nd turn						$____ . ____
3rd turn						$____ . ____
4th turn						$____ . ____
				Grand Total		$____ . ____

	Ⓟ	Ⓝ	Ⓓ	Ⓠ	$1	Total
1st turn						$____ . ____
2nd turn						$____ . ____
3rd turn						$____ . ____
4th turn						$____ . ____
				Grand Total		$____ . ____

	Ⓟ	Ⓝ	Ⓓ	Ⓠ	$1	Total
1st turn						$____ . ____
2nd turn						$____ . ____
3rd turn						$____ . ____
4th turn						$____ . ____
				Grand Total		$____ . ____

Copyright © SRA/McGraw-Hill

Use with Lesson 10.3.

Then-and-Now Poster

Now

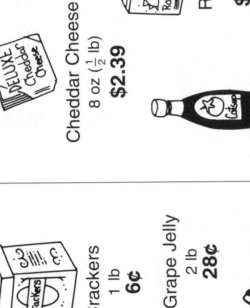

Crackers
1 lb
$1.38

Grape Jelly
2 lb
$2.08

Raisins
1 lb
$2.29

Cheddar Cheese
8 oz ($\frac{1}{2}$ lb)
$2.39

Catsup
32 oz/1 qt
$1.77

20-Inch Girl's Bicycle
$119.99

Harmonica
Ten Double Holes
$17.50

Child's Wagon
Medium Size—15$\frac{1}{2}$" × 34"
$47.99

1897

Crackers
1 lb
6¢

Grape Jelly
2 lb
28¢

Cheddar Cheese
$\frac{1}{2}$ lb
6¢

Raisins
1 lb
10¢

Catsup
32 oz/1 qt
25¢

20-Inch Girl's Bicycle
$29.00

Harmonica
Ten Double Holes
45¢

Child's Wagon
Large Size—15" × 30"
$1.65

Copyright © SRA/McGraw-Hill

Shopping at the Classroom Store

Choose items to buy from the Classroom Store. For each purchase:

- Record the items on the sales slip.

- Write the price of each item on the sales slip.

- Estimate the total cost and record it.

- Find the total cost and write it on the sales slip.

Purchase 1   **Classroom Store**

Items:

_____ $__ . _____

_____ $__ . _____   Estimated cost:

           Total: $__ . _____   about $_____

Purchase 2   **Classroom Store**

Items:

_____ $__ . _____

_____ $__ . _____   Estimated cost:

           Total: $__ . _____   about $_____

Purchase 3   **Classroom Store**

Items:

_____ $__ . _____

_____ $__ . _____   Estimated cost:

           Total: $__ . _____   about $_____

Copyright © SRA/McGraw-Hill

Math Message

Name: _____

Write in decimal notation:

1. 29 cents = $_____

2. 59¢ = $_____

3. 9 cents = $_____

4. a dollar forty-seven

    = $_____

5. 10 dollars and 2 cents

    = $_____

6. nine hundred thirty-three
    dollars and thirty cents

    = $_____

Challenge

7. three thousand five hundred
    forty-six dollars and
    sixteen cents

    = $_____

Name: _____

Write in decimal notation:

1. 29 cents = $_____

2. 59¢ = $_____

3. 9 cents = $_____

4. a dollar forty-seven

    = $_____

5. 10 dollars and 2 cents

    = $_____

6. nine hundred thirty-three
    dollars and thirty cents

    = $_____

Challenge

7. three thousand five hundred
    forty-six dollars and
    sixteen cents

    = $_____

Copyright © SRA/McGraw-Hill

Math Message

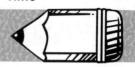

Name: _____

Count squares to find the area of each shaded figure.

1. 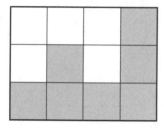 _____ square centimeters

2. 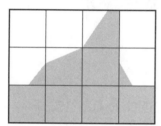 _____ sq cm

Name: _____

Count squares to find the area of each shaded figure.

1. 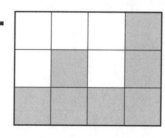 _____ square centimeters

2. 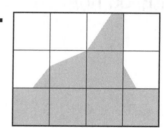 _____ sq cm

---

Name: _____

Count squares to find the area of each shaded figure.

1. 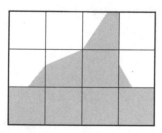 _____ square centimeters

2. 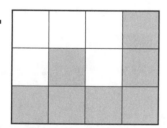 _____ sq cm

Name: _____

Count squares to find the area of each shaded figure.

1. 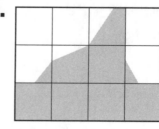 _____ square centimeters

2. 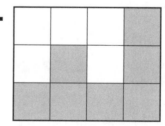 _____ sq cm

Copyright © SRA/McGraw–Hill

Use with Lesson 10.7.

My Handprint and Footprint Areas

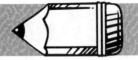

Work with a partner.

1. Trace your partner's hand onto his or her journal page 257. When your hand is traced, keep your fingers close together.

2. Count the number of whole square centimeters inside your handprint.

   • If more than half of a square centimeter is inside your handprint, count the whole square.

   • If less than half of a square centimeter is inside your handprint, do not count the square.

3. Record the area of your handprint at the bottom of that page.

4. Trace your partner's foot onto his or her journal page 258. (Keep your sock on your foot.)

5. Count to find the area of your footprint. Record the area of your footprint at the bottom of that page.

6. Exchange journals and check each other's counts. Count again if you don't agree with your partner.

Follow-Up

Work in a small group. Compare your hand to other group members'. Then compare your foot to others'. Predict the following:

   • Whose hand areas are about the same? Whose are larger? Smaller?

   • Whose foot areas are about the same? Larger? Smaller?

Compare your predictions to the areas you recorded.

Copyright © SRA/McGraw-Hill

Worktables

Work in a group.

Materials   ☐ trapezoid pattern blocks

☐ Pattern-Block Template (1 per person)

☐ *Math Journal 2,* p. 259

Pretend that each red trapezoid
pattern block is a small table.

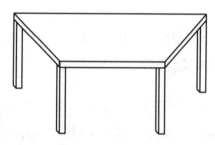

Your teacher wants to make larger
worktables by fitting these small tables
together.

Try each of the following problems. Use a Pattern-Block
Template to record the tables you make on journal page 259.

1. Make a worktable shaped like a hexagon.

2. Make a worktable shaped like a triangle.

3. Use more than 1 block to make a worktable
shaped like a trapezoid.

4. Make a worktable shaped like a parallelogram.

5. Make another parallelogram worktable that has
twice the area of the one you just made.

6. Make any other worktable shapes that you can with
the trapezoids.

Follow-Up

Compare your reports. Find all the different-size and
different-shape worktables your group made.

Copyright © SRA/McGraw-Hill

Use with Lesson 10.7.

Geoboard Fractions

Materials   ☐ geoboard   ☐ rubber bands

☐ *Math Journal 2,* p. 260

Work with a partner.

1. One partner makes a shape on the geoboard with one rubber band.

2. The other partner tries to divide the shape into equal parts using other rubber bands. The equal parts should be the same size and shape.

3. Take turns until each partner has made 3 shapes.

4. Record some of the shapes you divided on journal page 260. Show the equal parts.

5. Record some shapes on the journal page you could not divide into equal parts.

Work in a group.

6. Check one another's work.

7. Discuss these questions:

• Are shapes that can be divided equally special in some way?

• What about the shapes that cannot be divided equally?

Example

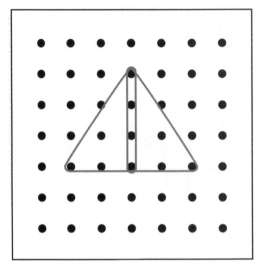

Copyright © SRA/McGraw–Hill

Place-Value Chart

Ten-Thousands	Thousands	Hundreds	Tens	Ones

Copyright © SRA/McGraw-Hill

         Use with Lesson 10.8.

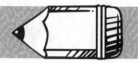

Place-Value Book

You will make a Place-Value Book that looks like the one below.

Place-Value Book

Tool-Kit Number _____

Ten-Thousands	Thousands	Hundreds	Tens	Ones

Cut out the pages of the Place-Value Book on *Math Masters*, pages 177–180. Cut on the dashed lines. Your teacher will show you how to make the book.

Place-Value Book

Tool-Kit Number _____

Page 1

Copyright © SRA/McGraw-Hill

Place-Value Book (cont.)

✂

Page 2

| 0 | 0 | 0 | 0 | 0 |

Page 3

| 1 | 1 | 1 | 1 | 1 |

Page 4

| 2 | 2 | 2 | 2 | 2 |

Page 5

| 3 | 3 | 3 | 3 | 3 |

Copyright © SRA/McGraw-Hill

　　　　　　　　　　　　　　　　Use with Lesson 10.9.

Place-Value Book (cont.)

Page 6

| 4 | 4 | 4 | 4 | 4 |

Page 7

| 5 | 5 | 5 | 5 | 5 |

Page 8

| 6 | 6 | 6 | 6 | 6 |

Page 9

| 7 | 7 | 7 | 7 | 7 |

Copyright © SRA/McGraw-Hill

Use with Lesson 10.9.

Place-Value Book (cont.)

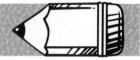

Page 10

8	8	8	8	8

Page 11

9	9	9	9	9

Page 12

Ten-Thousands	Thousands	Hundreds	Tens	Ones

Copyright © SRA/McGraw-Hill

Digit Cards

4	9
3	8
2	7
1	6
0	5

Copyright © SRA/McGraw-Hill

Place-Value Labels

Ten-Thousands	Ten-Thousands	Ten-Thousands
Thousands	Thousands	Thousands
Hundreds	Hundreds	Hundreds
Tens	Tens	Tens
Ones	Ones	Ones

Ten-Thousands	Ten-Thousands	Ten-Thousands
Thousands	Thousands	Thousands
Hundreds	Hundreds	Hundreds
Tens	Tens	Tens
Ones	Ones	Ones

Copyright © SRA/McGraw-Hill

Use with Lesson 10.9.

Place-Value Card Holder

Ones

Tens

Hundreds

Fold back on dotted line.

Thousands

Ten-Thousands

Copyright © SRA/McGraw-Hill

Use with Lesson 10.9.

Place-Value Book Cover

Page 1

Place-Value Book

Tool-Kit Number _____

Copyright © SRA/McGraw-Hill

Use with Lesson 10.9.

Place-Value Book 0–1

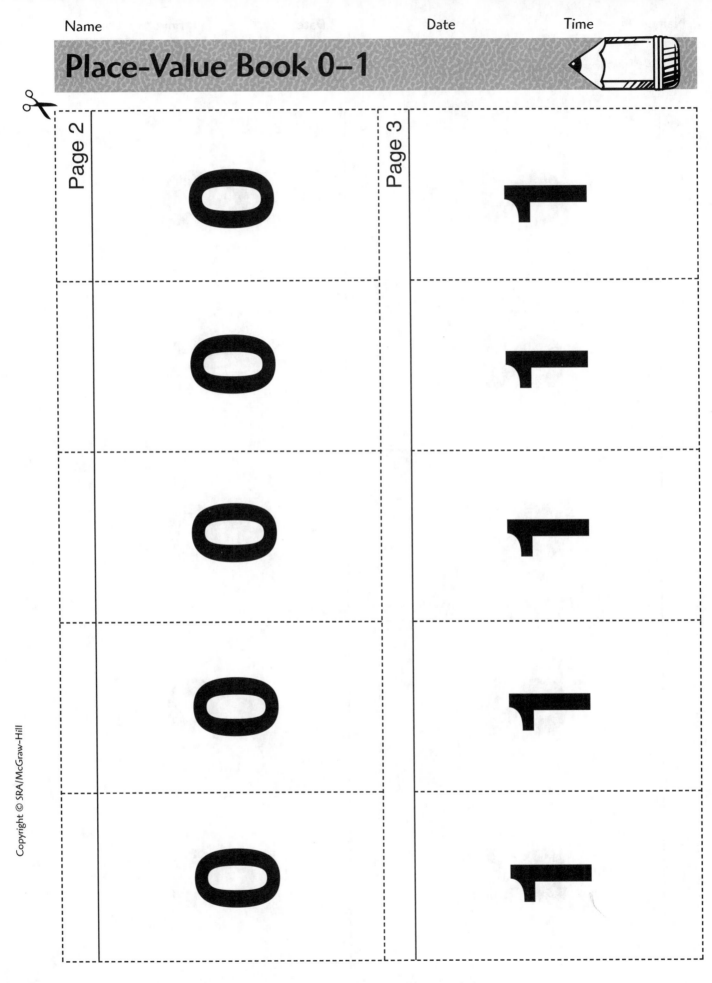

Page 2

Page 3

Copyright © SRA/McGraw–Hill

Use with Lesson 10.9.

Place-Value Book 2–3

Page 4

2 2

2 2

2

2 2

2 2

Page 5

3 3

3 3

3

3 3

3 3

Copyright © SRA/McGraw-Hill

Use with Lesson 10.9.

Place-Value Book 4–5

Page 6

4

4

4

4

4

Page 7

5

5

5

5

5

Copyright © SRA/McGraw-Hill

Use with Lesson 10.9.

Place-Value Book 6–7

Page 8

6

6

6

6

6

Page 9

7

7

7

7

7

Copyright © SRA/McGraw-Hill

Use with Lesson 10.9.

Place-Value Book 8–9

Page 10

8

8

8

8

8

Page 11

9

9

9

9

9

Copyright © SRA/McGraw–Hill

Use with Lesson 10.9.

Place Values for the Place-Value Book

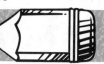

Page 12

Ten-Thousands	Thousands	Hundreds	Tens	Ones

Copyright © SRA/McGraw-Hill

Use with Lesson 10.9.

Copyright © SRA/McGraw–Hill

Name   Date   Time

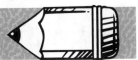

Areas of States

List the states in the table from largest area to smallest area.

State	Area (sq miles)
Arkansas	53,182
Florida	59,928
Georgia	58,977
Illinois	57,918
Iowa	56,276
New York	53,989

State	Area (sq miles)
largest:	
smallest:	

✂ -

Copyright © SRA/McGraw–Hill

Name   Date   Time

Areas of States

List the states in the table from largest area to smallest area.

State	Area (sq miles)
Arkansas	53,182
Florida	59,928
Georgia	58,977
Illinois	57,918
Iowa	56,276
New York	53,989

State	Area (sq miles)
largest:	
smallest:	

Use with Lesson 10.10.

Estimating Costs

Find the costs of 6 items that are sold in a supermarket. You might go to the supermarket, look at an ad in the newspaper, or find the items in your own home.

List the items and their costs. Estimate how many of each item you could buy with $3.00. Continue the chart on the back of this page.

Item	Cost per Item	Number of Items for $3.00
Loaf of Bread	$1.49	2

Copyright © SRA/McGraw-Hill

✂ -

Estimating Costs

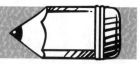

Find the costs of 6 items that are sold in a supermarket. You might go to the supermarket, look at an ad in the newspaper, or find the items in your own home.

List the items and their costs. Estimate how many of each item you could buy with $3.00. Continue the chart on the back of this page.

Item	Cost per Item	Number of Items for $3.00
Loaf of Bread	$1.49	2

Copyright © SRA/McGraw-Hill

Multiplication/Division Diagram

_____	_____ per _____	_____ in all

_____	_____ per _____	_____ in all

_____	_____ per _____	_____ in all

Copyright © SRA/McGraw-Hill

Use with Lesson 11.3.

Multiplication Draw

Materials ❏ number cards 1–5 and 10

❏ calculator (optional)

Players 2 to 4

Directions

1. Mix the cards. Place them facedown between the players.

2. Begin with the 1st Round (times-2 facts).

3. Each player …

- draws a card. This is a missing factor.

- writes this factor after "1st draw" in the 1st Round column on the next page.

- writes the product.

Example: A player …

- draws a 3.

- writes 3 in 2 × _____.

- solves 2 × __*3*__ = _____.

4. Players return their cards to the pile. Mix the cards and place them facedown.

5. Repeat Steps 3 and 4 for four more draws.

Copyright © SRA/McGraw-Hill

Use with Lesson 11.5.

Multiplication Draw (cont.)

6. After the 5th draw, players add their five products. They may use calculators.

7. The player with the largest sum wins the round.

8. Repeat the above steps for the 2nd Round (times-5 facts) and 3rd Round (times-10 facts).

	1st Round: 2s	**2nd Round: 5s**	**3rd Round: 10s**
1st draw	$2 \times \underline{\quad} = \underline{\quad}$	$5 \times \underline{\quad} = \underline{\quad}$	$10 \times \underline{\quad} = \underline{\quad}$
2nd draw	$\underline{\quad} \times 2 = \underline{\quad}$	$\underline{\quad} \times 5 = \underline{\quad}$	$\underline{\quad} \times 10 = \underline{\quad}$
3rd draw	$\underline{\quad} \times 2 = \underline{\quad}$	$\underline{\quad} \times 5 = \underline{\quad}$	$\underline{\quad} \times 10 = \underline{\quad}$
4th draw	$2 \times \underline{\quad} = \underline{\quad}$	$5 \times \underline{\quad} = \underline{\quad}$	$10 \times \underline{\quad} = \underline{\quad}$
5th draw	$\underline{\quad} \times 2 = \underline{\quad}$	$\underline{\quad} \times 5 = \underline{\quad}$	$\underline{\quad} \times 10 = \underline{\quad}$
Sum of products			

Copyright © SRA/McGraw-Hill

Use with Lesson 11.5.

Products Table

0×0 =**0**	0×1 =	0×2 =	0×3 =	0×4 =	0×5 =	0×6 =	0×7 =	0×8 =	0×9 =	0×10 =
1×0 =	1×1 =**1**	1×2 =	1×3 =	1×4 =	1×5 =	1×6 =	1×7 =	1×8 =	1×9 =	1×10 =
2×0 =	2×1 =	2×2 =**4**	2×3 =	2×4 =	2×5 =	2×6 =	2×7 =	2×8 =	2×9 =	2×10 =
3×0 =	3×1 =	3×2 =	3×3 =**9**	3×4 =	3×5 =	3×6 =	3×7 =	3×8 =	3×9 =	3×10 =
4×0 =	4×1 =	4×2 =	4×3 =	4×4 =**16**	4×5 =	4×6 =	4×7 =	4×8 =	4×9 =	4×10 =
5×0 =	5×1 =	5×2 =	5×3 =	5×4 =	5×5 =**25**	5×6 =	5×7 =	5×8 =	5×9 =	5×10 =
6×0 =	6×1 =	6×2 =	6×3 =	6×4 =	6×5 =	6×6 =**36**	6×7 =	6×8 =	6×9 =	6×10 =
7×0 =	7×1 =	7×2 =	7×3 =	7×4 =	7×5 =	7×6 =	7×7 =**49**	7×8 =	7×9 =	7×10 =
8×0 =	8×1 =	8×2 =	8×3 =	8×4 =	8×5 =	8×6 =	8×7 =	8×8 =**64**	8×9 =	8×10 =
9×0 =	9×1 =	9×2 =	9×3 =	9×4 =	9×5 =	9×6 =	9×7 =	9×8 =	9×9 =**81**	9×10 =
10×0 =	10×1 =	10×2 =	10×3 =	10×4 =	10×5 =	10×6 =	10×7 =	10×8 =	10×9 =	10×10 =**100**

Copyright © SRA/McGraw-Hill

Square Products

Work in a small group.

Materials   ❑ centimeter grid paper (*Math Masters,* p. 86)

                ❑ centimeter cubes or pennies (or both)

                ❑ tape

Directions

1. Each person chooses a different number from 2 to 10.

2. Build an array that shows your number multiplied by itself.
Use pennies or centimeter cubes.

3. Draw each array on centimeter grid paper.
Write a number model under each array.

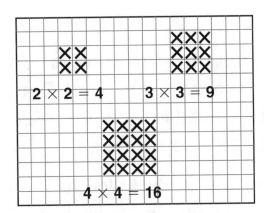

Copyright © SRA/McGraw–Hill

Square Products (cont.)

4. Make and record a few more arrays. On a blank sheet of paper, make a table like the one below. Begin with the smallest factors. Record them in order: 2 × 2, 3 × 3, 4 × 4, and so on.

Array (factors)	Total (products)
2 × 2	4
3 × 3	9
4 × 4	16

5. Continue working together. Build arrays with cubes or pennies for larger and larger numbers. Draw the arrays on grid paper. You may need to tape pieces of grid paper together for the larger arrays.

6. Record the factors and products for the larger numbers in your table. Look for number patterns in the list of products.

Copyright © SRA/McGraw-Hill

Use with Lesson 11.6.

×,÷ Fact Triangle

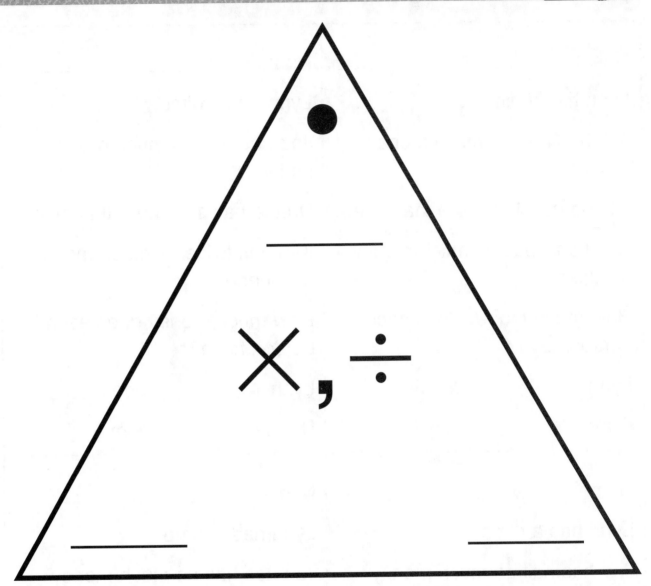

Copyright © SRA/McGraw–Hill

Use with Lesson 11.7.

Math Message

Name _____

Lynn has a dime.

Joe has half as much money as Lynn.

Duane has 15¢ more than Joe.

Kim has twice as much money as Duane.

How much money does each person have?

Lynn $_____   Joe $_____

Duane $_____   Kim $_____

Name _____

Lynn has a dime.

Joe has half as much money as Lynn.

Duane has 15¢ more than Joe.

Kim has twice as much money as Duane.

How much money does each person have?

Lynn $_____   Joe $_____

Duane $_____   Kim $_____

Name _____

Lynn has a dime.

Joe has half as much money as Lynn.

Duane has 15¢ more than Joe.

Kim has twice as much money as Duane.

How much money does each person have?

Lynn $_____   Joe $_____

Duane $_____   Kim $_____

Name _____

Lynn has a dime.

Joe has half as much money as Lynn.

Duane has 15¢ more than Joe.

Kim has twice as much money as Duane.

How much money does each person have?

Lynn $_____   Joe $_____

Duane $_____   Kim $_____

Use with Lesson 11.9.

Copyright © SRA/McGraw-Hill

Museum Store Poster

$0.72 Elephant

$1.86 Kite

$0.27 Plane

$1.39 Magnet

$0.30 Pen

$0.18 Ring

$0.48 Shell

Dinosaur $0.59

$0.75 Number Puzzle

Copyright © SRA/McGraw–Hill

Use with Lesson 11.10.

Math Message

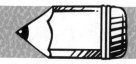

Name _____

Math Message

There are:

_____ months in 1 year.

_____ weeks in 1 year.

_____ days in 1 week.

_____ hours in 1 day.

_____ minutes in 1 hour.

_____ seconds in 1 minute.

Name _____

Math Message

There are:

_____ months in 1 year.

_____ weeks in 1 year.

_____ days in 1 week.

_____ hours in 1 day.

_____ minutes in 1 hour.

_____ seconds in 1 minute.

Name _____

Math Message

There are:

_____ months in 1 year.

_____ weeks in 1 year.

_____ days in 1 week.

_____ hours in 1 day.

_____ minutes in 1 hour.

_____ seconds in 1 minute.

Name _____

Math Message

There are:

_____ months in 1 year.

_____ weeks in 1 year.

_____ days in 1 week.

_____ hours in 1 day.

_____ minutes in 1 hour.

_____ seconds in 1 minute.

Copyright © SRA/McGraw-Hill

Use with Lesson 12.1.

Review: Telling Time

1. How many hours do clock faces show? _____ hours

2. How long does it take the hour hand to move from one
number to the next? _____

3. How long does it take the minute hand to move from one
number to the next? _____

4. How many times does the hour hand move around the
clock face in one day? _____ times

5. How many times does the minute hand move around the
clock face in one day? _____ times

Write the time shown by each clock.

6.    **7.**    **8.**

_____:_____   _____:_____   _____:_____

Draw the hour and minute hands to match the time.

9.    **10.** 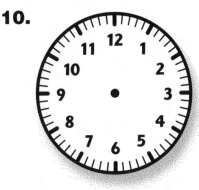   **11.**

8:00   6:45   4:10

Copyright © SRA/McGraw-Hill

Name _____   Date _____   Time _____

Blank Calendar Grid

Month _____

Sunday	Monday	Tuesday	Wednesday	Thursday	Friday	Saturday

Copyright © SRA/McGraw-Hill

Use with Lesson 12.1.

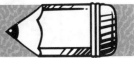

Telling Time to 5 Minutes

Write the time shown on each clock.

1.

_____ : _____

2.

_____ : _____

3.

_____ : _____

4.

_____ : _____

5.

_____ : _____

6.

_____ : _____

Draw the hour and minute hands to match the time.

7.

4:55

8.

7:25

9.

8:05

10.

1:50

11.

6:20

12.

10:40

Copyright © SRA/McGraw–Hill

Use with Lesson 12.2.

"Easier" Multiplication Facts

Name _____

2 × 4 = _____
3 × 5 = _____
2 × 2 = _____
4 × 3 = _____
5 × 5 = _____
6 × 2 = _____
6 × 5 = _____
3 × 3 = _____
4 × 5 = _____
3 × 6 = _____

7 × 3 = _____
5 × 2 = _____
6 × 4 = _____
2 × 7 = _____
3 × 2 = _____
4 × 4 = _____
4 × 0 = _____
4 × 7 = _____
7 × 5 = _____
0 × 2 = _____

Name _____

2 × 4 = _____
3 × 5 = _____
2 × 2 = _____
4 × 3 = _____
5 × 5 = _____
6 × 2 = _____
6 × 5 = _____
3 × 3 = _____
4 × 5 = _____
3 × 6 = _____

7 × 3 = _____
5 × 2 = _____
6 × 4 = _____
2 × 7 = _____
3 × 2 = _____
4 × 4 = _____
4 × 0 = _____
4 × 7 = _____
7 × 5 = _____
0 × 2 = _____

Copyright © SRA/McGraw-Hill

Use with Lesson 12.4.

Addition Card Draw

Materials   ❑ score sheet from *Math Masters,* p. 208

❑ 1 each of the number cards 0–20

❑ slate or scratch paper

Players   2

Directions

Shuffle the cards and place the deck with the numbers facing down. Take turns.

1. Draw the top 3 cards from the deck.

2. Record the numbers on the score sheet. Put the 3 cards in a separate pile.

3. Find the sum. Use your slate or paper to do the computation.

After 3 turns:

4. Check your partner's work. Use a calculator.

5. Find the total of the 3 answers. Write the total on the score sheet. The player with the higher total wins.

Copyright © SRA/McGraw–Hill

Addition Card Draw Score Sheet

Game 1

1st turn:

____ + ____ + ____ = ____

2nd turn:

____ + ____ + ____ = ____

3rd turn:

____ + ____ + ____ = ____

Total: _____

Game 2

1st turn:

____ + ____ + ____ = ____

2nd turn:

____ + ____ + ____ = ____

3rd turn:

____ + ____ + ____ = ____

Total: _____

Game 3

1st turn:

____ + ____ + ____ = ____

2nd turn:

____ + ____ + ____ = ____

3rd turn:

____ + ____ + ____ = ____

Total: _____

Game 4

1st turn:

____ + ____ + ____ = ____

2nd turn:

____ + ____ + ____ = ____

3rd turn:

____ + ____ + ____ = ____

Total: _____

Copyright © SRA/McGraw-Hill

Use with Lesson 12.5.

"What's My Rule?"

Complete the tables in Problems 1–3.

1.

Rule
×2

in	out
3	
5	
	14
8	
	12

2.

Rule
×10

in	out
2	
4	
	15
7	
	25

3.

Rule
×5

in	out
0	
3	
	50
8	
	100

Complete the table and write the rule.

Complete the table and write the rule.

Write a rule of your own. Fill in the table.

4.

Rule

in	out
1	2
2	4
	6
5	
8	16

5.

Rule

in	out
3	12
5	
2	8
6	24
	40

6.

Rule

in	out

Copyright © SRA/McGraw-Hill

Use with Lesson 12.5.

Coordinate Letters

1. Connect these points in order:

(1,1)

(1,6)

(3,4)

(5,6)

(5,1)

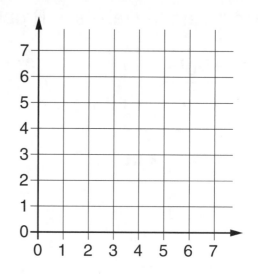

2. Connect these points in order:

(4,1)

(1,1)

(1,3)

(3,3)

(1,3)

(1,5)

(4,5)

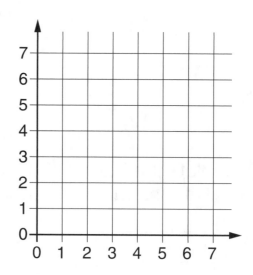

3. Make up points for another letter.
Trade with a partner.
Make your partner's letter.

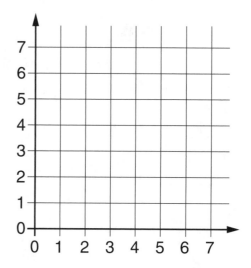

Copyright © SRA/McGraw-Hill

Use with Lesson 12.6.

Paper Thermometer

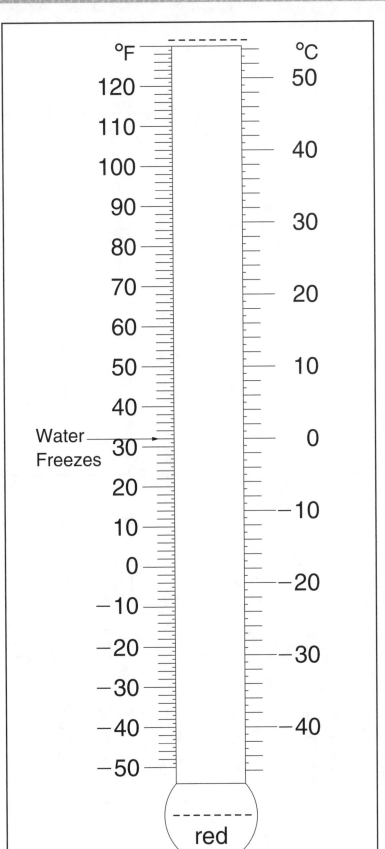

Color this red.

°F

120

110

100

90

80

70

60

50

40

Water Freezes 30

20

10

0

−10

−20

−30

−40

−50

°C

50

40

30

20

10

0

−10

−20

−30

−40

red

Leave this white

glue

Copyright © SRA/McGraw-Hill

A Week of Weather Observations

	Temp.	Cloud	Wind	Rain	Snow	Fog	Ice	Other
Monday Mon.	A.M. P.M.							
Tuesday Tues.	A.M. P.M.							
Wednesday Wed.	A.M. P.M.							
Thursday Thurs.	A.M. P.M.							
Friday Fri.	A.M. P.M.							
Totals	**A.M.** High ___ Low ___ **P.M.** High ___ Low ___	Clear ○ ___ Partly Cloudy ◑ ___ Cloudy ● ___						

Copyright © SRA/McGraw-Hill

Use with Project 2.

Chinese Calendar Animals

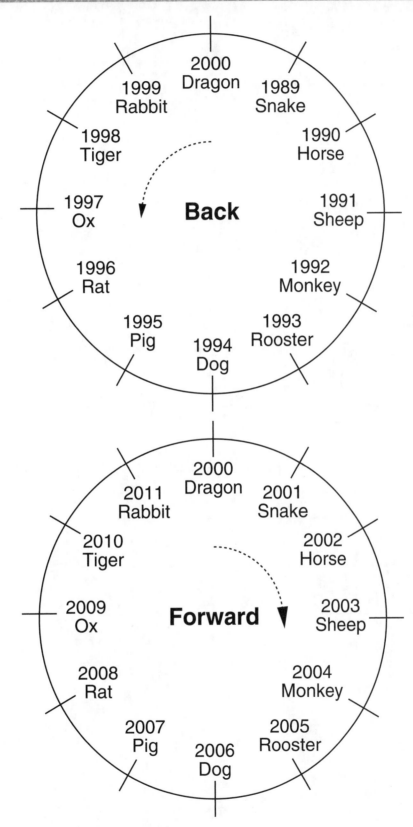

Back

2000 Dragon
1999 Rabbit
1989 Snake
1998 Tiger
1990 Horse
1997 Ox
1991 Sheep
1996 Rat
1992 Monkey
1995 Pig
1994 Dog
1993 Rooster

Forward

2000 Dragon
2011 Rabbit
2001 Snake
2010 Tiger
2002 Horse
2009 Ox
2003 Sheep
2008 Rat
2004 Monkey
2007 Pig
2006 Dog
2005 Rooster

Order of the animals beginning with the year of the rat: rat, ox, tiger, rabbit, dragon, snake, horse, sheep, monkey, rooster, dog, pig.

Copyright © SRA/McGraw-Hill

Chinese Calendar

Year of the

_____

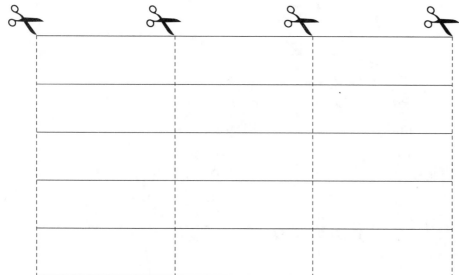

Copyright © SRA/McGraw-Hill

Use with Project 3.

How Far Can I Run in 10 Seconds?

1. Record the distance you ran in 10 seconds.

_____ feet

2. The range of 10-second running

distance for our class is _____ feet.

3. A middle 10-second running distance

for our class is _____ feet.

Follow-Up

Record your distance again on a stick-on note. Your teacher will use the notes to make a bar graph of the data on the wall. A sample is shown below.

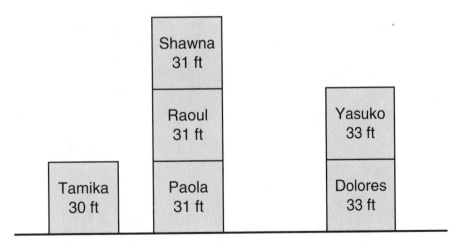

Copyright © SRA/McGraw–Hill

Math Boxes (6 cells)

1.

2.

3.

4.

5.

6.

Copyright © SRA/McGraw-Hill

Use as needed.

Math Boxes (5 cells)

1.

2.

3.

4.

5.

Copyright © SRA/McGraw–Hill

Use as needed.

Math Boxes (4 cells)

1.

2.

3.

4.

Copyright © SRA/McGraw-Hill

Use as needed.

Home Link Family Note

Family Note

Copyright © SRA/McGraw-Hill

Use as needed.

Copyright © SRA/McGraw–Hill

Pattern-Block Template

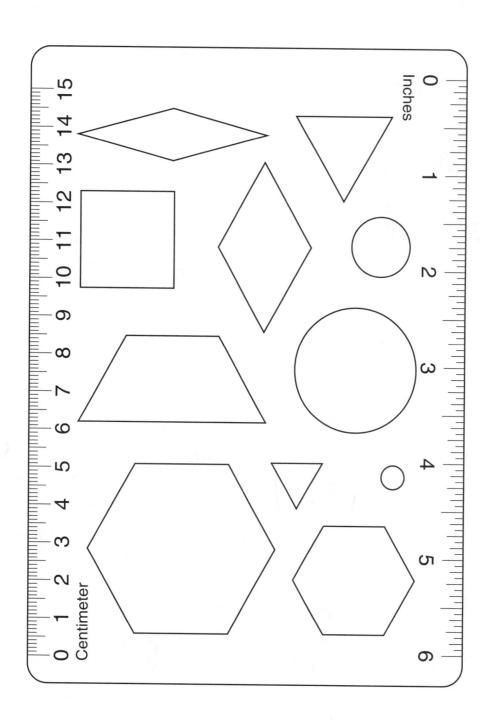

Copyright © SRA/McGraw-Hill

Use as needed.

Number Grids

Grid 1

-9	-8	-7	-6	-5	-4	-3	-2	-1	0
1	2	3	4	5	6	7	8	9	10
11	12	13	14	15	16	17	18	19	20
21	22	23	24	25	26	27	28	29	30
31	32	33	34	35	36	37	38	39	40
41	42	43	44	45	46	47	48	49	50
51	52	53	54	55	56	57	58	59	60
61	62	63	64	65	66	67	68	69	70
71	72	73	74	75	76	77	78	79	80
81	82	83	84	85	86	87	88	89	90
91	92	93	94	95	96	97	98	99	100
101	102	103	104	105	106	107	108	109	110

Grid 2

-9	-8	-7	-6	-5	-4	-3	-2	-1	0
1	2	3	4	5	6	7	8	9	10
11	12	13	14	15	16	17	18	19	20
21	22	23	24	25	26	27	28	29	30
31	32	33	34	35	36	37	38	39	40
41	42	43	44	45	46	47	48	49	50
51	52	53	54	55	56	57	58	59	60
61	62	63	64	65	66	67	68	69	70
71	72	73	74	75	76	77	78	79	80
81	82	83	84	85	86	87	88	89	90
91	92	93	94	95	96	97	98	99	100
101	102	103	104	105	106	107	108	109	110

Grid 3

-9	-8	-7	-6	-5	-4	-3	-2	-1	0
1	2	3	4	5	6	7	8	9	10
11	12	13	14	15	16	17	18	19	20
21	22	23	24	25	26	27	28	29	30
31	32	33	34	35	36	37	38	39	40
41	42	43	44	45	46	47	48	49	50
51	52	53	54	55	56	57	58	59	60
61	62	63	64	65	66	67	68	69	70
71	72	73	74	75	76	77	78	79	80
81	82	83	84	85	86	87	88	89	90
91	92	93	94	95	96	97	98	99	100
101	102	103	104	105	106	107	108	109	110

Grid 4

-9	-8	-7	-6	-5	-4	-3	-2	-1	0
1	2	3	4	5	6	7	8	9	10
11	12	13	14	15	16	17	18	19	20
21	22	23	24	25	26	27	28	29	30
31	32	33	34	35	36	37	38	39	40
41	42	43	44	45	46	47	48	49	50
51	52	53	54	55	56	57	58	59	60
61	62	63	64	65	66	67	68	69	70
71	72	73	74	75	76	77	78	79	80
81	82	83	84	85	86	87	88	89	90
91	92	93	94	95	96	97	98	99	100
101	102	103	104	105	106	107	108	109	110

Copyright © SRA/McGraw-Hill

Use as needed.

Domino Addition

 +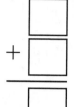

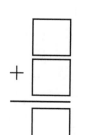 +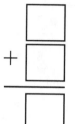

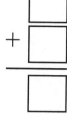 +

 +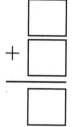

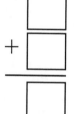 +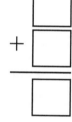

 +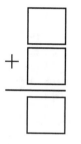

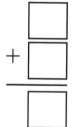 +

 +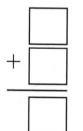

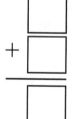 +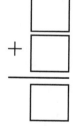

 +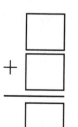

Copyright © SRA/McGraw-Hill

Use as needed.

Domino Subtraction

 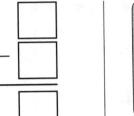  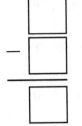  

 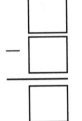  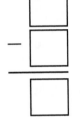  

 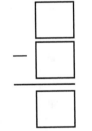  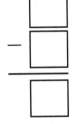  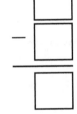

 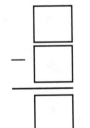  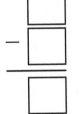  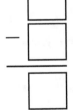

 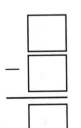  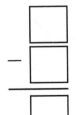  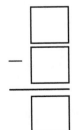

Copyright © SRA/McGraw–Hill

Use as needed.

Geoboard Dot Paper

Copyright © SRA/McGraw-Hill

Use as needed.

Money Exchange Game Mat

Copyright © SRA/McGraw–Hill

Use as needed.

Inch and Centimeter Rulers

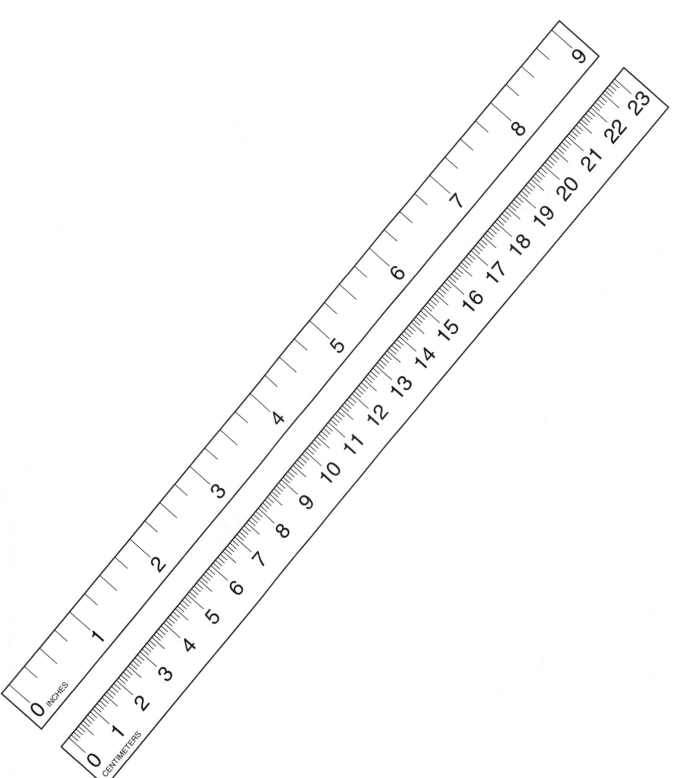

Copyright © SRA/McGraw-Hill

Use as needed.

Bar Graph

Title: _____

Copyright © SRA/McGraw–Hill

Use as needed.

Tic-Tac-Toe Addition

Draw a line through any three numbers whose sum is the target number in the square. The numbers may be in a row, in a column, or on a diagonal. Draw more than one line for each sum.

8		
5	2	1
1	3	7
6	2	0

14		
3	4	7
1	8	6
5	1	3

18		
6	4	9
5	8	5
7	6	4

20		
12	1	9
4	3	6
8	7	5

Think of some other Tic-Tac-Toe puzzles and write them below.

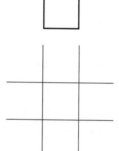
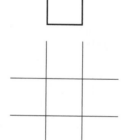
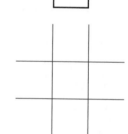

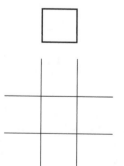
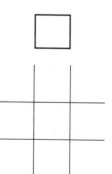
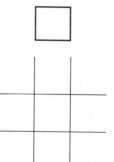
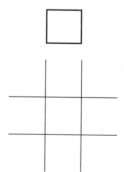

Copyright © SRA/McGraw-Hill

Use as needed.

Introduction to Second Grade Everyday Mathematics

Welcome to *Second Grade Everyday Mathematics*. It is a part of an elementary school mathematics curriculum developed by the University of Chicago School Mathematics Project.

Several features of the program are described below to help familiarize you with the structure and expectations of *Everyday Mathematics*.

A problem-solving approach based on everyday situations By making connections between their own knowledge and their experiences both in school and outside of school, children learn basic math skills in meaningful contexts so that the mathematics becomes "real."

Frequent practice of basic skills Instead of practice presented in a single, tedious drill format, children practice basic skills in a variety of more engaging ways. In addition to completing daily review exercises covering a variety of topics, patterning on the number grid, and working with addition and subtraction fact families in different formats, children will play games that are specifically designed to develop basic skills.

An instructional approach that revisits concepts regularly To enhance the development of basic skills and concepts, children regularly revisit previously learned concepts and repeatedly practice skills encountered earlier. The lessons are designed to take advantage of previously learned concepts and skills and to build on them throughout the year instead of treating them as isolated bits of knowledge.

A curriculum that explores mathematical content beyond basic arithmetic Mathematics standards around the world indicate that basic arithmetic skills are only the beginning of the mathematical knowledge children will need as they develop critical-thinking skills. In addition to basic arithmetic, *Everyday Mathematics* develops concepts and skills in the following topics—numeration; operations and computation; data and chance; geometry; measurement and reference frames; and patterns, functions, and algebra.

Copyright © SRA/McGraw-Hill

Use with Lesson 1.1.

Second Grade Everyday Mathematics emphasizes the following content:

Numeration Counting; reading and writing numbers; identifying place value; comparing numbers; working with fractions; using money to develop place value and decimal concepts

Operations and Computation Recalling addition and subtraction facts; exploring fact families (related addition and subtraction facts, such as $2 + 5 = 7$, $5 + 2 = 7$, $7 - 5 = 2$, and $7 - 2 = 5$); adding and subtracting with tens and hundreds; beginning multiplication and division; exchanging money amounts

Data and Chance Collecting, organizing, and interpreting data using tables, charts, and graphs

Geometry Exploring 2- and 3-dimensional shapes; classifying polygons

Measurement Using tools to measure length, weight, capacity, and volume; using U.S. customary and metric measurement units, such as feet, centimeters, ounces, and grams

Reference Frames Using clocks, calendars, thermometers, and number lines

Patterns, Functions, and Algebra Exploring number patterns, rules for number sequences, relations between numbers, and attributes

Everyday Mathematics provides you with ample opportunities to monitor your child's progress and to participate in your child's mathematics experiences.

Throughout the year, you will receive Family Letters to keep you informed of the mathematical content that your child will be studying in each unit. Each letter includes a vocabulary list, suggested Do-Anytime Activities for you and your child, and an answer guide to selected Home Link (homework) activities.

You will enjoy seeing your child's confidence and comprehension soar as he or she connects mathematics to everyday life.

We look forward to an exciting year!

Copyright © SRA/McGraw-Hill

232

Unit 1: Numbers and Routines

This unit reacquaints children with the daily routines of *Everyday Mathematics.* Children also review and extend mathematical concepts that were developed in *Kindergarten Everyday Mathematics* and *First Grade Everyday Mathematics.*

In Unit 1, children will ...

• Count in several different intervals—forward by 2s from 300, forward by 10s from 64, backward by 10s from 116, and so on.

• Practice addition facts, such as $5 + 4 = ?$ and $? = 7 + 5$.

• Review whole numbers by answering questions like "Which number comes after 57? After 98? After 234?" and "Which number is 10 more than 34? 67? 89?"

• Respond to prompts like "Write 38. Circle the digit in the 10s place. Put an X on the digit in the 1s place."

• Work with a number grid to reinforce place-value skills and observe number patterns.

									0
1	2	3	4	5	6	7	8	9	10
11	12	13	14	15	16	17	18	19	20
21	22	23	24	25	26	27	28	29	30

Children use number grids to learn about ones and tens digits and to identify number patterns, such as multiples of three.

• Review equivalent number names, such as $10 = 5 + 5$, $10 = 7 + 3$, $10 = 20 - 10$, and so on.

• Play games, such as *Addition Top-It,* to strengthen number skills.

• Practice telling time and using a calendar.

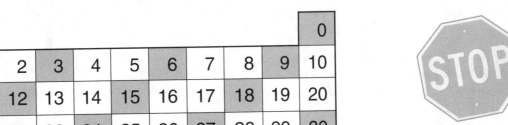

Do-Anytime Activities

To work with your child on the concepts taught in this unit, try these interesting and rewarding activities:

1 Discuss examples of mathematics in everyday life: television listings, road signs, money, recipe measurements, time, and so on.

2 Discuss rules for working with a partner or in a group.

    • Speak quietly.   • Be polite.   • Help each other.   • Share.

    • Listen to your partner.   • Take turns.   • Praise your partner.   • Talk about problems.

3 Discuss household tools that can be used to measure things or help solve mathematical problems.

Copyright © SRA/McGraw-Hill

Use with Lesson 1.1.

Vocabulary

Important terms in Unit 1:

math journal A book used by each child; it contains examples, instructions, and problems, as well as space to record answers and observations.

tool kits Individual zippered bags or boxes used in the classroom; they contain a variety of items, such as rulers, play money, and number cards, to help children understand mathematical ideas.

Math Message A daily activity children complete independently, usually as a lead-in to the day's lesson. For example: "Count by 10s. Count as high as you can in 1 minute. Write down the number you get to."

Mental Math and Reflexes A daily whole-class oral or written activity, often emphasizing computation done mentally.

number grid A table in which numbers are arranged consecutively, usually in rows of ten. A move from one number to the next within a row is a change of 1; a move from one number to the next within a column is a change of 10.

									0
1	2	3	4	5	6	7	8	9	10
11	12	13	14	15	16	17	18	19	20
21	22	23	24	25	26	27	28	29	30

Exploration A small-group, hands-on activity designed to introduce or extend a topic.

Math Boxes Math problems that provide opportunities for reviewing and practicing previously introduced skills.

Math Boxes 1.9

1. Which number is 10 more?

42 _____

57 _____

2. Solve.

_____ + 6 = 8

3. Write the amount.

Ⓝ Ⓝ Ⓟ Ⓟ Ⓓ

_____ ¢

4. Draw the hands so the clock shows 4:45.

5. Circle the digit in the 100s place.

8 4 9

6. Write these numbers in order. Start with the smallest number.

103   29   86

_____ _____ _____

Home Links Problems and activities intended to promote follow-up and enrichment at home.

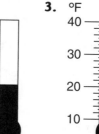

As You Help Your Child with Homework

As your child brings home assignments, you may want to go over the instructions together, clarifying them as necessary. The answers listed below will guide you through this unit's Home Links.

Home Link 1.12

1. <   **2.** >   **3.** >
4. =   **5.** <   **6.** <

Home Link 1.13

1. °F   **2.** °F   **3.** °F   **4.** °F

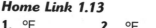

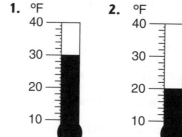

Copyright © SRA/McGraw-Hill

Use with Lesson 1.1.

Relations: $<$, $>$, $=$

**Family
Note**

In *Second Grade Everyday Mathematics*, children "do mathematics." We expect that children will want to share their enthusiasm for the mathematics activities they do in school with their families. Your child will bring home assignments and activities to do as homework throughout the year. These assignments, called "Home Links," will be identified by the house at the top right corner of this page. The assignments will not take very much time to complete, but most of them involve interaction with an adult or an older child.

There are many reasons for including Home Links in the second grade program:

· The assignments encourage children to take initiative and responsibility for completing them. As you respond with encouragement and assistance, you help your child build independence and self-confidence.

· Home Links reinforce newly learned skills and concepts. They provide opportunities for children to think and practice at their own pace.

· These assignments are often designed to relate what is done in school to children's lives outside school. This helps tie mathematics to the real world, which is very important in the *Everyday Mathematics* program.

· The Home Links assignments will help you get a better idea of the mathematics your child is learning in school.

Generally, you can help by listening and responding to your child's requests and comments about mathematics. You also can help by linking numbers to real life, pointing out ways in which you use numbers (time, TV channels, page numbers, telephone numbers, bus routes, shopping lists, and so on). Extending the notion that "children who are read to, read," *Everyday Mathematics* supports the belief that children who have someone do math with them will learn mathematics. Playful counting and thinking games that are fun for both you and your child are very helpful for such learning.

*Please return the **second page** of this Home Link to school tomorrow.*

Copyright © SRA/McGraw-Hill

Relations: $<$, $>$, $=$ (cont.)

> **Reminder**
>
> $=$ means *equals* or
>   *is the same as*
>
> $<$ means *is less than*
>
> $>$ means *is greater than*

$$3 < 5$$

$$5 > 3$$

Explain to someone at home how to do Problems 1–6.

Then write $<$, $>$, or $=$ in each blank.

1. 8 _____ 12

2. 25 _____ 18

3. 103 _____ 53

4. 79 _____ 79

5. 199 _____ 200

6. 56 _____ 88

7. Count by 2s for someone at home.

Count as high as you can. I counted to _____.

8. Make up a few of your own.

_____ $<$ _____   _____ $>$ _____   _____ $=$ _____

Copyright © SRA/McGraw-Hill

Temperatures

Family Note

In today's lesson, the class examined thermometers and practiced reading Fahrenheit temperatures. We began a daily routine of recording the outside temperature. If you have a nondigital thermometer at home (inside or outside), encourage your child to read the Fahrenheit temperatures to you. We will introduce Celsius temperatures in a later unit.

Please return this Home Link to school tomorrow.

1. Circle the thermometer that shows 30°F.

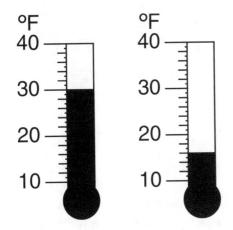

2. Circle the thermometer that shows 20°F.

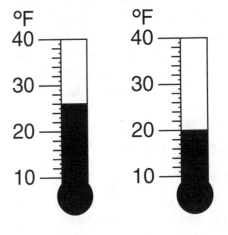

3. Circle the thermometer that shows 12°F.

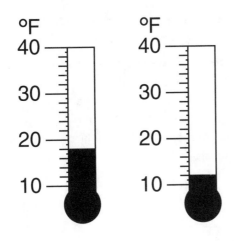

4. Circle the thermometer that shows 28°F.

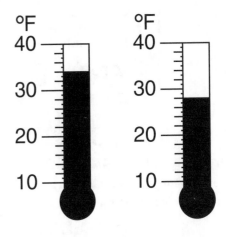

Copyright © SRA/McGraw-Hill

Use with Lesson 1.13.

Name

Date

Time

Family Letter

**Home Link
1.14**

Unit 2: Addition and Subtraction Facts

Unit 2 focuses on reviewing and extending addition facts and linking subtraction to addition. Children will solve basic addition and subtraction facts through real-life stories.

In *Everyday Mathematics*, the ability to recall number facts instantly is called "fact power." Instant recall of the addition and subtraction facts will become a powerful tool in computation with multidigit numbers, such as 29 + 92.

Math Tools

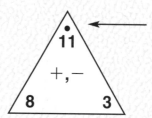

Your child will be using **Fact Triangles** to practice and review addition and subtraction facts. Fact Triangles are a "new and improved" version of flash cards; the addition and subtraction facts shown are made from the same three numbers, helping your child understand the relationships among those facts. The Family Note on Home Link 2.8, which you will receive later, provides a more detailed description of Fact Triangles.

The dot designates the largest number.

A Fact Triangle showing the fact family for 3, 8, and 11

Vocabulary

Important terms in Unit 2:

label A unit, descriptive word, or phrase used to put a number or numbers in context. Using a label reinforces the idea that numbers always refer to something.

unit box A box that contains the label or unit of measure for the numbers in a problem. For example, in number stories involving children in the class, the unit box would be as follows:

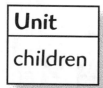

A unit box allows children to remember that numbers have a context without having to repeat the label in each problem.

number story A story made up by children, teachers, or parents. It contains a problem that can be solved by using one or more of the four basic operations.

number model A number sentence that shows how the parts of a number story are related. For example, 5 + 8 = 13 shows how the parts are related in this number story: "5 children skating. 8 children playing ball. How many children in all?"

fact power The ability to instantly recall basic number facts.

doubles fact The sum or product of the same two 1-digit numbers, such as 2 + 2 = 4 or 3 × 3 = 9.

turn-around facts A pair of addition (or multiplication) facts in which the order of the addends (or factors) is reversed, such as 3 + 5 = 8 and 5 + 3 = 8 (or 3 × 4 = 12 and 4 × 3 = 12). If you know an addition or multiplication fact, you also know its turnaround.

Copyright © SRA/McGraw-Hill

fact family A collection of addition and subtraction facts (and later, multiplication and division facts) made from the same three numbers. For example, the addition/subtraction fact family for the numbers 2, 4, and 6 consists of $2 + 4 = 6$, $4 + 2 = 6$, $6 - 4 = 2$, and $6 - 2 = 4$. The multiplication/division fact family for the numbers 2, 4, and 8 consists of $2 \times 4 = 8$, $4 \times 2 = 8$, $8 \div 2 = 4$, and $8 \div 4 = 2$.

Frames-and-Arrows diagram A diagram used to represent a number sequence, or a set of numbers that are ordered according to a rule. A Frames-and-Arrows diagram consists of frames connected by arrows to show the path from one frame to the next. Each frame contains a number in the sequence; each arrow represents a rule that determines which number goes in the next frame.

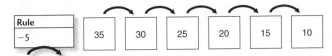

"What's My Rule?" table A list of number pairs in which the numbers in each pair are related according to the same rule. This relationship can be represented by a **function machine,** an imaginary device that processes numbers according to the rule. A number (input) is put into the machine and is transformed into a second number (output) through the application of the rule.

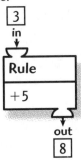

Function machine

in	out
3	8
5	10
8	13

"What's My Rule?" table

Do-Anytime Activities

To work with your child on the concepts taught in this unit and in previous units, try these interesting and rewarding activities:

1 Talk with your child about why it is important to learn basic facts.

2 Create addition and subtraction stories about given subjects.

3 Have your child explain how to use a facts table.

4 As you discover which facts your child is having difficulty mastering, make a Fact Triangle using the three numbers of that fact family.

5 Name a number and ask your child to think of several different ways to represent that number. For example, 10 can be represented as $9 + 1$, $5 + 5$, $14 - 4$, and so on.

10	
ten	$12 - 2$
$1 + 9$	$6 + 4$
diez	$10 - 0$

Copyright © SRA/McGraw-Hill

Use with Lesson 1.14.

Building Skills through Games

In Unit 2, your child will practice addition facts as well as find equivalent names for numbers by playing the following games.

Beat the Calculator

A "Calculator" (a player who uses a calculator to solve the problem) and a "Brain" (a player who solves the problem without a calculator) race to see who will be first to solve addition problems.

Addition Top-It

Each player turns over two cards and calls out their sum. The player with the higher sum then takes all the cards from that round.

Name That Number

Each player turns over a card to find a number that must be renamed using any combination of five faceup cards.

$$6 = 8 - 2$$
$$6 = 10 - 4$$
$$6 = 4 + 2$$

Copyright © SRA/McGraw-Hill

240

Use with Lesson 1.14.

As You Help Your Child with Homework

As your child brings home assignments, you may want to go over the instructions together, clarifying them as necessary. The answers listed below will guide you through this unit's Home Links.

Home Link 2.2

	2 +4 6	0 +0 0	5 +4 9	1 +4 5	2 +5 7	3 +2 5	1 +9 10	3 +6 9	4 +4 8	1 +1 2
	2 +0 2	3 +5 8	5 +1 6	1 +4 5	9 +2 11	0 +7 7	2 +3 5	2 +2 4	7 +2 9	3 +4 7	2 +8 10
	6 +2 8	1 +6 7	5 +5 10	0 +6 6	4 +3 7	0 +5 5	1 +8 9	4 +6 10	5 +3 8	4 +0 4	3 +1 4
	0 +8 8	6 +6 12	8 +2 10	9 +0 9	3 +3 6	7 +1 8	2 +6 8	1 +3 4	5 +2 7	6 +1 7	0 +4 4
	2 +1 3	2 +9 11	6 +2 8	6 +4 10	0 +1 1	4 +2 6	6 +3 9	0 +2 2	5 +1 6	1 +2 3	2 +7 9
	4 +5 9	7 +0 7	6 +2 8	9 +3 12	1 +5 6	0 +9 9	1 +7 8	1 +5 6	7 +3 10	0 +6 6	6 +5 11
	9 +1 10	8 +0 8	6 +2 8	8 +3 11	1 +0 1	6 +0 6	3 +3 6	0 +3 3	3 +8 11	3 +7 10	

Home Link 2.3

1. a. 4 **b.** 10 **c.** 0 **d.** 14 **e.** 6
   f. 16 **g.** 12 **h.** 18 **i.** 2 **j.** 8

3. a. 9 **b.** 9 **c.** 17 **d.** 13 **e.** 5
   f. 15 **g.** 11

Home Link 2.4

1. a. 7 **b.** 11 **c.** 7 **d.** 7 **e.** 11 **f.** 7

2. a. 8 **b.** 5 **c.** 6 **d.** 3 **e.** 7 **f.** 9

3. a. 11 **b.** 15 **c.** 16 **d.** 10 **e.** 14 **f.** 15
   g. 17 **h.** 14 **i.** 18 **j.** 16 **k.** 13 **l.** 17

Home Link 2.5

	2 +6 8	2 +5 7	1 +6 7	0 +8 8	5 +7 12	3 +9 12	7 +0 7	4 +4 8	1 +5 6	4 +3 7
	2 +7 9	6 +5 11	1 +7 8	3 +5 8	0 +9 9	8 +1 9	2 +8 10	0 +6 6	3 +3 6	8 +7 15
	4 +4 8	5 +4 9	9 +3 12	0 +9 9	4 +6 10	6 +1 8	5 +5 10	0 +8 8	9 +5 14	7 +6 13	1 +6 7
	6 +2 8	3 +8 11	7 +4 11	9 +2 11	5 +3 8	4 +4 8	2 +9 11	4 +8 12	4 +9 13	1 +1 2	5 +2 7
	3 +4 7	6 +6 12	8 +4 12	7 +5 12	7 +0 7	6 +2 8	3 +7 10	4 +5 9	7 +4 11	6 +8 14	5 +6 11
	8 +5 13	3 +6 9	4 +7 11	5 +2 7	1 +6 7	3 +5 8	6 +7 13	5 +7 12	8 +3 11	7 +7 14	9 +4 13
	6 +1 7	8 +4 12	2 +6 8	7 +7 14	4 +2 6	1 +4 5	0 +7 7	3 +9 12	4 +5 9	6 +4 10	

Home Link 2.6

2. $9 + 6 = 15$; $6 + 9 = 15$; $15 - 6 = 9$; $15 - 9 = 6$

3. $8 + 7 = 15$; $7 + 8 = 15$; $15 - 7 = 8$; $15 - 8 = 7$

4. $5 + 9 = 14$; $9 + 5 = 14$; $14 - 9 = 5$; $14 - 5 = 9$

5. 13 **6.** 14 **7.** 12 **8.** 16

Home Link 2.10

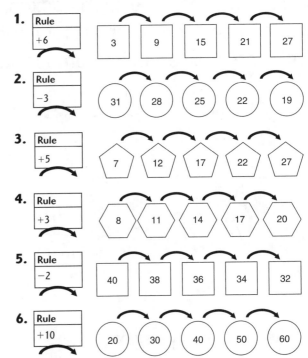

1. Rule +6 : 3, 9, 15, 21, 27

2. Rule −3 : 31, 28, 25, 22, 19

3. Rule +5 : 7, 12, 17, 22, 27

4. Rule +3 : 8, 11, 14, 17, 20

5. Rule −2 : 40, 38, 36, 34, 32

6. Rule +10 : 20, 30, 40, 50, 60

Home Link 2.11

1. Rule +9

in	out
1	10
4	13
6	15
8	17
5	14

2. Rule −8

in	out
10	2
12	4
9	1
14	6
8	0

3. Rule +6

in	out
4	10
6	12
3	9
9	15
0	6

4. Rule +5

in	out
8	13
4	9
13	18
5	10
Answers vary.	

5. 18; 5

Copyright © SRA/McGraw-Hill

Addition Number Stories

Family Note

Before beginning this Home Link, review with your child the vocabulary from the Unit 2 Family Letter: *number story, label, unit box,* and *number model.* Then, encourage your child to make up and solve number stories and to write number models for the stories. Stress that the answer to the question makes more sense if it has a label.

Please return this Home Link to school tomorrow.

Tell someone at home what you know about addition number stories, labels, unit boxes, and number models. Write an addition number story about each picture. Write the answer and a number model.

Unit
lions

1.

Story: _____

_____

_____

_____

_____

Answer the question: _____   Number model: __ + __ = __
                     (unit)

Unit
bricks

2.

Story: _____

_____

_____

_____

Answer the question: _____   Number model: ___ + ___ = ___
                     (unit)

Use with Lesson 2.1.

Copyright © SRA/McGraw-Hill

Addition Facts

Family Note

In class today, we continued working with addition stories. We reviewed shortcuts when adding 0 or 1 to a number. We also stressed the importance of memorizing the sum of two 1-digit numbers. Then we reinforced addition facts by playing a game called *Beat the Calculator*.

Please return this Home Link to school tomorrow.

Solve these addition fact problems.

	2 + 4	0 + 0	5 + 4	1 + 4	2 + 5	3 + 2	1 + 9	3 + 6	4 + 4	1 + 1
	2 + 0	3 + 5	5 + 1	1 + 4	9 + 2	0 + 7	2 + 3	2 + 2	7 + 2	3 + 4	2 + 8
	6 + 2	1 + 6	5 + 5	0 + 6	4 + 3	0 + 5	1 + 8	4 + 6	5 + 3	4 + 0	3 + 1
	0 + 8	6 + 6	8 + 2	9 + 0	3 + 3	7 + 1	2 + 6	1 + 3	5 + 2	6 + 1	0 + 4
	2 + 1	2 + 9	6 + 2	6 + 4	0 + 1	4 + 2	6 + 3	0 + 2	5 + 1	1 + 2	2 + 7
	4 + 5	7 + 0	6 + 2	9 + 3	1 + 5	0 + 9	1 + 7	1 + 5	7 + 3	0 + 6	6 + 5
	9 + 1	8 + 0	6 + 2	8 + 3	1 + 0	6 + 0	3 + 3	0 + 3	3 + 8	3 + 7	

Copyright © SRA/McGraw-Hill

Doubles Facts

Family Note

Today we worked with an Addition/Subtraction Facts Table and dominoes to practice with a special kind of addition problem called doubles facts. $3 + 3 = 6$, $4 + 4 = 8$, and $5 + 5 = 10$ are examples of doubles facts. We also worked with almost-doubles facts, such as $3 + 4 = 7$, $5 + 4 = 9$, and $7 + 8 = 15$. Review doubles facts and almost-doubles facts with your child.

Please return this Home Link to school tomorrow.

1. Write the sum for each doubles fact.

a. $2 + 2 =$ _____   **b.** _____ $= 5 + 5$ **c.** _____ $= 0 + 0$

d.   7   **e.**   3   **f.**   8   **g.**   6
  $+ 7$ $+ 3$ $+ 8$ $+ 6$

h. $9 + 9 =$ _____   **i.** _____ $= 1 + 1$ **j.** _____ $= 4 + 4$

2. Ask someone to give you doubles facts. You say the sums. Do this for about 10 minutes or until you know all the doubles facts.

3. Write each sum. Use doubles facts to help you.

a. $5 + 4 =$ _____   **b.** $4 + 5 =$ _____   **c.** _____ $= 9 + 8$

d.   6   **e.**   2   **f.**   7   **g.**   6
  $+ 7$ $+ 3$ $+ 8$ $+ 5$

Copyright © SRA/McGraw-Hill

Turn-Around, Doubles, and +9

Family Note

It is important for children to have instant recall of addition facts. They use shortcuts to help them learn the facts. For example, *turn-around facts* are facts that have the same sum, but the numbers being added are reversed or turned around. *Doubles facts* are facts in which the same number is added. When solving +9 facts, children are encouraged to think of the easier +10 combinations and then subtract 1 from the sum.

Please return this Home Link to school tomorrow.

1. Write the sums. Tell someone at home what you know about turn-around facts.

   a. $6 + 1 =$ _____   **b.** _____ $= 3 + 8$ **c.** $5 + 2 =$ _____

   d. $1 + 6 =$ _____   **e.** _____ $= 8 + 3$ **f.** $2 + 5 =$ _____

2. Fill in the missing numbers. Tell someone at home what you know about doubles facts.

   a. _____ $+ 8 = 16$ **b.** $5 +$ _____ $= 10$ **c.** $12 =$ _____ $+ 6$

   d. $6 =$ _____ $+ 3$ **e.** _____ $+ 7 = 14$ **f.** _____ $+ 9 = 18$

3. Write the sums. Tell someone what you know about +9 facts.

   a. $10 + 1 =$ _____   **b.** _____ $= 5 + 10$ **c.** $6 + 10 =$ _____

   d. $1 + 9 =$ _____   **e.** _____ $= 9 + 5$ **f.** $6 + 9 =$ _____

   g. $10 + 7 =$ _____   **h.** _____ $= 4 + 10$ **i.** $8 + 10 =$ _____

   j. $7 + 9 =$ _____   **k.** _____ $= 9 + 4$ **l.** $8 + 9 =$ _____

Copyright © SRA/McGraw-Hill

Addition Facts Maze

Family Note

For homework, your child will review addition facts like the ones we have been working on in class. To help identify the path from the child to the ice cream cone, have your child circle the sums of 9, 10, and 11.

Please return this Home Link to school tomorrow.

Help the child find the ice cream. Answer all the problems. Then draw the child's path by connecting facts with sums of 9, 10, or 11. You can move up, down, left, or right as you move between boxes.

	2 + 6	2 + 5	1 + 6	0 + 8	5 + 7	3 + 9	7 + 0	4 + 4	1 + 5	4 + 3
2 + 7	6 + 5	1 + 7	3 + 5	6 + 3	1 + 8	8 + 2	5 + 3	2 + 4	3 + 3	8 + 7
4 + 4	5 + 4	9 + 3	0 + 9	4 + 6	7 + 1	5 + 5	8 + 0	5 + 9	6 + 7	6 + 1
6 + 2	3 + 8	7 + 4	9 + 2	5 + 3	4 + 4	2 + 9	4 + 8	4 + 9	1 + 1	5 + 2
3 + 4	6 + 6	8 + 4	7 + 5	7 + 0	6 + 2	7 + 3	3 + 6	4 + 7	6 + 8	5 + 6
8 + 5	3 + 6	4 + 7	5 + 2	1 + 6	3 + 5	6 + 7	5 + 7	8 + 3	7 + 7	9 + 4
6 + 1	8 + 4	2 + 6	7 + 7	4 + 2	1 + 4	0 + 7	3 + 9	4 + 5	6 + 4	

Copyright © SRA/McGraw-Hill

Domino Facts

Family Note

Today we learned that addition problems and subtraction problems are related. For example, $5 + 3 = 8$ can be rewritten to show two related subtraction facts: $8 - 5 = 3$ and $8 - 3 = 5$.

Each domino shown below can be used to write 2 addition facts and 2 related subtraction facts.

Please return this Home Link to school tomorrow.

Write 2 addition facts and 2 subtraction facts for each domino.

1.

$$\begin{array}{r} 7 \\ +\ 3 \\ \hline 10 \end{array} \qquad \begin{array}{r} 3 \\ +\ 7 \\ \hline \end{array} \qquad \begin{array}{r} 10 \\ -\ 3 \\ \hline 7 \end{array} \qquad \begin{array}{r} 10 \\ -\ 7 \\ \hline \end{array}$$

2.

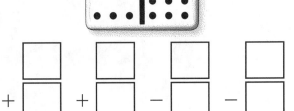

3.

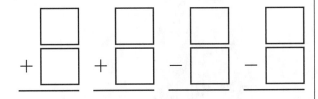

4.

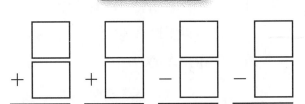

Write the sums. Tell someone at home what you know about doubles-plus-1 and doubles-plus-2 facts.

5. $6 + 7 =$ _____

6. _____ $= 8 + 6$

7. $5 + 7 =$ _____

8. $7 + 9 =$ _____

Copyright © SRA/McGraw-Hill

Weighing Things

Family Note

Today we worked with a pan balance to compare the weights of objects. We used a spring scale to weigh objects up to a pound. We introduced the word *ounce* as a unit of weight for light objects.

Please return the **second page** *of this Home Link to school tomorrow.*

1. Tell someone at home about how you used the pan balance to compare the weights of two objects.

2. Tell someone at home how you used the spring scale to weigh objects.

Copyright © SRA/McGraw-Hill

Use with Lesson 2.7.

Weighing Things (cont.)

3. Look at the pairs of objects below. In each pair, circle the object that you think is heavier.

a.

Shoe

b.

Sock

c.

Feather

Marble

Brick

Tape Measure

4. Look at the objects below. Circle the objects that you think weigh less than 1 pound.

Pattern-Block Template

Scissors   Egg   Chair

Television

Pencil   Glasses

Copyright © SRA/McGraw-Hill

Fact Triangles

Family Note

Fact Triangles are tools used to help build mental arithmetic skills. You might think of them as the *Everyday Mathematics* version of flash cards. Fact Triangles are more effective for helping children memorize facts, however, because of their emphasis on fact families. A **fact family** is a collection of related addition and subtraction facts that use the same 3 numbers. The fact family for the numbers 2, 4, and 6 consists of $2 + 4 = 6$, $4 + 2 = 6$, $6 - 4 = 2$, and $6 - 2 = 4$.

To use Fact Triangles to practice addition with your child, cover the number next to the large dot with your thumb.

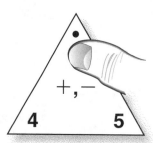

Your child tells you the addition fact: $4 + 5 = 9$ or $5 + 4 = 9$.

To use Fact Triangles to practice subtraction, cover one of the numbers in the lower corners with your thumb.

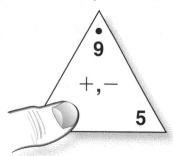 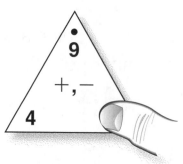

Your child tells you the subtraction facts: $9 - 5 = 4$ and $9 - 4 = 5$.

If your child misses a fact, flash the other two fact problems on the card and then return to the fact that was missed.

Example: Sue can't answer $9 - 5$. Flash $4 + 5$, then $9 - 4$, and finally $9 - 5$ a second time.

Make this activity brief and fun. Spend about 10 minutes each night over the next few weeks or until your child masters all of the facts. The work that you do at home will help your child develop an instant recall of facts and will complement the work that we are doing at school.

Copyright © SRA/McGraw-Hill

Fact Triangles (cont.)

Cut out the Fact Triangles. Show someone at home how you use them to practice adding and subtracting.

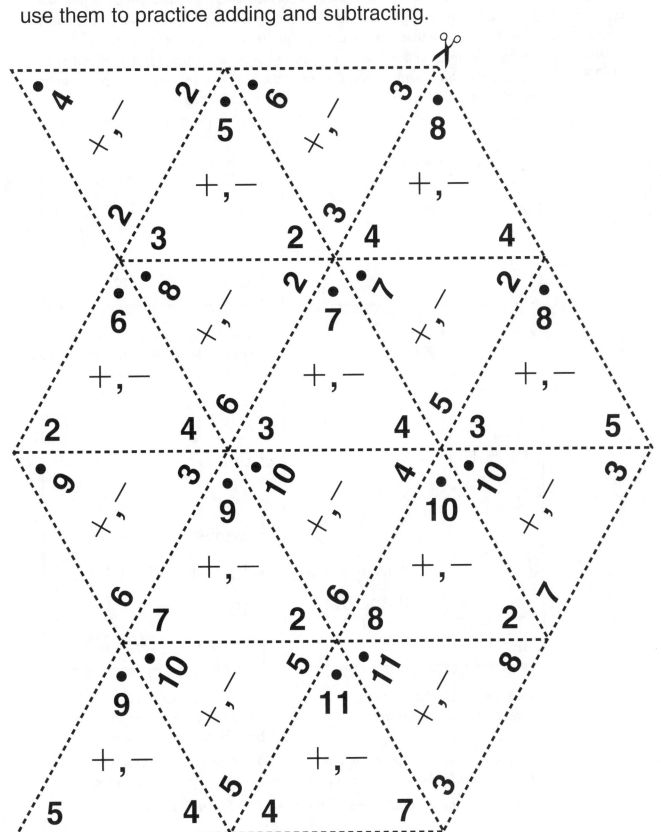

Copyright © SRA/McGraw-Hill

Name-Collection Boxes

Family Note

Beginning in *First Grade Everyday Mathematics*, children use **name-collection boxes** to help them collect equivalent names for the same number. These boxes help children appreciate the idea that numbers can be expressed in many different ways.

A name-collection box is an open box with a tag attached. The tag identifies the number whose names are collected in the box. In second grade, typical names include sums, differences, tally marks, and arrays. At higher grades, names may include products, quotients, and the results of several mathematical operations.

| **10** | ← Tag for box |

Name-collection box

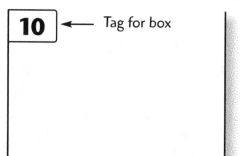

| **10** |
| ten |
| 12 − 2 |
| 6 + 4 |

‖‖‖‖ ‖‖‖‖

∷∷

Items in the name-collection box above represent the number 10. Some names contain numbers, and some do not.

| **9** |
| 19 − 10 |
| (15 − 7) |
| 3 + 3 + 3 |
| (8 + 0) |
| (5 + 4 + 1) |
| (‖‖‖‖ ‖‖‖) |

x x x
x x x
x x x

1 less
than 10

Sometimes we ask children to circle names that do not belong in the box.

| | |
| 6 + 6 |
| 12 + 0 |
| twelve |
| 15 − 1 − 2 |
| 18 − 6 |
| 12 − 0 |

x x x
x x x
x x x
x x x

1 less
than 13

‖‖‖‖ ‖‖‖‖ ‖

Sometimes we ask children to fill in the tag for the numbers shown in the box. The tag here should read 12.

Encourage your child to name a number in different ways—for example, use tally marks, write addition and subtraction problems, or draw pictures of objects.

*Please return the **second page** of this Home Link to school tomorrow.*

Copyright © SRA/McGraw-Hill

Use with Lesson 2.9.

Name-Collection Boxes (cont.)

1. Give the Family Note to someone at home. Show that person the name-collection box below. Explain what a name-collection box is used for.

8		
2 + 6	4 + 4	x x x x
eight	12 − 4	x x x x
ocho	10 − 2	8 − 0
8 + 0	3 + 5	⊬⊬ |||

2. Write 10 names in this 10-box.

10

3. Make up your own name-collection box. Write at least 10 names in the box.

Copyright © SRA/McGraw-Hill

Frames-and-Arrows Problems

Family Note

Today your child used **Frames-and-Arrows diagrams.** These diagrams show sequences of numbers—numbers that follow one after the other according to a rule. Frames-and-Arrows diagrams are made up of shapes called *frames* and arrows that connect the frames. Each frame contains one of the numbers in the sequence. Each *arrow* stands for a rule that tells which number goes in the next frame. Here is an example of a Frames-and-Arrows diagram. The arrow rule is "Add 2."

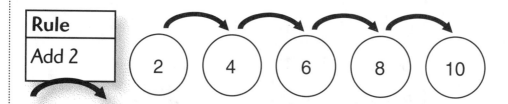

In a Frames-and-Arrows problem, some of the information is left out. To solve the problem, you have to find the missing information. Here are two examples of Frames-and-Arrows problems:

Example 1: Fill in the empty frames according to the rule.

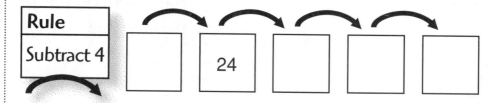

Solution: Write 28, 20, 16, and 12 in the empty frames.

Example 2: Write the arrow rule in the empty box.

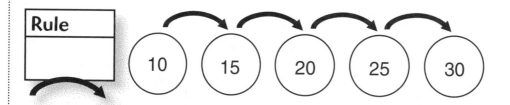

Solution: The arrow rule is Add 5, or +5.

Ask your child to tell you about Frames-and-Arrows diagrams. Take turns making up and solving Frames-and-Arrows problems like the examples above with your child.

*Please return the **second page** of this Home Link to school tomorrow.*

Copyright © SRA/McGraw-Hill

Frames and Arrows (cont.)

Give the Family Note to someone at home. Tell that person what you know about Frames and Arrows. Fill in the empty frames and rule boxes.

1.

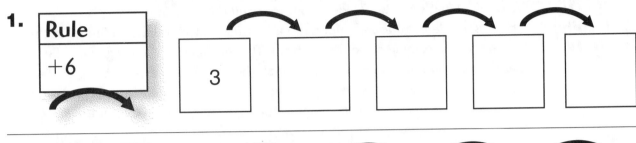

Rule
+6

3

2.

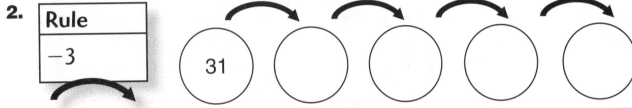

Rule
−3

31

3.

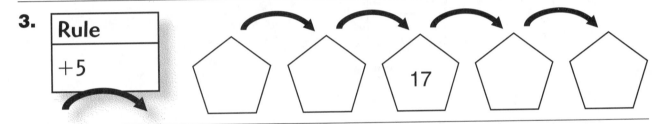

Rule
+5

17

4.

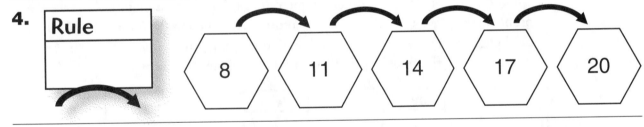

Rule

8   11   14   17   20

5.

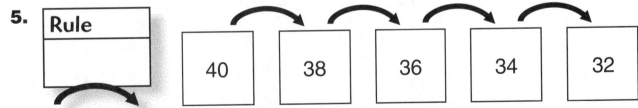

Rule

40   38   36   34   32

6.

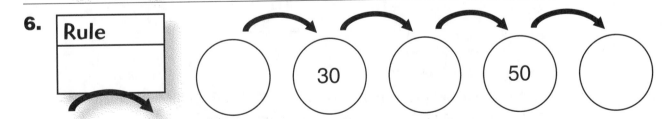

Rule

30   50

Now write your own Frames-and-Arrows problem on the back of this sheet. Ask someone at home to solve it.

Copyright © SRA/McGraw-Hill

"What's My Rule?"

Family Note

Today your child learned about a kind of problem you may not have seen before. We call it "What's My Rule?" Please ask your child to explain it to you.

   Here is a little background information: Imagine a machine with a funnel at the top and a tube coming out of the bottom. The machine can be programmed so that if a number is dropped into the funnel, the machine does something to the number, and a new number comes out the tube. For example, the machine could be programmed to add 5 to any number that is dropped in. If you put in 3, out would come 8. If you put in 7, out would come 12.

We call this device a *function machine*.

```
  ┌───┐
  │ 3 │
  └───┘
   in
    ↓
 ┌──────────┐
 │ Rule     │
 ├──────────┤
 │ +5       │
 └──────────┘
    ↓
   out
  ┌───┐
  │ 8 │
  └───┘
```

You can show the results of the rule "+5" in a table:

in	out
3	8
7	12
15	20

   In a "What's My Rule?" problem, some of the information is missing. To solve the problem, you have to find the missing information. The missing information could be the numbers that come out of a function machine, the numbers that are dropped in, or the rule for programming the machine. *For example:*

Rule	
Add 6	

in	out
3	
5	
8	

Missing:
"out" numbers

Rule	

in	out
6	3
10	5
16	8

Missing:
rule

Rule	
+4	

in	out
	6
	16
	11

Missing:
"in" numbers

Like Frames-and-Arrows problems, "What's My Rule?" problems help children practice facts (and extended facts) in a problem-solving format.

*Please return the **second page** of this Home Link to school tomorrow.*

Copyright © SRA/McGraw-Hill

Use with Lesson 2.11.

"What's My Rule?" (cont.)

Give the Family Note to someone at home. Show that person how you can complete "What's My Rule?" tables. Show that person how you can find rules.

1. Fill in the table.

Rule
+9

in	out
1	10
4	13
6	
8	
5	

2. Find the rule.

Rule

in	out
10	2
12	4
9	1
14	6
8	0

3. Fill in the table.

Rule
+6

in	out
4	10
	12
	9
	15
	6

4. Challenge Find the rule. Fill in the table.

Rule

in	out
8	13
4	9
13	
	10

5. Al read 5 more pages than Cindy.

If Cindy read 13 pages, how many pages did Al read?

_____ pages

If Al read 10 pages, how many pages did Cindy read?

_____ pages

Copyright © SRA/McGraw–Hill

Use with Lesson 2.11.

Subtraction Maze

Family Note

For homework, your child will practice subtraction facts like the ones we have been working on in class. To help identify the path from the dog to the ball, have your child circle the differences of 3, 4, and 5.

Please return this Home Link to school tomorrow.

Help the dog find her ball. Solve all of the problems. Then draw the dog's path by connecting facts with answers of 3, 4, or 5. You can move up, down, left, right, or diagonally as you move between boxes.

	8 − 4	12 − 6	8 − 8	4 − 0	5 − 4	9 − 7	10 − 3	5 − 2	6 − 0	18 − 9
8 − 7	16 − 8	6 − 1	7 − 3	4 − 2	12 − 3	5 − 1	9 − 8	8 − 6	6 − 3	7 − 6
5 − 1	3 − 3	9 − 2	11 − 0	7 − 2	3 − 2	12 − 6	8 − 3	3 − 1	8 − 0	6 − 4
10 − 2	5 − 0	7 − 1	9 − 3	11 − 2	10 − 5	12 − 1	7 − 0	4 − 3	14 − 7	3 − 0
5 − 3	12 − 0	2 − 1	8 − 1	6 − 5	12 − 2	6 − 2	2 − 2	7 − 5	10 − 9	9 − 0
11 − 3	4 − 1	9 − 1	2 − 0	10 − 1	9 − 9	8 − 5	3 − 0	11 − 1	10 − 7	11 − 8
10 − 0	5 − 5	10 − 9	8 − 2	10 − 8	11 − 9	6 − 6	12 − 3	9 − 6	7 − 4	

Copyright © SRA/McGraw-Hill

Use with Lesson 2.12.

Addition/Subtraction Facts

Family Note

For homework, your child will practice addition and subtraction facts like the ones we have been working on in class. Help your child solve the problems and identify the path from the bird to the seeds by circling all the cells with the answer 6.

Please return this Home Link to school tomorrow.

The bird wants to eat the seeds. Solve all of the problems below. Then draw the bird's path by connecting facts with an answer of 6. There are addition and subtraction facts. Watch for + or −!

	7 +3	5 +9	6 +3	16 −8	4 +3	5 +6	6 +6	6 +7	4 +6	11 −9
14 −8	7 +4	4 +5	8 +4	9 −0	6 +8	12 −8	6 +1	4 +4	5 +7	2 +5
15 −9	5 +3	5 +5	6 +4	15 −8	5 +0	7 +8	11 −8	4 +9	18 −9	5 +8
6 +9	8 −2	12 −9	7 +7	3 +6	10 −8	5 +4	13 −9	2 +2	7 +9	2 +7
7 +5	3 +4	11 −5	3 +8	13 −7	8 +8	6 +5	5 +3	8 +1	3 +9	17 −8
1 +3	7 +3	6 +2	12 −6	16 −9	9 −3	7 −1	9 +9	1 +9	3 +3	8 +2
17 −9	4 +2	4 +7	14 −9	7 +6	5 +2	13 −8	10 −4	6 +0	8 −0	Bird Seed

Copyright © SRA/McGraw-Hill

Addition/Subtraction Facts (cont.) Home Link 2.13

Cut out the Fact Triangles. Show someone at home how you use them to practice adding and subtracting.

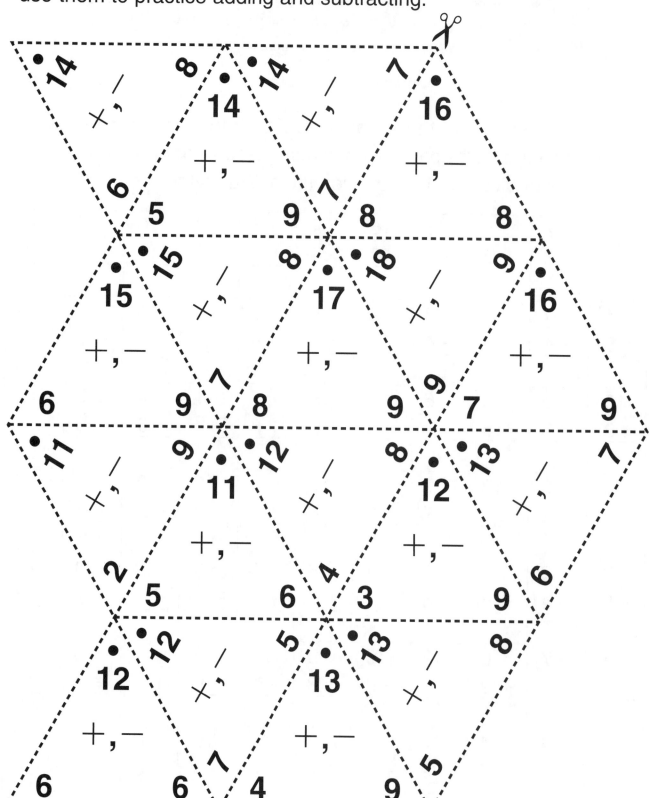

Copyright © SRA/McGraw–Hill

                                           Use with Lesson 2.13.

Unit 3: Place Value, Money, and Time

In Unit 3, children will read, write, and compare numbers from 0 through 999, working on concepts and skills built upon since *Kindergarten Everyday Mathematics*. Your child will review *place value*, or the meaning of each digit in a number. For example, in the number 52, the 5 represents 5 tens, and the 2 represents 2 ones.

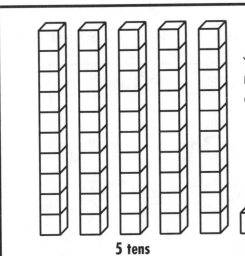

5 tens   **2 ones**

Your child will use base-10 blocks like these to help him or her understand the idea of place value.

Your child will also review money concepts, including finding the values of coins, identifying different coin combinations for the same amount, and making change.

43¢

43¢

43¢

Your child will read and record time using the hour and minute hands on an analog clock.

Use with Lesson 2.14.

Copyright © SRA/McGraw-Hill

Vocabulary

Important terms in Unit 3:

analog clock A clock that shows time by the position of the hour and minute hands.

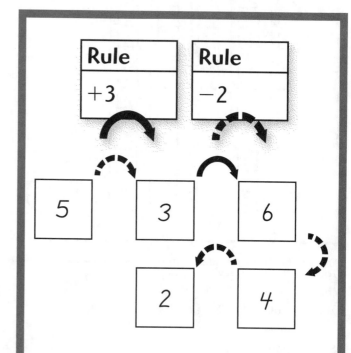

analog clock

digital clock A clock that shows time by using digits.

digital clock

data A collection of information, usually in the form of numbers. For example, the following data show the ages (in years) of six second graders: 6, 7, 6, 6, 7, 6.

middle number The number in the middle of a set of data when the data are organized in sequential order. For example, the numbers in this set of data are arranged from least to greatest:

2   3   ⑤   8   10

The number 5 is the middle number of this set. The middle number is also called the *median*.

two-rule Frames and Arrows A diagram that shows a sequence of numbers, or numbers that follow one after the other according to two rules. For example, see the Frames-and-Arrows diagram below.

Rule	Rule
+3	−2

5   3   6

2   4

To go from the first square to the second square, use the rule for the dashed arrow.

$$5 - \mathbf{2} = 3$$

To go from the second square to the third square, use the rule for the solid arrow.

$$3 + \mathbf{3} = 6$$

Copyright © SRA/McGraw-Hill

Use with Lesson 2.14.

Do-Anytime Activities

To work with your child on the concepts taught in this unit and in previous units, try these interesting and rewarding activities:

1 Have your child tell the time shown on an analog clock.

2 Draw an analog clock face without hands. Say a time and have your child show it on the clock face.

3 At the grocery store, give your child an item that costs less than $1.00. Allow your child to pay for the item separately. Ask him or her to determine how much change is due and to check that the change received is correct.

4 Gather a handful of coins with a value less than $2.00. Have your child calculate the total value.

5 Reinforce place value in 2- and 3-digit numbers. For example, in the number 694, the digit 6 means 6 hundreds, or 600; the digit 9 means 9 tens, or 90; and the digit 4 means 4 ones, or 4.

As You Help Your Child with Homework

As your child brings home assignments, you may want to go over the instructions together, clarifying them as necessary. The answers listed below will guide you through this unit's Home Links.

Home Link 3.1

1. a. 374   **b.** 507   **2.** 740

3. 936   **4.** 8; 0; 6   **5.** 2; 3; 1

Home Link 3.3

2. 6:30   **3.** 2:15   **4.** 9:00   **5.** 1:30

6.    **7.**

8.    **9.**

Home Link 3.4

1. | Rule | *Sample answers:*
| Add 12 |

In	Out	Out in a different way
I	II ..	I :: ....
II	III	II ::::: : .....
II	III	II ::::: ::: ..

2. | Rule |
| Add 16 |

In	Out	Out in a different way
IIII .	IIIII	IIII ::::: ::....
.....	I :....	II .

Home Link 3.6

1. 40¢; 50¢; 55¢   **2.** 50¢; 45¢; 55¢

Home Link 3.8

5¢; 35¢; 16¢; 5¢; 2¢; 52¢

Copyright © SRA/McGraw-Hill

Use with Lesson 2.14.

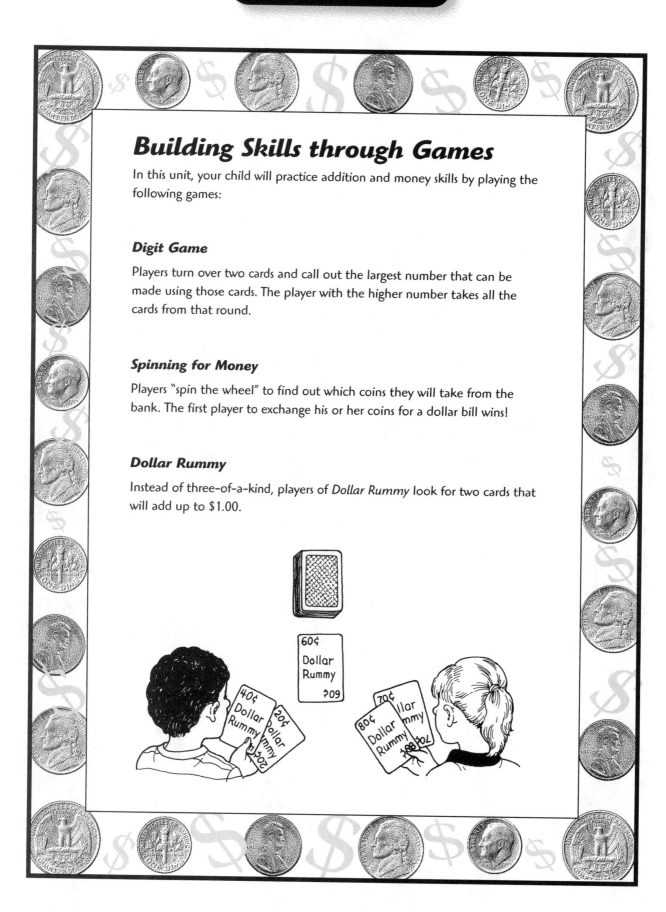

Building Skills through Games

In this unit, your child will practice addition and money skills by playing the following games:

Digit Game

Players turn over two cards and call out the largest number that can be made using those cards. The player with the higher number takes all the cards from that round.

Spinning for Money

Players "spin the wheel" to find out which coins they will take from the bank. The first player to exchange his or her coins for a dollar bill wins!

Dollar Rummy

Instead of three-of-a-kind, players of *Dollar Rummy* look for two cards that will add up to $1.00.

Copyright © SRA/McGraw-Hill

Use with Lesson 2.14.

Place Value

Family Note

All numbers are made up of digits. The value of a digit depends on its place in the number. In the number 704, the digit 7 means 7 hundreds, the digit 0 means 0 tens, and the digit 4 means 4 ones. This idea is called **place value.**

Your child has been using base-10 blocks to help him or her understand the idea of place value. Base-10 blocks are shown in Problems 1a and 1b below. A "cube" (with each side 1 unit long) represents 1. A "long" (a rod that is 10 units long) represents 10. And a "flat" (a square with each side 10 units long) represents 100.

Please return this Home Link to school tomorrow.

1. Which number do the base-10 blocks show?

a.

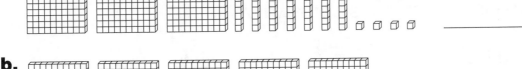

          _____

b.

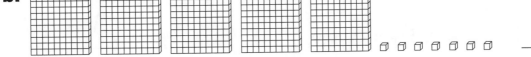

          _____

2. Write a number with
7 in the hundreds place,
0 in the ones place, and
4 in the tens place.

_____

3. Write a number with
3 in the tens place,
6 in the ones place, and
9 in the hundreds place.

_____

4. In 806, how
many hundreds? _____

How many tens? _____

How many ones? _____

5. In 231, how
many hundreds? _____

How many tens? _____

How many ones? _____

Copyright © SRA/McGraw-Hill

Use with Lesson 3.1.

How Much Does It Cost?

Family Note

In this activity, your child looks through advertisements, selects items that cost less than $2.00, and shows how to pay for those items in more than one way. For example, your child could pay for an item that costs 79¢ by drawing 3 quarters and 4 pennies or by drawing 7 dimes and 9 pennies. If you do not have advertisements showing prices, make up some items and prices for your child.

Please return this Home Link to school tomorrow.

Look at newspaper or magazine advertisements. Find items that cost less than $2.00. Write the name and price of each item.

Show someone at home how you would pay for these items with coins and a $1 bill. Write Ⓟ, Ⓝ, Ⓓ, Ⓠ, and $1. Try to show amounts in more than one way.

1. I would buy _____. It costs _____.

This is one way I would pay: _____

This is another way: _____

2. I would buy _____. It costs _____.

This is one way I would pay: _____

This is another way: _____

3. I would buy _____. It costs _____.

This is one way I would pay: _____

This is another way: _____

Copyright © SRA/McGraw-Hill

Times of Day

Family Note

Your child has been learning how to tell time by writing times shown on an analog clock (a clock with an hour hand and a minute hand) and by setting the hands on an analog clock to show a specific time. To complete the exercises on this page, your child will need a paper clock or a real clock with an hour hand and a minute hand. You can make a clock from *Math Masters,* page 40. Ask your child to show you other times on his or her clock.

Please return this Home Link to school tomorrow.

1. Use your clock to show someone at home the time you do the following activities. Write the time under each activity.

Eat dinner   Go to bed   Get up   Eat lunch

____:____   ____:____   ____:____   ____:____

Write the time.

2.

____:____

3.

____:____

Copyright © SRA/McGraw-Hill

Use with Lesson 3.3.

Times of Day (cont.)

4.

_____:_____

5.

_____:_____

Draw the hands to match the time.

6.

4:00

7.

9:30

8.

12:45

9.

10:15

Copyright © SRA/McGraw-Hill

"What's My Rule?" with Blocks

Family Note

Your child will complete the tables on this page by drawing tens and ones for 2–digit numbers. More than one picture can be drawn for a number. For example, to show 26, your child might draw 2 tens and 6 ones, 1 ten and 16 ones, or 26 ones. The symbol | stands for 10, and the symbol • stands for 1.

Please return this Home Link to school tomorrow.

1. Draw simple pictures of base-10 blocks to complete the table.

Rule
Add 12

In	Out	Out in a Different Way
•••	| •••••	:::::: •••••
|	|| ••	
|| ••••		
|| •••••• •		

2. Write the rule. Then complete the table.

Rule

In	Out	Out in a Different Way
||||| •••	||||| ••••• ••••	||||| :::::: :::::.
| ••••••• ••	|| :::::. •••••	| :::::: •••••
|||| •		
•••••		

Copyright © SRA/McGraw-Hill

Pockets Bar Graph

Family Note

Help your child to first fill in the table below and then display the data by making a **bar graph.**

Please return this Home Link to school tomorrow.

1. Pick five people. Count the number of pockets that each person's clothing has. Complete the table.

2. Draw a bar graph for your data. First, write the name of each person on a line at the bottom of the graph. Then, color the bar above each name to show how many pockets that person has.

Name	Number of Pockets

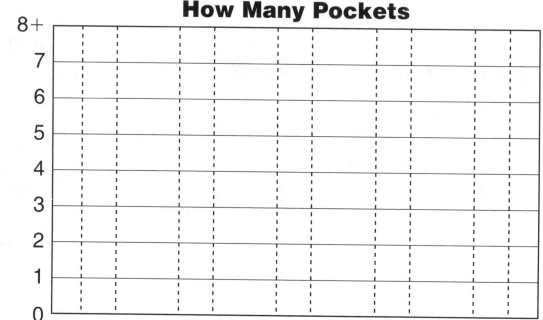

How Many Pockets

Number of Pockets

8+
7
6
5
4
3
2
1
0

Names

Copyright © SRA/McGraw-Hill

Use with Lesson 3.5.

Frames-and-Arrows Problems

Family Note

Frames-and-Arrows diagrams show sequences of numbers—numbers that follow one after the other according to a rule.

   The problems on this Home Link are a variation of the Frames-and-Arrows problems your child brought home in the last unit. In each of the problems below, two different rules are represented by two different arrows.

Please return this Home Link to school tomorrow.

Show someone at home how to solve these Frames-and-Arrows problems. Use coins to help you.

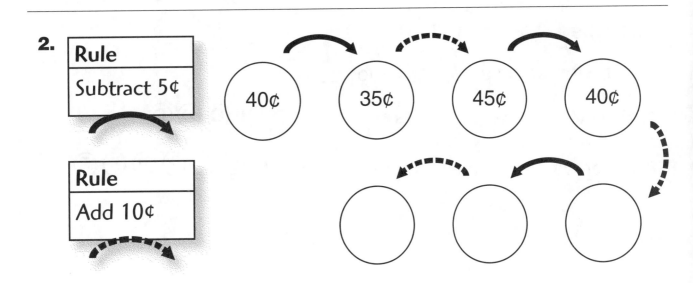

Copyright © SRA/McGraw-Hill

Change at a Garage Sale

**Family
Note**

Encourage your child to make change by counting up. Using real coins and dollar bills will make this activity easier. *For example:*

- Start with the cost of an item—65 cents.
- Count up to the money given—$1.00.

One way to make change: Put down a nickel and say "70." Then put down 3 dimes and say "80, 90, 1 dollar." *Another way:* Put down 3 dimes and say "75, 85, 95." Then put down 5 pennies and say "96, 97, 98, 99, 1 dollar."

Please return this Home Link to school tomorrow.

Pretend you are having a garage sale. Do the following:

- Find small items in your home to "sell."

- Give each item a price less than $1.00.
  Give each item a different price.

- Pretend that customers pay for each item with a $1 bill.

- Show someone at home how you would make change by counting up. Use Ⓟ, Ⓝ, Ⓓ, and Ⓠ.

- Show another way you could make change for the same item.

Example

The customer buys ___*a pen*___ for ___*65¢*___.

One way I can make change: _____ Ⓝ Ⓓ Ⓓ Ⓓ

Another way I can make change: _____ Ⓓ Ⓓ Ⓓ Ⓟ Ⓟ Ⓟ Ⓟ Ⓟ

Copyright © SRA/McGraw-Hill

Change at a Garage Sale (cont.)

1. The customer buys _____ for _____ .

One way I can make change: _____

Another way I can make change: _____

2. The customer buys _____ for _____ .

One way I can make change: _____

Another way I can make change: _____

3. The customer buys _____ for _____ .

One way I can make change: _____

Another way I can make change:_____

4. The customer buys _____ for _____ .

One way I can make change: _____

Another way I can make change: _____

5. The customer buys _____ for _____ .

One way I can make change: _____

Another way I can make change: _____

Copyright © SRA/McGraw-Hill

Counting up to Make Change

Family Note

Help your child identify the amount of change that he or she would receive by "counting up" from the price of the item to the amount of money that was used to pay for the item. It may be helpful to act out the problems with your child using real coins and bills.

Please return this Home Link to school tomorrow.

Complete the table.

I buy:	It costs:	I pay with:	My change is:
a bag of potato chips	70¢	Q Q Q	_____ ¢
a box of crayons	65¢	$1	_____ ¢
a pen	59¢	Q Q Q	_____ ¢
an apple	45¢	D D D D D	_____ ¢
a notebook	73¢	Q Q D D N	_____ ¢
a ruler	48¢	$1	_____ ¢
	_____	_____	_____ ¢
	_____	_____	_____ ¢

Copyright © SRA/McGraw-Hill

Use with Lesson 3.8.

Unit 4: Addition and Subtraction

In Unit 4, children will use addition and subtraction stories to develop mental-arithmetic skills. Mental arithmetic is computation done in one's head or by drawing pictures, making tallies, or using manipulatives (counters, money, number lines, and number grids—no calculators, though). Children can also use their own solution strategies.

A second grader uses a number grid to solve $5 + 9$.

1	2	3	4	⑤	6	7	8	9	10
11	12	13	⑭	⑮	16	17	18	19	20
21	22	23	24	25	26	27	28	29	30

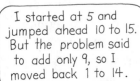

I started at 5 and jumped ahead 10 to 15. But the problem said to add only 9, so I moved back 1 to 14.

Addition has two basic meanings: *putting together* and *changing to more.* In this unit, children will use **parts-and-total diagrams** and **change diagrams** to help them organize information in addition stories that either "put together" or "change to more." See the vocabulary section on page 276 to learn more about these diagrams.

Parts-and-Total Diagram

Total	
?	
Part	Part
20	16

Change Diagram

Start	Change	End
20	+6	?

Children will also develop estimation skills by solving problems that involve purchases. For example, your child will estimate whether $5.00 is enough to buy a pen that costs $1.69, a notebook that costs $2.25, and a ruler that costs 89¢.

In the last part of this unit, children will learn paper-and-pencil strategies for addition and will continue to gain hands-on experience with thermometers, money, tape measures, and rulers. Home Links 4.8 and 4.9, which you will receive later, will give you more information on the paper-and-pencil strategies that your child will be learning.

Please keep this Family Letter for reference as your child works through Unit 4.

Copyright © SRA/McGraw-Hill

Vocabulary

Important terms in Unit 4:

change-to-more number story A number story having a starting quantity that is increased so that the ending quantity is more than the starting quantity.

For example: *Nick has 20 comic books. He buys 6 more. How many comic books does Nick have now?*

change diagram A device used to organize information in a change-to-more or change-to-less number story. The change diagram below illustrates the above change-to-more number story.

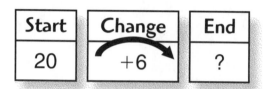

Start	Change	End
20	+6	?

mental arithmetic Computation done totally or partially in one's head, using a variety of strategies.

parts-and-total number story A number story in which two or more quantities (parts) are combined to form a total quantity. For example: *Carl baked 20 cookies. Sam baked 16 cookies. How many cookies did Carl and Sam bake in all?*

parts-and-total diagram A device used to organize information in a parts-and-total number story. The parts-and-total diagram below, for example, illustrates the previous example described under "parts-and-total number story."

Total	
?	
Part	**Part**
20	16

estimate An educated guess, or an answer in the right "ballpark," rather than an exact answer.

algorithm A step-by-step set of instructions for doing something—for example, for solving addition or subtraction problems.

Building Skills through Games

In Unit 4, your child will practice addition skills by playing the following game:

Addition Spin
A "Spinner" and a "Checker" take turns adding two numbers and checking the sum. After five turns, each player uses a calculator to find the sum of his or her scores. The player with the higher total wins!

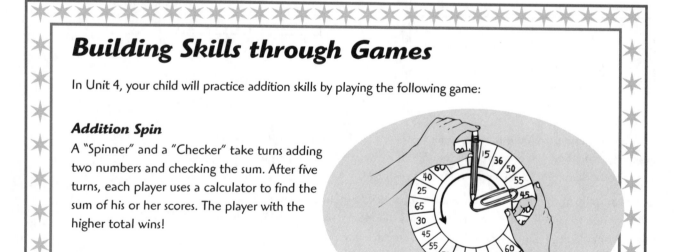

Copyright © SRA/McGraw-Hill

Do-Anytime Activities

To work with your child on the concepts taught in this unit and in previous units, try these interesting and rewarding activities:

1 Encourage your child to show you addition and subtraction strategies as these are developed during the unit.

2 Make up number stories involving estimation. For example, pretend that your child has $2.00 and that he or she wants to buy a pencil marked 64¢, a tablet marked 98¢, and an eraser marked 29¢. Help your child to estimate the total cost of the three items (without tax) and to determine if there is enough money to buy them. If appropriate, you can also ask your child to estimate the amount of change due.

3 Look at weather reports in the newspaper and on television and discuss differences between high and low temperatures. Also note the differences between the Fahrenheit and Celsius scales.

Copyright © SRA/McGraw-Hill

As You Help Your Child with Homework

As your child brings home assignments, you may want to go over the instructions together, clarifying them as necessary. The answers listed below will guide you through this unit's Home Links.

Home Link 4.1

1. 18 grapes; 11 + 7 = 18

2. 38 cards; 30 + 8 = 38

3. 52 pounds; 42 + 10 = 52

4. 27   **5.** 80   **6.** 83

7. 10   **8.** 17   **9.** 70

10. 30   **11.** 66   **12.** 80

Home Link 4.2

1. 47 pounds; 17 + 30 = 47

2. 75 pounds; 45 + 30 = 75

3. 60 pounds; 15 + 45 = 60

4. 92 pounds; 17 + 45 + 30 = 92

Home Link 4.3

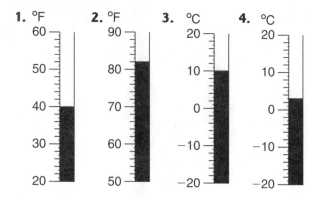

1. °F   **2.** °F   **3.** °C   **4.** °C

Home Link 4.4

1. 20°F   **2.** 34°F   **3.** 52°F

4. 96°F   **5.** 48°F   **6.** 73°F

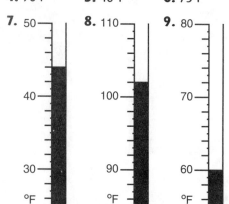

7. 50   **8.** 110   **9.** 80

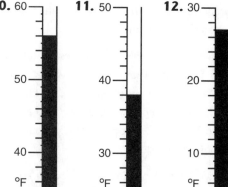

10. 60   **11.** 50   **12.** 30

13. 70   **14.** 35   **15.** 97

16. 26   **17.** 50   **18.** 68

Home Link 4.5

1. no   **2.** yes   **3.** no   **4.** yes

5. 100   **6.** 46   **7.** 47

Home Link 4.6

1. 30 marbles; 20 + 10 = 30

2. 54 cookies; 30 + 24 = 54

3. 100   **4.** 140   **5.** 79   **6.** 83

7. 94   **8.** 77

Home Link 4.7

2. About 20 inches

Home Link 4.8

1. 76   **2.** 100   **3.** 83   **4.** 120

5. 98   **6.** 90   **7.** 93   **8.** 85

9. 71   **10.** 83   **11.** 169   **12.** 544

Home Link 4.9

1. 89   **2.** 108   **3.** 83   **4.** 94

5. 77   **6.** 92   **7.** 185   **8.** 363

Copyright © SRA/McGraw–Hill

Use with Lesson 3.9.

Change Number Stories

Family Note

Your child has learned about a device called a "change diagram," and it is shown in the example below. Diagrams like this can help your child organize the information in a problem. When the information is organized, it is easier to decide which operation $(+, -, \times, \div)$ to use to solve the problem. Change diagrams are used to represent problems in which a starting quantity is increased or decreased. For the number stories on this Home Link, the starting quantity is always increased.

*Please return the **second page** of this Home Link to school tomorrow.*

Do the following for each number story on the next page:

- Write the numbers you know in the change diagram.

- Write ? for the number you need to find.

- Answer the question.

- Write a number model.

Example: Twenty-five children are riding on a bus.
At the next stop, 5 more children get on.
How many children are on the bus now?

Start	Change	End
25	+5	?

The starting number of children has been increased.

Answer: There are 30 children on the bus now.

Possible number model: 25 + 5 = 30

Copyright © SRA/McGraw-Hill

Change Number Stories (cont.)

1. Becky ate 11 grapes.
Later in the day she ate
7 more grapes.
How many grapes did she

eat in all? _____ grapes

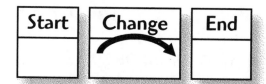

Number model:

_____

2. Bob has 30 baseball cards.
He buys 8 more.
How many baseball
cards does Bob

have now? _____ cards

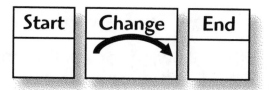

Number model:

_____

3. A large fish weighs 42 pounds.
A small fish weighs 10 pounds.
The large fish swallows the
small fish.
How much does the large fish

weigh now? _____ pounds

Number model:

_____

Add or subtract.

4. $20 + 7 =$ _____

5. _____ $= 40 + 40$

6. $3 + 80 =$ _____

7. $30 - 20 =$ _____

8. $47 - 30 =$ _____

9. $50 + 20 =$ _____

10. _____ $= 90 - 60$

11. $86 - 20 =$ _____

12. _____ $= 83 - 3$

Copyright © SRA/McGraw-Hill

Use with Lesson 4.1.

Parts-and-Total Number Stories

Family Note

Today your child learned about another device to use when solving number stories. We call it a "parts-and-total diagram." Parts-and-total diagrams are used to organize the information in problems in which two or more quantities (parts) are combined to form a total quantity.

*Please return the **second page** of this Home Link to school tomorrow.*

Large Suitcase
45 pounds

Small Suitcase
30 pounds

Backpack
17 pounds

Package
15 pounds

Use the weights shown in these pictures. Then do the following for each number story on the next page:

- Write the numbers you know in each parts-and-total diagram.

- Write ? for the number you want to find.

- Answer the question.

- Write a number model.

Example: Twelve fourth graders and 23 third graders are on a bus. How many children in all are on the bus?

The parts are known. The total is to be found.

Total	
?	
Part	Part
12	23

Answer: 35 children

Possible number model: 12 + 23 = 35

Copyright © SRA/McGraw-Hill

Number Stories (cont.)

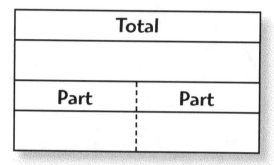

1. You wear the backpack and carry the small suitcase. How many pounds do you

carry in all? _____ pounds

Total	
Part	**Part**

Number model:

_____

2. You carry the large suitcase and the small suitcase. How many pounds do you

carry in all? _____ pounds

Total	
Part	**Part**

Number model:

_____

3. You carry the package and the large suitcase. How many pounds do you

carry in all? _____ pounds

Total	
Part	**Part**

Number model:

_____

4. You wear the backpack and carry both of the suitcases. How many pounds do you

carry in all? _____ pounds

Total		
Part	**Part**	**Part**

Number model:

_____

Copyright © SRA/McGraw-Hill

Use with Lesson 4.2.

Reading a Thermometer

Family Note

In today's lesson, your child read temperatures on a real thermometer and on a thermometer pictured on a poster. The thermometers on this page show three different-size degree marks. The longest marks show 10-degree intervals, the medium-size marks show even-number degree intervals, and the shortest marks show odd-number degree intervals.

Help your child find the temperature shown by each thermometer by starting at a degree mark showing tens, counting the medium-size marks by 2s, and, if the temperature is at a short mark, counting 1 more.

Please return this Home Link to school tomorrow.

Circle the thermometer that shows the correct temperature.

1. 40°F

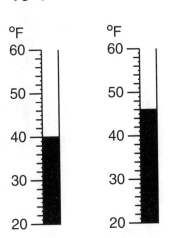

2. 82°F

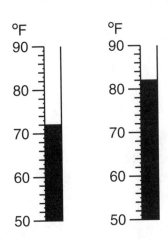

3. 10°C

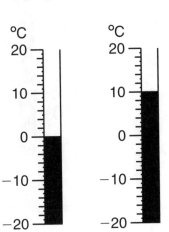

4. 3°C

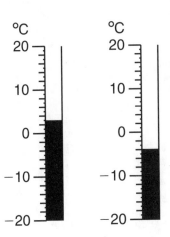

Copyright © SRA/McGraw-Hill

Name ___ Date ___ Time ___

Temperature

Family Note

In today's lesson, your child solved problems involving temperatures. On the thermometers on this Home Link, the longer degree marks are spaced at 2-degree intervals. Point to these degree marks while your child counts by 2s; "40, 42, 44, 46, 48, 50 degrees."

Problems 6 and 12 involve temperatures that are an "odd" number of degrees. Help your child use the shorter degree marks to get the correct answers.

Please return this Home Link to school tomorrow.

Write the temperature shown on each thermometer.

1. 30 20 10 °F

_____

2. 40 30 20 °F

_____

3. 60 50 40 °F

_____

4. 110 100 90 °F

_____

5. 60 50 40 °F

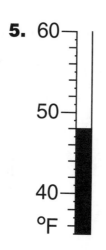

_____

6. 80 70 60 °F

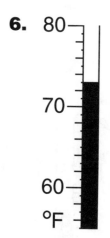

_____

Copyright © SRA/McGraw-Hill

Use with Lesson 4.4.

Fill in each thermometer to show the temperature.

7. Show 44°F.

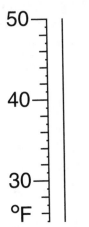

8. Show 102°F.

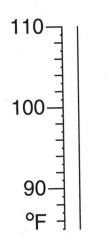

9. Show 60°F.

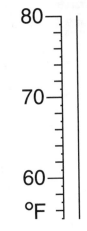

10. Show 56°F.

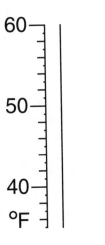

11. Show 38°F.

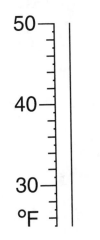

12. Show 27°F.

Add or subtract.

13. 30 + 40 = _____

14. 75 − 40 = _____

15. _____ = 7 + 90

16. _____ = 46 − 20

17.   53
      − 3

18.   60
      + 8

Copyright © SRA/McGraw-Hill

Shopping at the Grocery Store

**Family
Note**

Many problems in and out of the classroom require estimates rather than exact
answers. In Problems 1–5 below, you need to know only whether the total cost is
greater than $1.00 or less than $1.00; you do not need to know the exact total
cost. In Problem 1, for example, help your child notice that the price of the can
of frozen orange juice (98¢) is almost $1.00. Since a lemon is 10¢, your child
could not buy both items.

Please return this Home Link to school tomorrow.

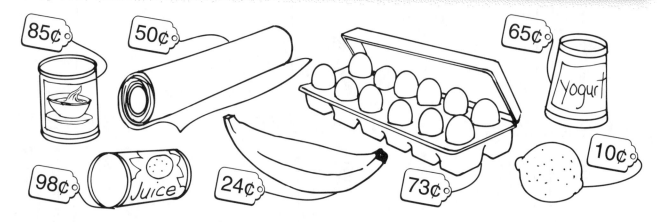

You have $1.00 to spend at the grocery store. Use estimation to
answer each question.

Can you buy:	**Circle *Yes* or *No*.**	
1. a can of frozen orange juice and a lemon?	Yes	No
2. a banana and a dozen eggs?	Yes	No
3. a container of yogurt and a roll of paper towels?	Yes	No
4. a lemon and a can of soup?	Yes	No

Add or subtract.

5. 50 + 50 = _____   **6.** _____ = 6 + 40   **7.** _____ = 67 − 20

Copyright © SRA/McGraw-Hill

Name   Date   Time

Addition Number Stories

Family Note

In today's lesson, your child solved problems by adding 2-digit numbers mentally. For example, to find 34 + 23, you might first add the tens: 30 + 20 = 50. Then add the ones: 4 + 3 = 7. Finally, combine the tens and ones: 50 + 7 = 57.

Please return this Home Link to school tomorrow.

Try to solve Problems 1 and 2 mentally. Fill in the diagrams. Then write the answers and number models.

1. Ruth had 20 marbles in her collection. Her brother gave her 10 more. How many marbles does Ruth have now?

Start	Change	End

Answer: _____
(unit)

Number model:

_____

2. Tim baked 30 ginger snaps and 24 sugar cookies. How many cookies did he bake?

Total	
Part	Part

Answer: _____
(unit)

Number model:

_____

Try to do each problem mentally. Then write the answer.

Unit
raisins

3. _____ = 40 + 60

4. 90 + 50 = _____

5. _____ = 70 + 9

6. 80 + 3 = _____

7. 30 + 64 = _____

8. _____ = 27 + 50

Use with Lesson 4.6.

287

Measuring to the Nearest Inch

Family Note

In today's lesson, your child measured the length, width, or height of objects to the nearest inch and centimeter. In later lessons, your child will make more precise measurements (such as measuring to the nearest half-inch).

Ask your child to show you how to measure the sections of the path on this page. If you do not have a ruler at home, you may wish to buy an inexpensive one (preferably one having both inches and centimeters). Encourage your child to measure objects in your home.

Please return this Home Link to school tomorrow.

1. The ant will take this path to get to the picnic. Measure each part of the path to the nearest inch. If you do not have a ruler at home, cut out and use the ruler at the bottom of the page.

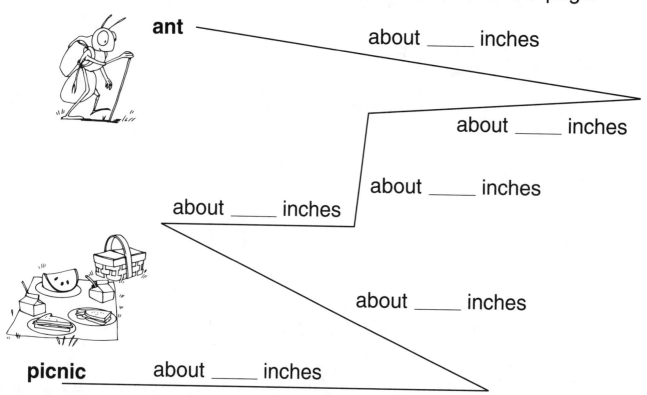

ant

about _____ inches

about _____ inches

about _____ inches

about _____ inches

about _____ inches

picnic   about _____ inches

2. What is the total length of the path? about _____ inches

Copyright © SRA/McGraw-Hill

INCHES   0   1   2   3   4   5   6

Use with Lesson 4.7.

Addition Strategies

Family Note

Everyday Mathematics encourages children to use a variety of strategies to solve computation problems. By doing so, children are developing a sense for numbers and operations rather than simply memorizing a series of steps.

We suggest that you give your child an opportunity to explore and choose addition strategies that he or she feels comfortable using. At some point, you may want to share the method that you know from your own school experience. But please allow your child some time to use his or her own methods before doing so.

Below are three examples of methods that your child might use to solve 2-digit addition problems.

Counting On

47 + 33 = ?   ←——— "My problem"

47 57 67 77   ←——— "Start at 47. Count up 30 more."

$\underline{+\ 3}$ ←——— "Add on 3 more."

80   ←——— "The answer is 80."

Combining Groups (1s, 10s, ...) Separately

29 + 37 = ?   ←——— "My problem"

20 + 30 = 50   ←——— "Add the tens."

9 + 7 = $\underline{16}$ ←——— "Add the ones."

66   ←——— "Put these together. The answer is 66."

Adjusting and Compensating

52 + 29 = ?   ←——— "My problem"

30   ←——— "30 is close to 29, just 1 more."

52 + 30 = 82   ←——— "52 plus 30 is 82."

$\underline{-\ 1}$ ←——— "Take away 1, because I added 30 instead of 29."

81   ←——— "The answer is 81."

Encourage your child to use a "ballpark estimate" as a way to check whether or not an answer to a computation problem makes sense. For example, in 34 + 59, 34 is close to 30 and 59 is close to 60. 30 + 60 = 90 is your ballpark estimate. "90 is close to my answer 93, so 93 is a reasonable answer."

*Please return the **second page** of this Home Link to school tomorrow.*

Copyright © SRA/McGraw-Hill

Addition Strategies (cont.)

Add.

1. 40 + 36 = _____ **2.** 20 + 80 = _____ **3.** _____ = 53 + 30

4. 60 + 60 = _____ **5.** _____ = 50 + 48 **6.** _____ = 70 + 20

Add. Show your work in the workspaces.

Check your work. Write a number model to show your ballpark estimate.

7.
```
   34
 + 59
```
Answer

Ballpark estimate:

_____

8. 17 + 68

Answer

Ballpark estimate:

_____

9. 46 + 25

Answer

Ballpark estimate:

_____

10. 56 + 27

Answer

Ballpark estimate:

_____

11. 123 + 46

Answer

Ballpark estimate:

_____

12.
```
   318
 + 226
```
Answer

Ballpark estimate:

_____

Copyright © SRA/McGraw-Hill

Use with Lesson 4.8.

Place Value

Family Note

Your child is learning a method for addition that focuses on place value. Find 68 + 24.

	10s	1s
	6	8
+	2	4
	8	0
+	1	2
	9	2

Add the tens (60 + 20 = 80) and write the sum.

Add the ones (8 + 4 = 12) and write the sum.

Combine the tens and ones (80 + 12 = 92) to find the final sum.

Encourage your child to use the correct place-value language when using this method. For example, when adding tens in the example, say "60 + 20 = 80," not "6 + 2 = 8." We only recently introduced this method, so allow plenty of time for practice before expecting your child to be able to use it easily.

Please return this Home Link to school tomorrow.

Find each sum.

1. 53
     + 36

2. 27
     + 81

3. 45
     + 38

4. 18
     + 76

5. 29
     + 48

6. 53
     + 39

7. 154
     + 31

8. 126
     + 237

Copyright © SRA/McGraw-Hill

Family Letter

Unit 5: 3-D and 2-D Shapes

Geometry is an important component of *Everyday Mathematics*. Studying geometry helps develop spatial sense and the ability to represent and describe the world. Instead of waiting until ninth or tenth grade, *Everyday Mathematics* introduces geometric fundamentals in Kindergarten and develops them over time. Children are thus prepared to study more advanced geometric topics later.

In Unit 5, children will consider five basic kinds of 3-dimensional shapes: prisms, pyramids, cylinders, cones, and spheres. To sort the shapes, children will explore similarities and differences among them. They will become familiar with both the names of shapes and the terms for parts of shapes.

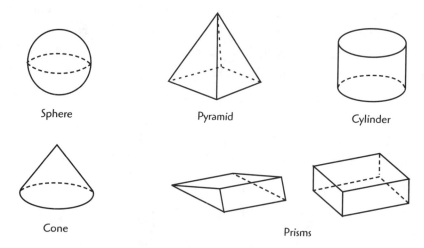

Sphere   Pyramid   Cylinder

Cone   Prisms

Children will also study **polygons,** or 2-dimensional shapes that form the flat surfaces of prisms and pyramids, as they look for examples in real life.

Later in the unit, children will explore **line symmetry** as they experiment with folding 2-dimensional shapes and matching the halves. Children will also cut out shapes and look for lines of symmetry in each shape. When children are given half of a shape, they will draw the missing half. Children will be asked to find symmetrical objects at home and in other places.

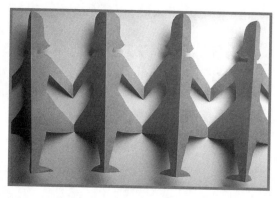

Please keep this Family Letter for reference as your child works through Unit 5.

Copyright © SRA/McGraw-Hill

Use with Lesson 4.10.

Vocabulary

The purpose of introducing children to the various shapes is to explore the characteristics of the shapes, not to teach vocabulary. This list is presented simply to acquaint you with some of the terms your child will be hearing in context in the classroom.

line segment Part of a straight line connecting two points.

Line segment *AB* or *BA*

angle (of a polygon) A figure formed by any two sides that have a common endpoint.

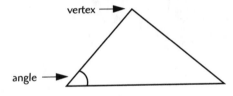

parallel Always the same distance apart; never meeting.

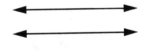

Two parallel lines

polygon A 2-dimensional figure with straight sides (line segments) connected end to end and no side crosses another side. *Poly-* means *many,* and *-gon* means *angle.*

polyhedron A 3-dimensional geometric shape with flat surfaces. The following shapes are regular polyhedrons:

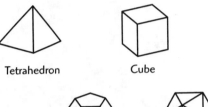

Tetrahedron   Cube   Octahedron

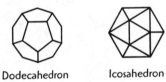

Dodecahedron   Icosahedron

face A flat surface on a 3-dimensional shape.

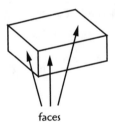

faces

vertex (corner) The point at which the sides of a polygon meet; the point at which the edges of a polyhedron meet.

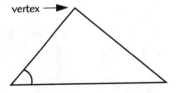

line symmetry The exact matching of two halves of a shape.

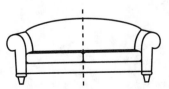

Copyright © SRA/McGraw-Hill

Use with Lesson 4.10.

Do-Anytime Activities

To work with your child on the concepts taught in this unit and in previous units, try these interesting and rewarding activities:

1 Together, look for 2-dimensional and 3-dimensional shapes in your home and neighborhood. Explore and name shapes and brainstorm about their characteristics. For example, compare a soup can and a tissue box. Talk about the differences between the shapes of the surfaces.

2 Use household items, such as toothpicks and marshmallows, straws and twist-ties, sticks, and paper to construct shapes like those shown below.

3 Look for geometric patterns in tile floors, quilts, buildings, and so on.

Copyright © SRA/McGraw-Hill

Use with Lesson 4.10.

As You Help Your Child with Homework

As your child brings home assignments, you may want to go over the instructions together, clarifying them as necessary. The answers listed below will guide you through this unit's Home Links.

Home Link 5.1

1.

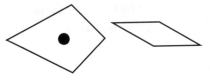

2. The shapes all have 4 sides.

Home Link 5.2

1. **2.** **3.**

Home Link 5.4

1. **2.** **3.**

6 triangles

Home Link 5.5

1.
A   B

X (blue)

D   X   C
   (red)

2.   ;no
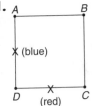

Home Link 5.6

1. the trapezoid   **2.** the square

3. the rectangle

Building Skills through Games

In Unit 5, your child will practice addition, time-telling, and money skills by playing the following games:

Addition Spin

Players "spin the wheel" twice and add the two selected numbers. Players check their partners' addition with a calculator.

Dollar Rummy

Instead of three-of-a-kind, players look for two cards that will add up to $1.00.

Clock Concentration

Players match pairs of cards showing the time on analog and digital clocks, or with words.

Copyright © SRA/McGraw-Hill

Use with Lesson 4.10.

"What's My Attribute Rule?"

Family Note

Your child has been classifying shapes according to such rules as *only large shapes, only small red shapes,* or *only triangles.* Help your child determine which shapes in Problem 1 fit the rule by checking those shapes against the shapes below. What do all of the shapes that fit the rule have in common? (They all have 4 sides.) Once your child thinks that she or he knows the rule, check that rule against the shapes that do NOT fit the rule. Do any of those shapes follow the proposed rule?

Please return this Home Link to school tomorrow.

These shapes fit the rule.

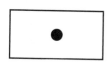 

These shapes do NOT fit the rule.

   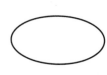

1. Which of these shapes fit the rule? Circle them.

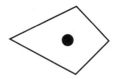  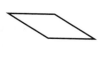 

2. What is the rule? _____

3. Draw a new shape that fits the rule.

Copyright © SRA/McGraw-Hill

Use with Lesson 5.1.

Attributes

Family Note

In this lesson, your child identified one or two ways in which blocks are different—by size, shape, or color. In each problem below, three of the shapes have something in common that is not a feature of the fourth shape. For example, in Problem 1, three of the shapes are squares, and the fourth shape is a circle. Help your child decide which shape is different. The attributes considered are *size* (small or large), *shape* (square, circle, or triangle), and *face* (smile or frown).

Please return this Home Link to school tomorrow.

1. Which shape does NOT belong? Circle it.

2. Which shape does NOT belong? Circle it.

3. Which shape does NOT belong? Circle it.

Copyright © SRA/McGraw-Hill

Polygons

Family Note

In this lesson, your child has been learning the names of different polygons. A polygon is a closed figure made up of straight sides, and you can trace and come back to where you started without retracing or crossing any part. Different types of polygons are shown below. Examples of polygons can be found in real-life objects. For example, a stop sign is an octagon and this page is a rectangle. As your child cuts out pictures of polygons, discuss each shape. Count the sides and angles and try to name the polygons. Talk about how the polygons are alike and different.

Please return this Home Link to school tomorrow or as requested by the teacher.

1. Cut out pictures from newspapers and magazines that show triangles, quadrangles, and other polygons. Ask an adult for permission first.

2. Paste each picture on a sheet of paper.

3. Write the names of some of the polygons under the pictures.

4. Bring your pictures to school.

Triangles	**Quadrangles or Quadrilaterals**
Pentagons	**Hexagons**
Heptagons	**Octagons**

These are NOT polygons.

Copyright © SRA/McGraw-Hill

Use with Lesson 5.3.

Family Note

In this lesson, your child learned to name points and line segments with capital letters. Using a straightedge, your child drew line segments to create shapes. Provide your child with a ruler, a piece of stiff cardboard, or another object having a straight edge. Observe as your child draws line segments. Ask your child to name the shapes that he or she draws in Problems 1 and 2 below (a 6-pointed star and a hexagon).

Please return this Home Link to school tomorrow.

Use a straightedge to draw line segments.

1. Draw these line segments:

$\overline{AC}$

$\overline{CE}$

$\overline{EA}$

$\overline{BF}$

$\overline{BD}$

$\overline{DF}$

A

B   F

C   D   E

2. Draw these line segments:

$\overline{AB}$

$\overline{BC}$

$\overline{CD}$

$\overline{DE}$

$\overline{EF}$

$\overline{FA}$

A

B   F

C   D   E

---

3. Draw the following line segments:

$\overline{AB}$, $\overline{BC}$

$\overline{CD}$, $\overline{DE}$

$\overline{EF}$, $\overline{FA}$

$\overline{AD}$, $\overline{FC}$

$\overline{BE}$

B

A   C

F   E   D

How many triangles are

there? _____

4. Draw points on the back of this page. Label each point with a letter. Use a straightedge to connect the points with line segments to make polygons.

Copyright © SRA/McGraw-Hill

Use with Lesson 5.4.

Parallel Line Segments

Family Note

Parallel line segments are always the same distance apart. They would never meet, even if they were extended forever in either or both directions. In Problem 1, line segment DC is parallel to line segment AB, and line segment AD is parallel to line segment BC. There are no parallel line segments in Problem 2.

*Please return the **top part** of this Home Link to school tomorrow.*

Copyright © SRA/McGraw–Hill

1. Draw line segments *AB, BC, CD,* and *DA.*

A •   • B

Put a red **X** on the line segment that is parallel to line segment *AB.*

Put a blue **X** on the line segment that is parallel to line segment *BC.*

D •   • C

2. Draw line segments *AB, BC,* and *CA.*

A
•

Is any line segment in your drawing parallel to line segment *AB?* _____

C •   • B

- -

Special Family Note

In Lesson 5.7, your child will be studying 3-dimensional shapes. Help your child gather 3-dimensional objects for a class collection that we call the "Shapes Museum." You and your child might want to separate the objects you collect according to shape.

Copyright © SRA/McGraw–Hill

Shapes Museum

For the next few days, your class will collect things to put into a Shapes Museum. Starting tomorrow, bring items like boxes, soup cans, party hats, pyramids, and balls to school. Ask an adult for permission before bringing in these items. Make sure that the things you bring are clean.

Quadrangles

Family Note

In this lesson, your child has been learning about different types of quadrangles, or polygons that have 4 sides. Quadrangles are also called *quadrilaterals*. In each problem below, three shapes have a common attribute that the fourth shape does not have. Encourage your child to use the hint given with each problem. In Problem 1, the trapezoid is different, because it has only 1 pair of parallel sides. In Problem 2, the square is different, because it is the only quadrangle with 4 square corners. In Problem 3, the rectangle is different, because it is the only quadrangle that doesn't have 4 equal sides.

Please return this Home Link to school tomorrow.

1. Which quadrangle is different from the other three?

_____

(*Hint:* Look at the number of pairs of parallel sides.)

rhombus

rectangle

square

trapezoid

2. Which quadrangle is different from the other three?

_____

square

kite

trapezoid

rhombus

(*Hint:* Look at the number of square corners.)

3. Which quadrangle is different from the other three?

_____

rhombus

rhombus

square

rectangle

(*Hint:* Look at the lengths of the sides.)

Copyright © SRA/McGraw-Hill

Use with Lesson 5.6.

3-D Shapes

Family Note

In this lesson, children have identified and compared 3-dimensional shapes. Our class also has created a Shapes Museum using the objects that children brought to school. Read your child's list of shapes. Together, find shapes to complete the list.

Please return this Home Link to school tomorrow.

On your way home, look for things that have these five shapes.

Make a list of things you see. Show your list to someone at home. Can you find any more shapes in your home? Add them to your list.

Prisms

Prisms

Cones

Cone

Pyramids

Pyramids

Spheres

Sphere

Cylinders

Cylinder

Copyright © SRA/McGraw-Hill

Make a Triangular Pyramid

Family Note

Your child has used straws and twist-ties to construct pyramids with different-shape bases. The *base* can be a triangle, a rectangle, a pentagon, or another shape. Help your child construct a triangular pyramid (a pyramid with a triangle as the base) by using the cutout pattern below. After constructing the pyramid, ask your child the following questions:

· What is the shape of the base? *(A triangle)*
· How many edges does the pyramid have? *(6)*
· How many faces does the pyramid have? *(4)*
· How many vertices does the pyramid have? *(4)*

Please return this Home Link to school tomorrow.

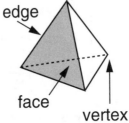

Ask someone at home to help you make a triangular pyramid out of this pattern.

1. Cut on the dashed lines.

2. Fold on the dotted lines.

3. Tape or glue tabs "inside" or "outside."

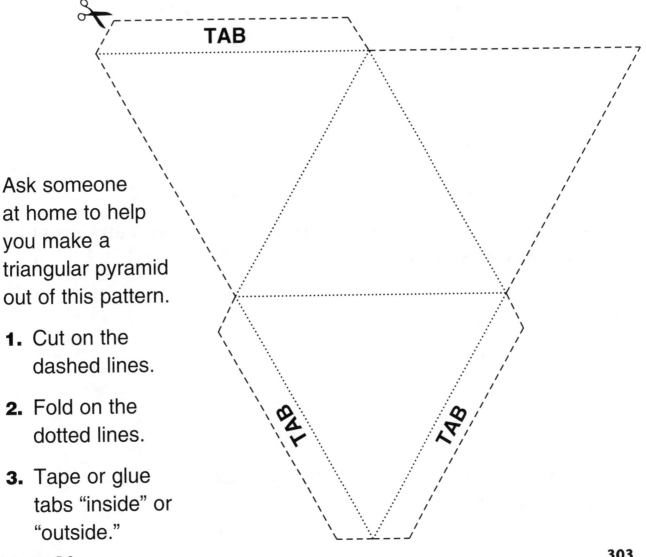

TAB

TAB

TAB

Copyright © SRA/McGraw-Hill

Symmetry Hunt

Home Link 5.9

Family Note

In this lesson, your child has been determining if shapes are symmetrical. A shape has *symmetry* if it has two halves that look alike but face in opposite directions. A *line of symmetry* divides the shape into two matching parts. Lines of symmetry are shown in the objects below. Help your child find other objects that are symmetrical. Remember that some shapes, such as the mirror below, may be symmetrical in more than one way.

Please return this Home Link to school tomorrow.

1. Ask someone to help you make a list of things at home that have symmetry. For example, you might list a window, a sofa, or a mirror.

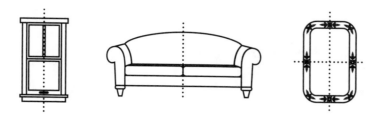

My List: _____

_____

2. Draw a picture of one thing on your list. Draw as many lines of symmetry as you can.

3. If you find pictures in books or magazines that show symmetry, bring them to school.

Copyright © SRA/McGraw-Hill

Use with Lesson 5.9.

Family Letter

Unit 6: Review and Extension of Whole-Number Operations

In Unit 6, children will take another look at the addition and subtraction diagrams that were introduced in Unit 4.

Children will also learn a procedure for subtraction called the *trade-first method.* You will receive more information about this method when we begin to use it in class.

Later in this unit, children will strengthen their understanding of multiplication and division as they act out number stories using manipulatives and arrays; complete diagrams to show the relationships in multiplication problems; and then begin to record corresponding number models.

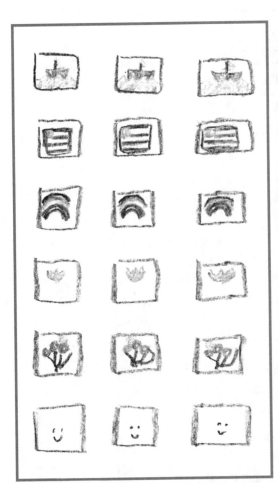

Start	Change	End
9	+3	?

Total	
50	
Part	**Part**
18	?

Quantity
35

Quantity	Difference
20	?

above: addition and subtraction diagrams

left: A child uses an array to solve the following problem: A sheet of stamps has 6 rows. Each row has 3 stamps. How many stamps are on a sheet?

below: multiplication diagram

boxes	marbles per box	marbles in all
3	7	?

Please keep this Family Letter for reference as your child works through Unit 6.

Copyright © SRA/McGraw-Hill

Vocabulary

Important terms in Unit 6:

comparison number story A number story that involves the difference between two quantities. For example: Ross sold 12 cookies. Anthony sold 5 cookies. How many more cookies did Ross sell?

comparison diagram A convenient way to represent a comparison number story. The following diagram, for example, represents the number story in the previous paragraph:

Quantity
12

Quantity	Difference
5	?

trade-first method (algorithm) A procedure for subtracting multidigit numbers. The trade-first method is similar to the traditional subtraction method; however, all of the "regrouping" or "borrowing" is done before the problem is solved.

array A rectangular arrangement of objects in rows and columns. For example, 20 pencils could be arranged in 4 rows of 5 pencils each. Arrays are an important learning link in understanding the connection between multiplication and division.

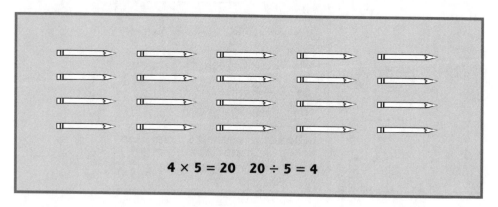

$$4 \times 5 = 20 \quad 20 \div 5 = 4$$

multiples Repeated groups of the same amount. Multiples of a number are the products of that number and whole numbers. For example, 2, 4, 6, 8, and 10 are all multiples of 2 because $2 \times 1 = 2$, $2 \times 2 = 4$, $2 \times 3 = 6$, and so on.

remainder The amount left over when things are divided into equal parts. If 20 pencils are shared equally by 6 people, each person gets 3 pencils, and 2 are left over. The remainder is 2.

Copyright © SRA/McGraw-Hill

Use with Lesson 5.10.

Do-Anytime Activities

To work with your child on the concepts taught in this unit and in previous units,
try these interesting and rewarding activities:

1 Have your child show you how making an array or making equal groups can help solve multiplication
number stories. Use common objects, such as buttons or pennies, to act out the stories.

2 Also try the opposite: Draw or make arrays and multiples of equal groups. Have your child make up
and solve number stories to go with them.

3 Discuss equal-sharing (division) stories. For example, use objects (such as pennies) to portray a
situation like the following: We have 7 cookies to divide equally among 3 people. How many
whole cookies will each person get? (2) How many cookies will be left over? (1)

Building Skills through Games

In Unit 6, your child will practice addition, subtraction, and multiplication skills by
playing the following games:

Three Addends

Players draw three cards, write addition models of the numbers they've picked, and solve
the problems.

Addition Top-It

Each player turns over two cards and calls out their sum. The player with the higher sum
then takes all the cards from that round.

Array Bingo

Players roll the dice and find an
Array Bingo card with the same
number of dots. Players then turn
that card over. The first player to
have a row, column, or diagonal of
facedown cards calls out "Bingo!"
and wins the game.

Copyright © SRA/McGraw-Hill

Use with Lesson 5.10.

As You Help Your Child with Homework

As your child brings home assignments, you may want to go over the instructions together, clarifying them as necessary. The answers listed below will guide you through this unit's Home Links.

Home Link 6.2

1. $19; 29 − 10 = 19

2. 15 fewer laps; 20 + 15 = 35

3. June 22; 10 + 12 = 22

4.
$$\begin{array}{r} 90 \\ + 11 \\ \hline 101 \end{array}$$

5.
$$\begin{array}{r} 40 \\ + 15 \\ \hline 55 \end{array}$$

6.
$$\begin{array}{r} 80 \\ + 7 \\ \hline 87 \end{array}$$

Home Link 6.3

1.

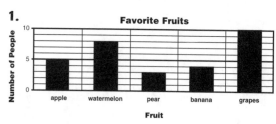

Favorite Fruits

2. grapes; pear

Home Link 6.5

1. 58; 41 cubes left; 58 − 17 = 41

2. 26; 8 cubes left; 26 − 18 = 8

3. 43; 18 cubes left; 43 − 25 = 18

4. 39; 7 cubes left; 39 − 32 = 7

5. 61; 14 cubes left; 61 − 47 = 14

Home Link 6.6

1. 31 **2.** 23 **3.** 29

4. 17 **5.** 16

Home Link 6.8

1. 3; 18 **2.** 4; 16 **3.** 10; 80

Home Link 6.10

1. Total = 21; $7 \times 3 = 21$

2. Total = 60; $6 \times 10 = 60$

3. 5 rows; 6 dots in each row; 30

4. 3 rows; 9 squares per row; 27

5. 6 rows; 6 squares in each row; 36

Home Link 6.11

3. by 2 people: 9¢ per person; 1¢ remaining
by 3 people: 6¢ per person; 1¢ remaining
by 4 people: 4¢ per person; 3¢ remaining

Copyright © SRA/McGraw-Hill

Use with Lesson 5.10.

Adding Three Numbers

Home Link 6.1

Family Note

Sometimes the order in which you add numbers can make it easier to find the sum. For example, when adding 17, 19, and 23, some people may first calculate 17 + 23 *(which equals 40)* and then add 19 *(40 + 19 = 59)*. For Problems 1–4, help your child look for easy combinations. Before working on Problems 5–10, you might go over the example with your child.

Please return this Home Link to school tomorrow.

For each problem:

- Think about an easy way to add the numbers.

- Write a number model to show the order in which you are adding the numbers.

- Find each sum. Tell someone at home why you added the numbers in that order.

1.

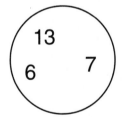

Number model:

____ + ____ + ____ = ____

2.

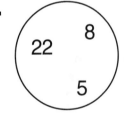

Number model:

____ + ____ + ____ = ____

3.

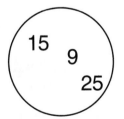

Number model:

____ + ____ + ____ = ____

4.

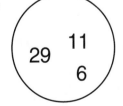

Number model:

____ + ____ + ____ = ____

Copyright © SRA/McGraw–Hill

Use with Lesson 6.1.

Adding Three Numbers (cont.)

Add. Use the partial-sums method.

Example

$$
\begin{array}{r}
33 \\
42 \\
+\ 11 \\
\hline
\end{array}
$$

Add the tens.	→ (30 + 40 + 10) →	80
Add the ones.	→ (3 + 2 + 1) →	6
Add the partial sums.	→ (80 + 6) →	86

5.
$$
\begin{array}{r}
23 \\
32 \\
+\ 14 \\
\hline
\end{array}
$$

6.
$$
\begin{array}{r}
14 \\
29 \\
+\ 27 \\
\hline
\end{array}
$$

7.
$$
\begin{array}{r}
8 \\
19 \\
+\ 35 \\
\hline
\end{array}
$$

8.
$$
\begin{array}{r}
46 \\
25 \\
+\ 12 \\
\hline
\end{array}
$$

9.
$$
\begin{array}{r}
40 \\
45 \\
+\ 63 \\
\hline
\end{array}
$$

10.
$$
\begin{array}{r}
9 \\
85 \\
+\ 96 \\
\hline
\end{array}
$$

Copyright © SRA/McGraw-Hill

Comparison Number Stories

Family Note

Today your child learned about a device that is useful when solving number stories. We call it a "comparison diagram." Diagrams like these can help your child organize the information in a problem. When the information is organized, it is easier to decide which operation ($+$, $-$, $\times$, or $\div$) to use to solve the problem. Comparison diagrams are used to represent problems in which two quantities are given, and the question is how much more or less one quantity is than the other (the difference).

Example 1: There are 49 fourth graders and 38 third graders. How many more fourth graders are there than third graders?

Note that the number of fourth graders is being compared with the number of third graders.

· *Answer:* There are 11 more fourth graders than third graders.

· *Possible number models:* Children who think of the problem in terms of subtraction will write $49 - 38 = 11$. Other children may think of the problem in terms of addition: "Which number added to 38 will give me 49?" They will write the number model as $38 + 11 = 49$.

Quantity	
49 fourth graders	

Quantity	Difference
38 third graders	?

Your child may write words in the diagram as a reminder of what the numbers mean.

Example 2: There are 53 second graders. There are 10 more second graders than first graders. How many first graders are there?

Note that sometimes the difference is known, and one of the two quantities is to be found.

· *Answer:* There are 43 first graders.

· *Possible number models:*
$53 - 10 = 43$ or $10 + 43 = 53$

Quantity	
53	

Quantity	Difference
?	10

For Problems 1 and 2, ask your child to explain the number model that he or she wrote. Also ask your child to explain the steps needed to solve Problems 4–6.

*Please return the **second page** of this Home Link to school tomorrow.*

Copyright © SRA/McGraw-Hill

Comparison Stories (cont.)

Home Link 6.2

In each number story:

- Write the numbers you know in the comparison diagram.
- Write ? for the number you want to find.
- Solve the problem. Then write a number model.

---

1. Ross has $29 in his bank account. Omeida has $10.

Ross has $_____ more than Omeida.

Number model: _____

Quantity

Quantity	Difference

---

2. Omar swam 35 laps in the pool. Anthony swam 20 laps.

Anthony swam _____ fewer laps than Omar.

Number model: _____

Quantity

Quantity	Difference

---

3. Claudia's birthday is June 10. Tisha's birthday is 12 days later.

Tisha's birthday is June _____.

Number model: _____

Quantity

Quantity	Difference

Add. Use the partial-sums method.

4.   39
   + 62

5.   48
    + 7

6.   33
   + 54

Use with Lesson 6.2.

Copyright © SRA/McGraw-Hill

Name   Date   Time

Graphing Data

**Family
Note**

The class has been collecting and graphing data about favorite foods. Ask your
child about the graph he or she made in class. In the table below, help your child
count the tally marks below the name of each fruit. To decide how high up to
color each bar, your child could lay a straightedge across the columns.

Please return this Home Link to school tomorrow.

In a survey, people were asked to name their favorite fruit.
The table below shows the results.

apple	watermelon	pear	banana	grapes
ⅢⅡ	ⅢⅡ ///	///	////	ⅢⅡ ⅢⅡ

1. Make a bar graph that shows how many people chose each fruit.
The first bar has been colored for you.

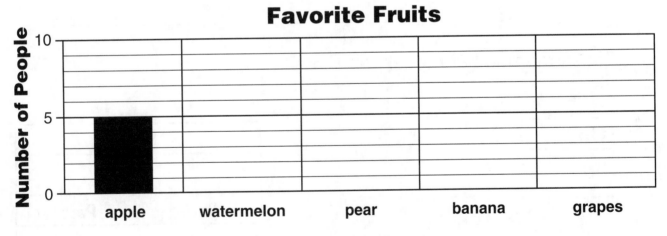

Favorite Fruits

2. Which fruit is the most popular? _____

Which fruit is the least popular? _____

What is your favorite kind of fruit? _____

Use with Lesson 6.3.

Copyright © SRA/McGraw-Hill

Number Stories and Diagrams

Family Note

In today's lesson, your child used diagrams to solve number stories. Listen to your child's stories. Ask your child to explain how each story relates to both the diagram and the number model. (See Home Link 5.10: *Unit 6 Family Letter* for information about number stories and diagrams.)

Please return this Home Link to school tomorrow.

Write number stories to match each diagram. Then finish the number model. Tell your stories to someone at home.

1.

Unit
building blocks

Start	Change	End
24	+6	?

_____

_____

Finish the number model: 24 + 6 = _____

2.

Unit
books

Total	
Part	Part

_____

_____

Finish the number model: 15 + 13 = _____

Copyright © SRA/McGraw-Hill

Use with Lesson 6.4.

Stories and Diagrams (cont.)

3.

Unit
bananas

Quantity

Quantity	Difference

Finish the number model: $28 - 8 =$ _____

4.

Unit
baseball cards

Total	

Part	Part

Write a number model for your story.

Number model: _____

Copyright © SRA/McGraw-Hill

Subtracting with Base-10 Blocks   Home Link 6.5

Family Note

In this lesson, your child found the answers to subtraction problems by using longs and cubes to represent tens and ones.
   Doing this will help your child understand the concept of subtraction before he or she learns to subtract using a step-by-step procedure, or algorithm, with paper and pencil. It is understandable that when you see the problems on this Home Link, you may be eager to teach your child to subtract the way you were taught. But please try to wait—the introduction of a formal algorithm for subtraction will be taught later in this unit.

Please return this Home Link to school tomorrow.

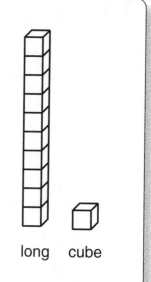

long   cube

Show subtraction by crossing out cubes.

Example

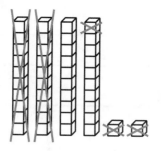

How many cubes are shown—both as separate cubes and as part of the longs? __42__

Cross out (subtract) 23 cubes. How many cubes are left? __19__

Number model:

__42__ – __23__ = __19__

1.

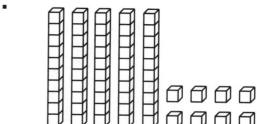

How many cubes are shown in all? _____

Cross out (subtract) 17 cubes. How many cubes are left? _____

Number model:

_____ – _____ = _____

Copyright © SRA/McGraw-Hill

Subtracting with Blocks (cont.)

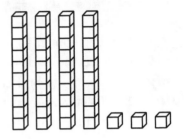

2.

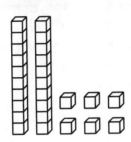

How many cubes
are shown in all? _____

Cross out (subtract)
18 cubes. How
many cubes are left? _____

Number model:

_____ − _____ = _____

3.

How many cubes
are shown in all? _____

Cross out (subtract)
25 cubes. How
many cubes are left? _____

Number model:

_____ − _____ = _____

4.

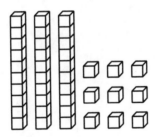

How many cubes
are shown in all? _____

Cross out (subtract)
32 cubes. How
many cubes are left? _____

Number model:

_____ − _____ = _____

5.

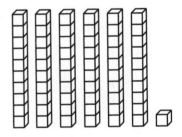

How many cubes
are shown in all? _____

Cross out (subtract)
47 cubes. How
many cubes are left? _____

Number model:

_____ − _____ = _____

Copyright © SRA/McGraw-Hill

Trade-First Subtraction

**Family
Note**

Today your child learned about subtracting multidigit numbers using a procedure
called the trade-first method. Your child also used "ballpark estimates" to
determine whether or not his or her answers made sense.

The **trade-first** method is similar to the traditional subtraction method that you
may be familiar with. However, all of the "regrouping" or "borrowing" is done
before the problem is solved—which gives the method its name, "trade-first."

Example

longs | cubes
10s | 1s

4 | 6
−3 | 9

· Are there enough tens and ones to remove exactly 3 tens and 9 ones from 46?
(*No; there are enough tens, but there aren't enough ones.*)

· Trade 1 ten for 10 ones.

longs | cubes
10s | 1s

3 | 16
4̶ | 6̶
−3 | 9

· Solve. 3 tens minus 3 tens
leaves 0 tens. 16 ones minus
9 ones leaves 7 ones. The
answer is 7.

longs | cubes
10s | 1s

3 | 16
4̶ | 6̶
−3 | 9
 | 7

· Make a ballpark estimate to see whether the answer makes sense: 46 is close
to 50, and 39 is close to 40. $50 - 40 = 10$. 10 is close to the answer of 7, so 7
is a reasonable answer.

The trade-first method is one of many ways people solve subtraction problems.
Your child may choose this method or may prefer to use a different procedure.
What is most important is that your child can successfully solve subtraction
problems using a method that makes sense to him or her.

*Please return the **second page** of this Home Link to school tomorrow.*

Copyright © SRA/McGraw-Hill

Trade-First Subtraction (cont.)

Make a ballpark estimate for each problem and write a number model for your estimate.

Use the trade-first method of subtraction to solve each problem.

Example:

longs 10s	cubes 1s	Answer
1	16	**8**

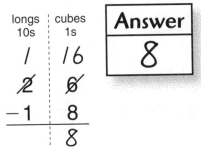

Ballpark estimate:

$$30 - 20 = 10$$

1.

longs 10s	cubes 1s	Answer
7	3	
−4	2	

Ballpark estimate:

_____

2.

longs 10s	cubes 1s	Answer
4	9	
−2	6	

Ballpark estimate:

_____

3.

longs 10s	cubes 1s	Answer
8	5	
−5	6	

Ballpark estimate:

_____

4.

longs 10s	cubes 1s	Answer
3	2	
−1	5	

Ballpark estimate:

_____

5. 34 − 18

Answer

Ballpark estimate:

_____

Copyright © SRA/McGraw-Hill

How Many?

Family Note

Your child has been working with arrays—rectangular arrangements of objects having the same number of objects in each row—to develop readiness for multiplication. Since this is a readiness activity, children have not yet written number models for multiplication, such as $4 \times 5 = 20$. Your child will do this in later lessons in this unit.

Please return this Home Link to school tomorrow.

---

1. Show someone at home this array.

X X X X X
X X X X X
X X X X X
X X X X X

How many rows? _____

How many **X**s in each row? _____

How many **X**s in all? _____

2. Draw an array of 16 **X**s.

How many rows? _____

How many **X**s in each row? _____

---

3. Draw an array of 24 **X**s.

How many rows? _____

How many **X**s in each row? _____

4. Draw a different array of 24 **X**s.

How many rows? _____

How many **X**s in each row? _____

Copyright © SRA/McGraw-Hill

Use with Lesson 6.7.

How Many?

Family Note

In today's lesson, your child learned that multiplication is an operation used to find the total number of things in several equal groups. As you help your child solve the following problems, emphasize that each group has the same number of things. Your child can use objects, draw pictures, count, or use any other helpful devices to find the answers.

Please return this Home Link to school tomorrow.

Example

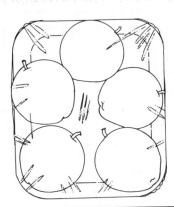

How many apples in 4 packages?

ⅢⅠ   ⅢⅠ   ⅢⅠ   ⅢⅠ
5 + 5 + 5 + 5 = 20

There are 20 apples in 4 packages.

---

1. △ △ △ △ △ △

How many sides on each triangle? _____ sides

How many sides in all? _____ sides

2.

How many tires on each car? _____ tires

How many tires in all? _____ tires

3.

How many fingers for each person?

_____ fingers

How many fingers in all?

_____ fingers

Copyright © SRA/McGraw-Hill

Use with Lesson 6.8.

Arrays

Family Note

In this lesson, your child solved multiplication problems about arrays, which are rectangular arrangements of objects in rows and columns. Encourage your child to use counters, such as pennies or buttons, while working on the following exercises.

Please return this Home Link to school tomorrow.

Tell someone at home what you know about arrays.

1. Look at the array and fill in the blank. • • • • • • • • • • • • • • • • • • • • • • • • 4 rows of dots 6 dots in each row _____ dots in all	**2.** Draw an array of dots. Your array should have 5 rows of dots 7 dots in each row That's _____ dots in all.	**3.** Draw an array of 12 dots.

Telephone:
a 4-by-3 array

Muffins:
a 3-by-2 array

Muffins:
a 4-by-3 array

Tic-tac-toe Grid:
a 3-by-3 array

Checkerboard:
an 8-by-8 array

Eggs:
a 2-by-6 array

Copyright © SRA/McGraw-Hill

Arrays

Family Note

In this lesson, your child continued to work with arrays to develop multiplication concepts. Your child described each array by naming the number of rows, the number of items in each row, and the total number of items in the array. Your child wrote number models to describe arrays. In the example, an array with 2 rows of 4 dots can be described using the number model $2 \times 4 = 8$.

Please return this Home Link to school tomorrow.

Show an array for the numbers that are given. Find the total number of dots in the array. Complete the number model.

Example

Numbers: 2, 4

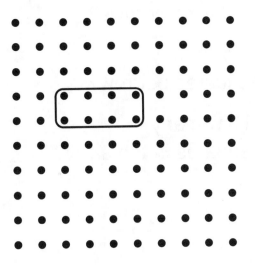

Total: _8_

Number model:

$2 \times 4 = 8$

1. Numbers: 7, 3

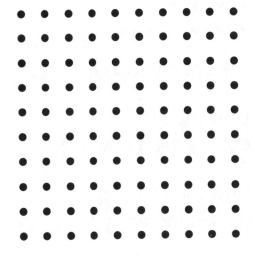

Total: _____

Number model:

____ × ____ = ____

Copyright © SRA/McGraw-Hill

Use with Lesson 6.10.

Arrays (cont.)

2. Numbers: 6, 10

Total: _____

Number model:

_____ × _____ = _____

Answer the questions about each array.

3.

How many rows? _____

How many
dots in each row? _____

How many
dots in the array? _____

4.

How many rows? _____

How many
squares per row? _____

How many
squares in the array? _____

5.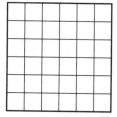

How many rows? _____

How many squares in each row? _____

How many squares in the array? _____

Copyright © SRA/McGraw-Hill

Division

Family Note

In this lesson, your child worked on the concept of division by putting objects into equal groups and sharing objects equally among several people. Objects that are left over are called the *remainder*. If 9 books are shared equally among 4 people, each person gets 2 books, and the 1 book that is left over is the remainder.

Watch as your child divides things equally among family members. Try to use groups of objects that can be divided with no remainder as well as groups that have remainders.

Please return this Home Link to school tomorrow.

1. Have someone at home give you a group or handful of small items, such as raisins, buttons, or popcorn. Show how you can divide the items equally among your family members. Are any items left over?

Make a record of what you did. Be ready to tell about it in class.

I shared _____ (how many?) items equally among _____ people.

Each person got _____. There were _____ left over.

2. Do this again with some other kind of item.

I shared _____ items equally among _____ people.

Each person got _____. There were _____ left over.

3. 19 cents shared equally

by 2 people   by 3 people   by 4 people

_____¢ per person   _____¢ per person   _____¢ per person

_____¢ remaining   _____¢ remaining   _____¢ remaining

Copyright © SRA/McGraw-Hill

Family Letter

Unit 7: **Patterns and Rules**

In Unit 7, children will concentrate on number patterns, computational skills, and the application of mathematics through the use of data. They will continue to use the 100-grid as a means of reinforcing numeration skills. Children will also explore the patterns of doubling and halving numbers, which will help prepare them for multiplication and division.

Computational work will be extended to several 2-digit numbers and to the subtraction of 1- and 2-digit numbers from multiples of 10.

Children will learn to find complements of tens; that is, they will answer such questions as "What must I add to 4 to get to 10? What must I add to 47 to get to 50?" or "How many tens are needed to get from 320 to 400?"

Children will also collect and interpret real-life data about animals, adults, and themselves. For example, they will collect data by measuring the lengths of their standing long jumps and then find the median jump length for the class.

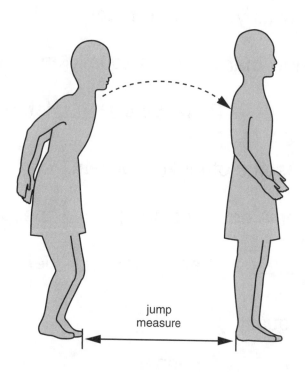

jump
measure

Please keep this Family Letter for reference as your child works through Unit 7.

Copyright © SRA/McGraw-Hill

Vocabulary

Important terms in Unit 7:

arrow-path puzzles Pieces of the number grid used to reinforce the structure of our base-ten numeration system.

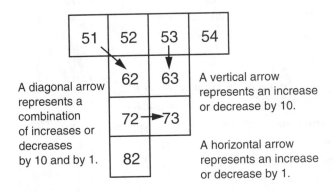

A diagonal arrow represents a combination of increases or decreases by 10 and by 1.

A vertical arrow represents an increase or decrease by 10.

A horizontal arrow represents an increase or decrease by 1.

median The number in the middle when a set of data is organized in sequential order; also called the *middle value.* For example, in the set of data below, 35 is the median.

30, 32, 32, 35, 36, 38, 40

frequency The number of times an event or value occurs in a set of data. For example, in the set of data above, 32 has a frequency of 2.

Do-Anytime Activities

To work with your child on the concepts taught in this unit and in previous units, try these interesting and rewarding activities:

1 If you have a calculator at home, practice making (and breaking) tens.

For example:

Making tens: Enter 33. What needs to be done to display 50? $33 + \underline{\hspace{1cm}} = 50$

Breaking tens: Enter 60. What needs to be done to display 52? $60 - \underline{\hspace{1cm}} = 52$

Or, for more challenging practice, try the following:

Enter 27. What needs to be done to display 40?

Enter 90. What needs to be done to display 66?

Try other similar numbers.

2 Make a game out of doubling, tripling, and quadrupling small numbers. For example, using the number 2, first double it. What number do you get? Continue the doubling process five more times. Then start again with the number 2 and triple it; then quadruple it. Discuss the differences among the final numbers.

3 Collect a simple set of data from family and friends. For example, how high can different people's fingertips reach while the people are standing flat on the floor? Order the data to find the median.

Copyright © SRA/McGraw-Hill

Use with Lesson 6.12.

Building Skills through Games

In Unit 7, your child will practice addition and subtraction skills by playing the following games:

Array Bingo

Players roll the dice and find an *Array Bingo* card with the same number of dots. Players then turn that card over. The first player to have a row, column, or diagonal of facedown cards calls out "Bingo!" and wins the game.

Hit the Target

Players choose a 2-digit multiple of ten as a "target number." One player enters a "starting number" on a calculator and tries to change the starting number to the target number by adding a number to it on the calculator. Children practice finding differences between 2-digit numbers and higher multiples of tens.

Copyright © SRA/McGraw-Hill

Use with Lesson 6.12.

As You Help Your Child with Homework

As your child brings home assignments, you may want to go over the instructions together, clarifying them as necessary. The answers listed below will guide you through this unit's Home Links.

Home Link 7.3

1. 6; 7; 5; 9; 2   **2.** 6; 7; 5; 9; 8

3. 32 + 38; 65 + 5; 10 + 60; 43 + 27; 19 + 51; 51 + 19; 27 + 43

Home Link 7.4

1. Team A: 35; Team B: 25; A

2. Team A: 30; Team B: 35; B

3. Team A: 29; Team B: 40; B

4. Team A: 45; Team B: 59; B

Home Link 7.5

1.

in	out
12	6
50	25
40	20
30	15
16	8
18	9

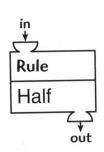

in → Rule **Half** → out

2. 1, 2, 4, 8, 16, 32, 64

3. 3, 6, 12, 24, 48, 96, 192

4. 127 pennies, or $1.27

Home Link 7.6

1. 8 pounds **2.** 20 pounds **3.** 5 pounds

4. 65 pounds **5.** 11,000 pounds

Home Link 7.7

1. 13 centimeters   **2.** 2 inches

3. 3 inches   **4.** 17 centimeters

5. 9 centimeters

Home Link 7.8

1. 3 points 7 points 9 points (12 points) 15 points 20 points 21 points

2. 56 in. 66 in. (68 in.) 70 in. 73 in.

3. 142 cm 168 cm (173 cm) 178 cm 185 cm

Home Link 7.9

1. 2   **2.** 0   **3.** 46   **4.** 52

5. 9   **6.** 48   **7.** 49

Copyright © SRA/McGraw-Hill

Use with Lesson 6.12.

Count by 2s, 5s, and 10s

Family Note

In this lesson, your child has been counting by 2s, 5s, and 10s. After your child has completed these problems, help him or her look for patterns in the ones digits of the answers. In the example, the ones digits repeat: 0, 2, 4, 6, 8, 0, 2, 4, and so on. If your child is successful with these problems, ask him or her to count backward by 2s, 5s, or 10s. Start from a number that is a multiple of 10, such as 200.

Please return this Home Link to school tomorrow.

Example

Count by 2s. Begin at 100. Write down your first 10 counts.

<u>100</u>, <u>102</u>, <u>104</u>, <u>106</u>, <u>108</u>, <u>110</u>, <u>112</u>, <u>114</u>, <u>116</u>, <u>118</u>

1. Count by 2s. Begin at 200. Write down your first 10 counts.

<u>200</u>, _____, _____, _____, _____, _____, _____, _____, _____, _____

2. Count by 5s. Begin at 500. Write down your first 10 counts.

_____, _____, _____, _____, _____, _____, _____, _____, _____, _____

3. Count by 10s. Begin at 550. Write down your first 10 counts.

_____, _____, _____, _____, _____, _____, _____, _____, _____, _____

Look at your counts. Tell someone at home about any patterns that you find in the counts.

Copyright © SRA/McGraw-Hill

Number-Grid Puzzle

Family Note

In this lesson, your child solved a special type of puzzle called a *number-grid puzzle*. Solving number-grid puzzles promotes place-value awareness that will help your child develop addition and subtraction skills. In the number grid shown below, the numbering starts at 100, and then the numbers increase by 1 as you move from left to right in each row. The shaded cells of the number grid should not be filled in. However, if your child is having difficulty, you might fill in a few of the shaded cells to provide some additional clues.

Please return this Home Link to school tomorrow.

Fill in the blank (unshaded) cells of the number grid.

									100
101	102								

Copyright © SRA/McGraw-Hill

Use with Lesson 7.2.

Missing Addends

Family Note

In this lesson, your child found the difference between a number and a multiple of 10. In Problems 1 and 2, your child will find the difference between a number and the next-higher multiple of 10. For example, your child will determine which number added to 62 equals 70 (8). In Problem 3, your child will find different combinations of numbers that add to 70. If your child has difficulty with this problem, suggest changing the first number in each combination to the next-higher multiple of 10. For example, add 2 to 48 to make 50 and then add 20 to 50 to make 70. 2 + 20 = 22, so 48 + 22 = 70.

Please return this Home Link to school tomorrow.

1. 4 + _____ = 10

10 = 3 + _____

_____ + 5 = 10

10 = _____ + 1

8 + _____ = 10

2. 54 + _____ = 60

90 = 83 + _____

75 + _____ = 80

40 = 31 + _____

_____ + 62 = 70

3. Make 70s. Show someone at home how you did it.

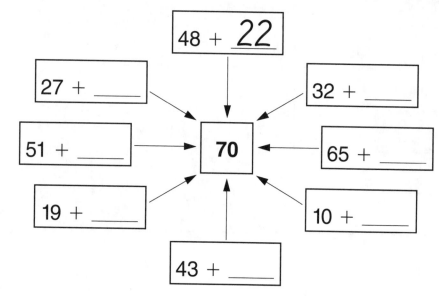

48 + 22

27 + _____

32 + _____

51 + _____   →   **70**   ←   65 + _____

19 + _____

10 + _____

43 + _____

Copyright © SRA/McGraw-Hill

Who Scored More Points?

Family Note

In this lesson, your child added three or more 1-digit and 2-digit numbers. As your child completes the problems below, encourage him or her to share the different ways in which the points can be added. Your child might add all of the tens first and then add all of the ones. For example, $20 + 5 + 4 + 6 = 20 + 15 = 35$. Your child may also look for combinations of numbers that are easier to add. In Game 1, for example, first add 14 and 6 to get 20 and then add 15 to get 35.

Please return this Home Link to school tomorrow.

Do the following for each problem:

- Add the points for each team.

- Decide which team scored more points. The team with the greater number of points wins the game.

- Circle your answer.

Unit
points

1. Game 1

Team A:
$15 + 14 + 6 =$ _____

Team B:
$5 + 13 + 7 =$ _____

Who won?   A   or   B

2. Game 2

Team A:
$12 + 6 + 4 + 8 =$ _____

Team B:
$5 + 10 + 19 + 1 =$ _____

Who won?   A   or   B

3. Game 3

Team A:
$17 + 4 + 5 + 3 =$ _____

Team B:
$2 + 11 + 9 + 18 =$ _____

Who won?   A   or   B

4. Game 4

Team A:
$7 + 4 + 16 + 13 + 5 =$ _____

Team B:
$22 + 9 + 8 + 3 + 17 =$ _____

Who won?   A   or   B

Copyright © SRA/McGraw-Hill

Doubles and Halves

Family Note

In today's lesson, your child heard a story and used a calculator to double numbers and find halves of numbers repeatedly. Help your child solve the doubling and halving problems below. When appropriate, have your child use money or counters to help solve the problems. In Problem 1, for example, your child might display 40 counters, divide them into two equal groups, and then count to find that half of 40 is 20.

Please return this Home Link to school tomorrow.

1. Write a rule in the rule box.
Then complete the table.

in
↓

Rule

↓
out

in	out
12	6
50	25
40	
30	
	8
	9

2. Fill in the frames using the rule in the rule box.

Rule
Double

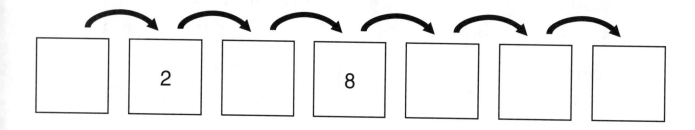

| | 2 | | 8 | | | |

Copyright © SRA/McGraw-Hill

Use with Lesson 7.5.

Doubles and Halves (cont.)

Home Link 7.5

3. Fill in the frames using the rule in the rule box.

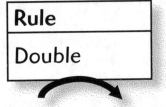

Rule
Double

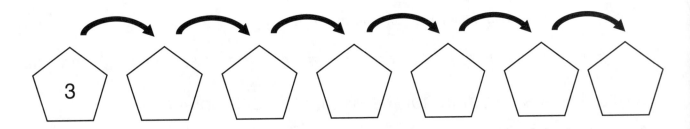

Challenge

4. Jay finds 1 penny under his pillow when he wakes up on Monday morning. On Tuesday, he finds 2 pennies. On Wednesday, he finds 4 pennies. So, on Wednesday, he has a total of 7 cents.

On Thursday, Friday, Saturday, and Sunday, Jay finds double the amount of money he found under his pillow the day before. How much money does Jay have on Sunday?

_____

Copyright © SRA/McGraw-Hill

Estimating Weights

Family Note

In today's lesson, your child practiced reading weights, in pounds, on a bath scale. One purpose of this activity is to improve your child's perception of weight so that he or she can make more realistic estimates of weights. To help develop your child's ability to read a bath scale, take every opportunity at home to use your bath scale to determine the weights of objects.

Please return this Home Link to school tomorrow.

Circle the best estimate for the weight of each object.

1. newborn baby

8 pounds

20 pounds

70 pounds

2. Thanksgiving turkey

$\frac{1}{2}$ pound

20 pounds

70 pounds

3. bag of apples

5 pounds

35 pounds

65 pounds

4. adult Golden Retriever

6 pounds

20 pounds

65 pounds

5. An adult bull African elephant (the largest animal on land)

100 pounds

500 pounds

11,000 pounds

Copyright © SRA/McGraw-Hill

Line Segment Lengths

Family Note

In today's lesson, your child measured his or her standing long jump in centimeters and his or her arm span in inches. Help your child draw and measure each line segment below.

Please return this Home Link to school tomorrow.

Draw and measure line segments. If necessary, cut out and use the ruler at the bottom of the next page.

1. Draw a line segment that is 5 inches long.

Measure the segment to the nearest centimeter.

The segment is about _____ centimeters long.

2. Draw a line segment that is 5 centimeters long.

Measure the segment to the nearest inch.

The segment is about _____ inches long.

Copyright © SRA/McGraw-Hill

Line Segment Lengths (cont.)

Home Link 7.7

3. Draw a line segment that is 8 centimeters long.

Measure the segment to the nearest inch.

The segment is about _____ inches long.

4. Draw a line segment that is $6\frac{1}{2}$ inches long.

Measure the segment to the nearest centimeter.

The segment is about _____ centimeters long.

5. Draw a line segment that is $3\frac{1}{2}$ inches long.

Measure the segment to the nearest centimeter.

The segment is about _____ centimeters long.

Copyright © SRA/McGraw-Hill

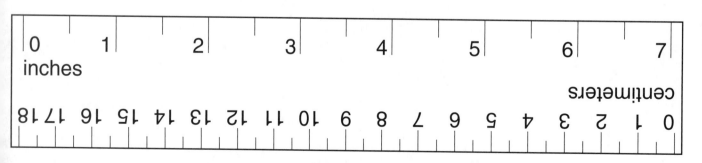

Use with Lesson 7.7.

Find the Middle Value

Family Note

In this lesson, your child has sorted data in order to find the median. *Median* is a term used for the middle value. To find the median of a set of data, arrange the data in ascending or descending order. Count from either end to the number in the middle. The middle value is the median. As your child finds the median in Problems 2 and 3, remind him or her that "in." is the abbreviation for inches and "cm" is the abbreviation for centimeters.

Please return this Home Link to school tomorrow.

List the data in order from smallest to largest.

Draw a circle around the median in your list.

1.

12 points	3 points	21 points	15 points	20 points	7 points	9 points

_____ points   _____ points   _____ points   _____ points   _____ points   _____ points   _____ points

smallest   **largest**

Copyright © SRA/McGraw-Hill

Find the Middle Value (cont.)

Home Link 7.8

2.

Bob: 66 in. tall	Amy: 70 in. tall	Peter: 56 in. tall	Kate: 73 in. tall	Andy: 68 in. tall

_____ in.   _____ in.   _____ in.   _____ in.   _____ in.

smallest   **largest**

3.

Bob: 168 cm tall	Amy: 178 cm tall	Peter: 142 cm tall	Kate: 185 cm tall	Andy: 173 cm tall

_____ cm   _____ cm   _____ cm   _____ cm   _____ cm

smallest   **largest**

Copyright © SRA/McGraw-Hill

Use with Lesson 7.8.

Interpreting Data

Family Note

Today your child represented data using a bar graph and a frequency table. The table below is called a *frequency table* because it shows how often different heights occurred. Help your child use the data to answer the questions. Remind your child that to find the median of a set of data, he or she should arrange the data in ascending or descending order and then count from either end to the number in the middle. The middle value is the median.

Please return this Home Link to school tomorrow.

Mr. Wilson is a basketball coach. He measured the height of each player. Then he made the data table shown below.

1. How many players are

50 inches tall? _____ players

2. How many players are

47 inches tall? _____ players

3. The shortest player is

_____ inches tall.

4. The tallest player is

_____ inches tall.

5. How many players did Mr. Wilson

measure? _____ players

6. Which height occurs most often? _____ inches

7. Find the middle (median) height. _____ inches

Players' Heights

Height (inches)	Number of Players
46	1
47	0
48	3
49	1
50	2
51	1
52	1

Copyright © SRA/McGraw-Hill

Family Letter

Unit 8: Fractions

In Unit 8, children will review and extend concepts of fractions. Specifically, they will recognize fractions as names for parts of a whole, or ONE.

Children will see that, as with whole numbers, many different fractions can name the same quantity. For example, $\frac{2}{4}$ and $\frac{6}{12}$ are both names for $\frac{1}{2}$.

Children will also explore relationships among fractions as they work with pattern-block shapes and Fraction Cards that show shaded regions.

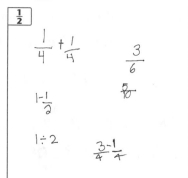

Children use Fraction Cards to compare fractions by looking at the shaded areas.

Copyright © SRA/McGraw-Hill

Please keep this Family Letter for reference as your child works through Unit 8.

Vocabulary

Important terms in Unit 8:

fraction A number that names equal parts of a whole, or ONE.

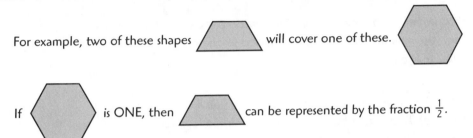

For example, two of these shapes will cover one of these.

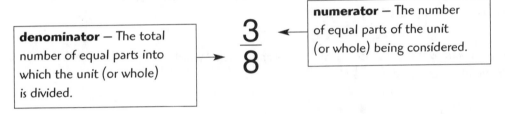

If is ONE, then can be represented by the fraction $\frac{1}{2}$.

denominator — The total number of equal parts into which the unit (or whole) is divided.

$$\frac{3}{8}$$

numerator — The number of equal parts of the unit (or whole) being considered.

It is not necessary for children to use the words numerator *and* denominator *now. They will learn them over time with repeated exposure. Do, however, use these words, as well as the informal "number on the top" and "number on the bottom," when you discuss fractions with your child.*

equivalent fractions Different fractions that represent the same quantity. For example, $\frac{1}{2}$ and $\frac{2}{4}$ are equivalent fractions.

Copyright © SRA/McGraw-Hill

Use with Lesson 7.10.

Do-Anytime Activities

To work with your child on the concepts taught in this unit and in previous units, try these interesting and rewarding activities:

1 Review fraction notation. For example, ask: "In a fraction, what does the number on the bottom (the denominator) tell you?" "What does the number on the top (the numerator) tell you?"

2 Draw a picture of a rectangular cake, a circular pizza, or a similar food (better yet, have the real thing). Discuss ways to cut the food in order to feed various numbers of people so that each person gets an equal portion.

3 Read a recipe and discuss the fractions in it. For example, ask: "How many $\frac{1}{4}$ cups of sugar would we need to get 1 cup of sugar?"

4 Compare two fractions and tell which is larger. For example, ask: "Which would give you more of a pizza: $\frac{1}{8}$ of it, or $\frac{1}{4}$?"

Copyright © SRA/McGraw-Hill

Use with Lesson 7.10.

As You Help Your Child with Homework

As your child brings home assignments, you may want to go over the instructions together, clarifying them as necessary. The answers listed below will guide you through this unit's Home Links.

Home Link 8.2

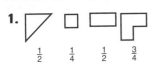

Home Link 8.4

1. $\frac{1}{2} = \frac{2}{4}$ 2. $\frac{1}{2} = \frac{4}{8}$ 3. $\frac{1}{4} = \frac{4}{16}$ 4. $\frac{1}{4} = \frac{2}{8}$

5. $\frac{1}{2} = \frac{3}{6}$ 6. $\frac{1}{5} = \frac{4}{20}$

Home Link 8.5

Home Link 8.3

1. 4; 4; 8

Home Link 8.7

1. $\frac{4}{7}$ 2. 4 tulips   3. $\frac{2}{12}$, or $\frac{1}{6}$ 4. 4 pages

5. $\frac{1}{3}$

Building Skills through Games

In Unit 8, your child will practice multiplication and fraction skills by playing the following games:

Array Bingo

Players roll the dice and find an *Array Bingo* card with the same number of dots. Players then turn that card over. The first player to have a row, column, or diagonal of facedown cards calls "Bingo!" and wins the game.

Equivalent Fractions Game

Players take turns turning over Fraction Cards and try to find matching cards that show equivalent fractions.

Fraction Top-It

Players turn over two Fraction Cards and compare the shaded parts of the cards. The player with the larger fraction keeps both of the cards. The player with more cards at the end wins!

Copyright © SRA/McGraw-Hill

Use with Lesson 7.10.

Equal Parts

Family Note

Help your child collect things that can be easily folded into equal parts. As your child works with fractions, remind him or her that the number under the fraction bar, the *denominator*, gives the total number of equal parts into which the whole is divided. The number over the fraction bar, the *numerator*, tells the number of equal parts that are being considered. Don't expect your child to use these words. They will be learned over time with repeated exposure.

Please return this Home Link to school tomorrow.

Use a straightedge.

1. Divide the shape into 2 equal parts. Color 1 part.

Part colored = $\dfrac{\square}{\square}$ Part not colored = $\dfrac{\square}{\square}$

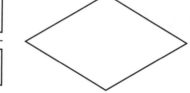

2. Divide the shape into 4 equal parts. Color 3 parts.

Part colored = $\dfrac{\square}{\square}$ Part not colored = $\dfrac{\square}{\square}$

3. Fold some things into equal parts.

Examples: paper napkin, paper plate, magazine picture

Label each part with a fraction. Show your folded things to someone at home. Talk about what the fractions mean.

Bring the things you folded to school for the Fractions Museum.

I folded a _____ into _____ equal parts.

Each part shows _____.

Copyright © SRA/McGraw-Hill

Fractions of Shapes

Family Note

As you work on this activity with your child, keep in mind that the shapes below the ONE are fractional parts of the ONE. Remind your child that the size of a fractional part of a whole depends on the size of the whole. It may be helpful for your child to separate the ONE into parts that are the size of the fractional part. For example, in Problem 1, your child can divide the square in half diagonally to determine that the triangle is $\frac{1}{2}$ of the square.

Please return this Home Link to school tomorrow.

1.   If this is ONE,

then what are these?

Write a fraction for each shape.   ___ ___ ___ ___

2.   If this is ONE,

then what are these?

Write a fraction for each shape.   ___ ___ ___ ___

3.   If this is ONE,

then what are these?

Write a fraction for each shape.   ___ ___ ___ ___

Copyright © SRA/McGraw-Hill

Fractions of Collections

Family Note

In this lesson, your child learned to use fractions to name part of a collection of objects. For example, your child could identify 2 out of 4 objects as $\frac{2}{4}$ or $\frac{1}{2}$. Show your child how to use pennies to act out Problem 1. Help your child collect household items that can be separated into fractional parts—or any other items that have fractions written on them. Encourage your child to bring these items to school for the class's Fractions Museum.

Please return this Home Link to school tomorrow.

1.

Three people share 12 pennies. Circle each person's share.

How many pennies does each person get? _____ pennies

$\frac{1}{3}$ of 12 pennies = _____ pennies

$\frac{2}{3}$ of 12 pennies = _____ pennies

2. Ask someone at home to help you find more things to bring to school for the Fractions Museum. Here are some ideas:

- Things that can be easily divided into equal parts, such as small collections of dried beans, buttons, or pasta; pieces of string, ribbon, or yarn; pictures of pies, bread, or pizza

- Ads, pictures, milk cartons, or measuring cups that have fractions written on them

- Objects that come in sets, such as a group of buttons or a box of watercolors

Copyright © SRA/McGraw-Hill

Use with Lesson 8.3.

Shading Fractional Parts

Family Note

In this lesson, your child learned that a fractional part of a whole can be named in many different ways with *equivalent* fractions. For example, $\frac{2}{4}$, $\frac{4}{8}$, and $\frac{3}{6}$ are names for $\frac{1}{2}$, and $\frac{2}{8}$ and $\frac{4}{16}$ are names for $\frac{1}{4}$. Help your child shade each of the shapes below to show the appropriate fraction. Make sure that your child understands that the fractions are equivalent because they name the same part of the shape.

Please return this Home Link to school tomorrow.

1. Shade $\frac{1}{2}$ of the rectangle.

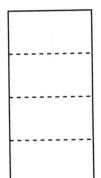

$$\frac{1}{2} = \frac{\square}{4}$$

2. Shade $\frac{1}{2}$ of the rectangle.

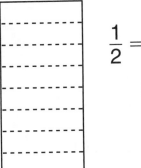

$$\frac{1}{2} = \frac{\square}{8}$$

3. Shade $\frac{1}{4}$ of the square.

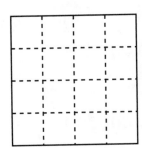

$$\frac{1}{4} = \frac{\square}{16}$$

4. Shade $\frac{1}{4}$ of the square.

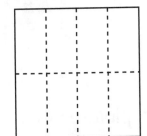

$$\frac{1}{4} = \frac{\square}{8}$$

5. Shade $\frac{1}{2}$ of the rectangle.

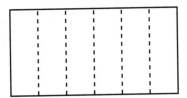

$$\frac{1}{2} = \frac{\square}{6}$$

6. Shade $\frac{1}{5}$ of the rectangle.

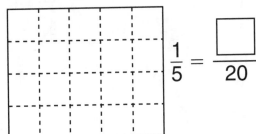

$$\frac{1}{5} = \frac{\square}{20}$$

Copyright © SRA/McGraw-Hill

Use with Lesson 8.4.

Fractions of Regions

 Family Note

In today's lesson, your child played a game in which he or she matched pictures of equivalent fractions. Stress the idea to your child that equivalent fractions show different ways to name a fractional part of a whole.

Please return this Home Link to school tomorrow.

1. Circle the pictures that show $\frac{1}{2}$ of the rectangle shaded.

   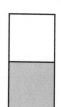      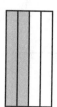

2. Circle the pictures that show $\frac{3}{4}$ of the rectangle shaded.

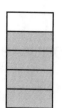      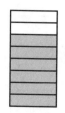   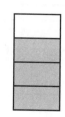

3. Circle the pictures that show $\frac{2}{3}$ of the rectangle shaded.

   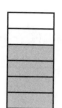   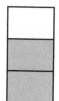   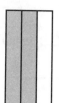

Copyright © SRA/McGraw-Hill

Use with Lesson 8.5.

More or Less Than $\frac{1}{2}$?

Family Note

The class has begun to compare fractions by identifying fractions that are less than, more than, or equal to $\frac{1}{2}$. To do the activity below, ask your child to draw a fraction bar on a sheet of paper. Your child might want to use the bar to create fractions by positioning the number tiles above and below the bar.

Please return this Home Link to school tomorrow.

Cut out the number tiles.

1. Use the tiles to make fractions that are less than $\frac{1}{2}$.

Make as many fractions as you can. Record the fractions you make.

Example

$$\frac{1}{3}$$

_____

2. Use the tiles to make fractions that are more than $\frac{1}{2}$.

Make as many fractions as you can. Record the fractions you make.

Example

$$\frac{2}{3}$$

_____

_____

Challenge

3. Use all 10 tiles to make 5 fractions that are less than $\frac{1}{2}$.

Record the fractions you make.

_____

| 0 |
| 1 |
| 2 |
| 3 |
| 4 |
| 5 |
| 6 |
| 7 |
| 8 |
| 9 |

Copyright © SRA/McGraw-Hill

Fractions

Family Note

In this lesson, your child has been completing number stories about fractions. Encourage your child to draw pictures or use small objects, such as pennies, to help him or her complete fraction number stories.

Please return this Home Link to school tomorrow.

1. 7 children are waiting for the school bus.

4 of them are girls.

What fraction of the children are girls? _____

2. There are 16 tulips in the garden.

$\frac{1}{4}$ of the tulips are red.

How many tulips are red? _____ tulips

3. 12 dogs were in the park.

2 of them were dalmatians.

What fraction of the dogs were dalmatians? _____

4. There are 20 pages in Jamal's book.

He read $\frac{1}{5}$ of the book.

How many pages did he read? _____ pages

5. There are 15 cupcakes.

5 of the cupcakes are chocolate.

What fraction of the cupcakes are chocolate? _____

Copyright © SRA/McGraw-Hill

Unit 9: Measurement

In Unit 9, children will explore measurements of various types. Your child will be asked to look for examples of measurements and tools for measuring and to bring them to school to put in our Measures All Around Museum. The examples will help children appreciate the important role that measurement plays in everyday life.

try square and level

stopwatch

Children will both estimate lengths of distances and actually measure lengths of distances by inch, foot, and yard, as well as centimeter, decimeter, and meter. Children will learn that measurements are always approximations; they will use terms like *close to, between,* and *about* when describing measurements. For more accurate measurements, children will measure to the nearest half–inch and half–centimeter.

In addition to measures of length, children will explore the areas of shapes using square inches and square centimeters. Children will also begin to develop a sense for the size of units of capacity and weight, such as cups and liters and pounds and kilograms.

Everyday Mathematics uses both U.S. customary and metric units of measure. While children make conversions within each system (length, capacity, or weight), they will not yet make conversions from one system to the other.

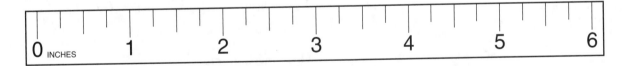

Please keep this Family Letter for reference as your child works through Unit 9.

Copyright © SRA/McGraw-Hill

Vocabulary

Important terms in Unit 9:

linear measure A measure used to designate length.

weight A measure of the force of gravity on an object or of how heavy something is.

capacity A measure of pourable substances that take the shape of their containers, such as liquids, sand, and rice.

perimeter The distance around a bounded surface. (The peRIMeter measures the "rim.")

area The number of units (usually squares) that can fit into a bounded surface.

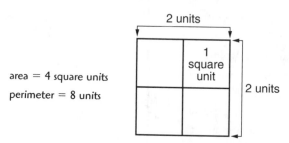

area = 4 square units

perimeter = 8 units

Metric System

Units of Length

1 meter (m)	= 10 decimeters (dm)
	= 100 centimeters (cm)
1 decimeter	= 10 centimeters
1 kilometer (km)	= 1,000 meters

Units of Weight

| 1 kilogram (kg) | = 1,000 grams (g) |

Units of Capacity

| 1 liter (L) | = 1,000 milliliters (mL) |
| $\frac{1}{2}$ liter | = 500 milliliters |

U.S. Customary System

Units of Length

1 yard (yd)	= 3 feet (ft)
	= 36 inches (in.)
1 foot	= 12 inches
1 mile (mi)	= 1,760 yards
	= 5,280 feet

Units of Weight

| 1 pound (lb) | = 16 ounces (oz) |
| 2,000 pounds | = 1 ton (T) |

Units of Capacity

1 cup (c)	= $\frac{1}{2}$ pint (pt)
1 pint	= 2 cups
1 quart (qt)	= 2 pints
1 half-gallon ($\frac{1}{2}$ gal)	= 2 quarts
1 gallon (gal)	= 4 quarts

Copyright © SRA/McGraw-Hill

Use with Lesson 8.8.

Do-Anytime Activities

To work with your child on the concepts taught in this unit and in previous units, try these interesting and rewarding activities:

1 Gather a tape measure, a yardstick, a ruler, a cup, a gallon container, and a scale. Discuss the various things you and your child can measure—for example, the length of a room, how many cups are needed to fill a gallon container, and your child's weight alone and when holding objects, such as books. Record the data and continue to measure and weigh different items periodically.

2 Mark out certain routes on a road map and together figure the distance between two points in both miles and kilometers.

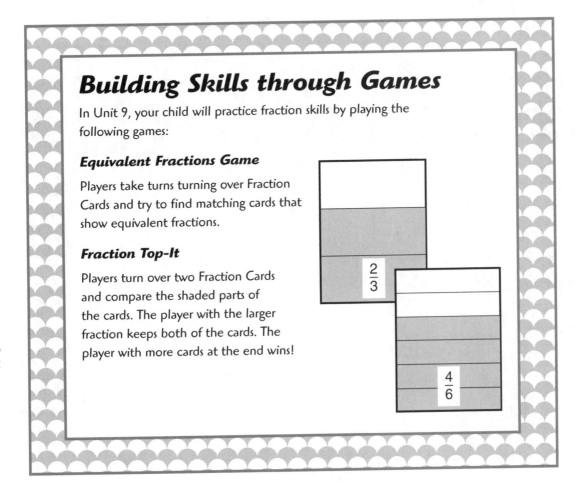

Building Skills through Games

In Unit 9, your child will practice fraction skills by playing the following games:

Equivalent Fractions Game

Players take turns turning over Fraction Cards and try to find matching cards that show equivalent fractions.

Fraction Top-It

Players turn over two Fraction Cards and compare the shaded parts of the cards. The player with the larger fraction keeps both of the cards. The player with more cards at the end wins!

$\frac{2}{3}$

$\frac{4}{6}$

Copyright © SRA/McGraw-Hill

Use with Lesson 8.8.

As You Help Your Child with Homework

As your child brings home assignments, you may want to go over the instructions together, clarifying them as necessary. The answers listed below will guide you through this unit's Home Links.

Home Link 9.2

3. 12 inches   **4.** 3 feet

5. 10 centimeters   **6.** 100 centimeters

7. 24 inches   **8.** 9 feet

9. 40 centimeters   **10.** 700 centimeters

Home Link 9.3

1. $2\frac{1}{2}$ inches   **2.** 4 inches

3. 3 centimeters   **4.** 9 centimeters

Home Link 9.4

1. Perimeter: 6 or 7 inches

2. Perimeter: $4\frac{1}{2}$ or 5 inches

3. Answer: 47 feet. Sample number models:

$14 + 14 + 9\frac{1}{2} + 9\frac{1}{2} = 47$ or

$2 \times 14 + 2 \times 9\frac{1}{2} = 47$

Home Link 9.6

1. mile   **2.** centimeter   **3.** foot

4. meter   **5.** inch   **6.** foot, yard

Home Link 9.7

2.
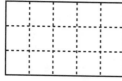
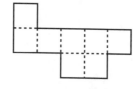

15 square centimeters   8 square centimeters

3.
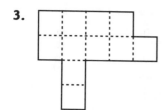

Home Link 9.8

1. 9 sq cm

2. 11 sq cm

3. 10 sq cm

4. I: 20 cm

U: 24 cm

J: 22 cm

Home Link 9.9

Rule	
1 gal = 4 qt	

gal	qt
2	8
4	16
6	24
10	40
Answers	vary.

Rule	
1 pt = 2 c	

pt	c
2	4
3	6
5	10
7	14
Answers	vary.

Rule	
1 qt = 2 pt	

qt	pt
2	4
4	8
6	12
8	16
Answers	vary.

Copyright © SRA/McGraw-Hill

Using Measurement

Family Note

In class today, your child measured distances by using a yardstick. Talk with your child about measurements that you use at your job, around the house, in sports, or in other activities. If you don't have measuring tools to show your child, you might find pictures of measuring tools in a catalog, magazine, or book. Discuss with your child how these tools are used.

Please return this Home Link to school tomorrow.

1. Talk with people at home about how they use measurements at home, at their jobs, or in other activities.

2. Ask people at home to show you the tools they use for measuring. Write the names of some of these tools. Be ready to talk about your list in class.

_____   _____

_____   _____

_____   _____

3. Look for measures in pictures in newspapers or magazines. For example, an ad might name the height of a bookcase or tell how much a container holds. Ask an adult if you may bring the pictures to school for our Measures All Around Museum. Circle the measures.

4. Bring one or two small boxes shaped like rectangular prisms to school. The boxes should be small enough to fit on a sheet of paper.

Copyright © SRA/McGraw-Hill

Use with Lesson 9.1.

Linear Measurements

Family Note

Today your child reviewed how to use a ruler to measure objects and distances in inches and feet and in centimeters and decimeters. Your child's class also began making a Table of Equivalencies for both the U.S. customary and the metric systems. Ask your child to show you how to measure some of the objects or distances that he or she selects to complete the tables below.

Please return this Home Link to school tomorrow.

1. Cut out the 6-inch ruler on the next page. Measure two objects or distances. Measure to the nearest foot. Then measure again to the nearest inch. Some things you might measure are the width of the refrigerator door, the length of the bathtub, or the height of a light switch from the floor.

Object *or* Distance	Nearest Foot	Nearest Inch
	about ____ ft	about ____ in.
	about ____ ft	about ____ in.

2. Cut out the 10-centimeter ruler on the next page. Measure the same objects or distances. Measure to the nearest decimeter. Then measure again to the nearest centimeter.

Object *or* Distance	Nearest Decimeter	Nearest Centimeter
	about ____ dm	about ____ cm
	about ____ dm	about ____ cm

Copyright © SRA/McGraw-Hill

Use with Lesson 9.2.

Linear Measurements (cont.)

Complete each sentence.

3. One foot is equal to _____ inches.

4. One yard is equal to _____ feet.

5. One decimeter is equal to _____ centimeters.

6. One meter is equal to _____ centimeters.

7. Two feet are equal to _____ inches.

8. Three yards are equal to _____ feet.

9. Four decimeters are equal to _____ centimeters.

10. Seven meters are equal to _____ centimeters.

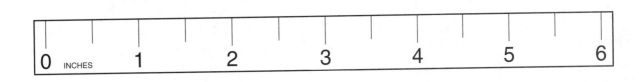

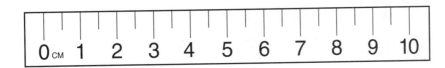

Copyright © SRA/McGraw-Hill

Measuring Lengths

Home Link 9.3

Family Note

Today your child measured life-size pictures of objects to the nearest half-inch and half-centimeter. Take turns with your child measuring objects to the nearest half-inch and half-centimeter. Check to see if your measurements are the same.

Please return this Home Link to school tomorrow.

Cut out the 6-inch ruler on the next page. Measure each line segment to the nearest half-inch. Write the measurement in the blank to the right of each segment.

1. _____ _____ inches

2. _____ _____ inches

Cut out the 15-centimeter ruler on the next page. Measure each line segment to the nearest half-centimeter. Write the measurement in the blank to the right of each segment.

3. _____ _____ centimeters

4. _____ _____ centimeters

Measure some things in your home to the nearest half-inch or half-centimeter. List the things and their measurements below.

Thing	**Measurement**
5. _____	_____
6. _____	_____
7. _____	_____
8. _____	_____

Copyright © SRA/McGraw-Hill

Measuring Lengths (cont.)

9. Draw pictures of two things you measured. Mark the parts you measured. Record the measurements under the pictures.

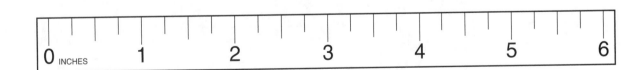

Copyright © SRA/McGraw-Hill

Perimeter

Family Note

In class today, your child found the perimeter of different shapes and the distance around his or her thumb, wrist, neck, and ankle. Perimeter is the measure around something. Finding perimeters also gives your child practice in measuring to the nearest half-inch and half-centimeter.

Please return this Home Link to school tomorrow.

Measure the side of each figure to the nearest $\frac{1}{2}$ inch. Write the length next to each side. Then find the perimeter.

1.

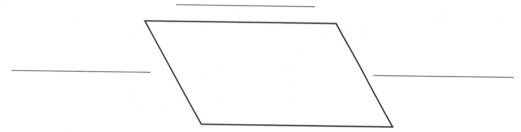

Perimeter:

_____ inches

2.

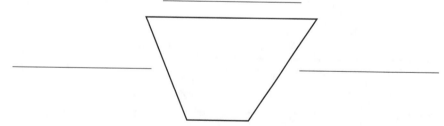

Perimeter:

_____ inches

Copyright © SRA/McGraw-Hill

Perimeter (cont.)

Solve the number story. Write a number model.

3. Mr. McGreggor is putting a fence around his vegetable garden. The garden is shaped liked a rectangle. The longer sides are 14 feet long and the shorter sides are $9\frac{1}{2}$ feet long. How much fencing should Mr. McGreggor buy?

Answer: _____ feet

Number model: _____

_____

4. Draw a quadrangle below. Measure the sides to the nearest $\frac{1}{2}$ inch. Write the length next to each side. Find the perimeter.

The perimeter of my quadrangle is _____ inches.

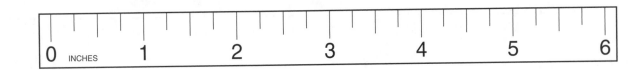

Copyright © SRA/McGraw-Hill

Travel Interview

Family Note

Our class is studying measurement of longer distances. If the traveler your child talks to had experiences with the metric system in another country, have your child include this information to share with the class.

Please return this Home Link to school tomorrow.

Ask someone at home to tell you about the longest trip he or she ever took. Write about the trip. Here are some questions you might want to ask that person:

- When did you take the trip?

- Where did you go?

- What interesting or unusual things did you see or do?

- How did you travel? By car? By plane? By train?

- How long did the trip take?

- How far did you travel?

_____

_____

_____

_____

_____

Copyright © SRA/McGraw-Hill

Units of Measure

Family Note

Today in class, your child identified appropriate measuring tools and units of measure for various items. All of the items below may be measured with any of the given units. There are, however, some units that are best suited for measuring short distances and some units that are best suited for measuring longer distances. Help your child decide which unit is best for each situation.

Please return this Home Link to school tomorrow.

Circle the unit that you would use to measure each item.

1. distance from Orlando, Florida, to Boston, Massachusetts

inch

foot

mile

2. length of a paper clip

centimeter

meter

kilometer

3. height of your teacher

yard

foot

mile

4. perimeter of your bedroom

centimeter

meter

kilometer

5. width of a deck of cards

inch

foot

yard

6. length of a bus

inch

foot

yard

Copyright © SRA/McGraw–Hill

Capacity and Area

Family Note

Today your child explored the ideas of *capacity* and *area*. Before your child is exposed to formal work with these measures (such as equivalent units of capacity or formulas for finding area), it is important that he or she have an informal understanding of these measures.

In Problem 1, help your child see that although the glasses may have different dimensions, they can still hold about the same amount of water. In Problems 2 and 3, the number of squares that your child counts is the area in square centimeters.

Please return this Home Link to school tomorrow.

1. Find two different glasses at home that you think hold about the same amount of water. Test your prediction by pouring water from one glass into the other. Do they hold about the same amount of water? Does one glass hold more than the other? Explain to someone at home how you know.

2. Count squares to find the area of each figure.

_____ square centimeters   _____ square centimeters

3. Circle the shape that has the larger area.

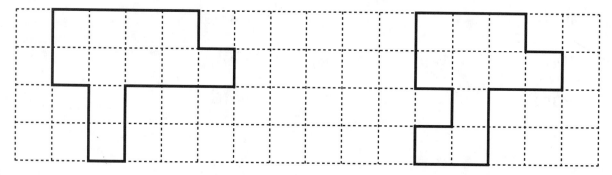

Copyright © SRA/McGraw-Hill

Use with Lesson 9.7.

Area and Perimeter

Family Note

Today children discussed the concept of finding the area of a surface. Area is measured by finding the number of square units needed to cover the surface inside of a shape. Make sure your child understands that, when he or she is finding the perimeter of the letters in Problem 4, he or she is finding the distance around the outside of the letters. Help your child find things at home that have square patterns and together find the areas of those items in square units.

Please return this Home Link to school tomorrow.

Find the area of each letter.

1.

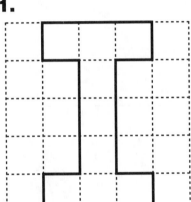

Area = _____ sq cm

2.

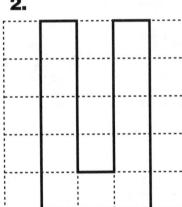

Area = _____ sq cm

3.

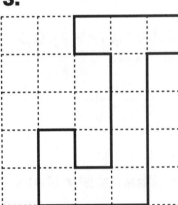

Area = _____ sq cm

4. What is the perimeter of each letter?

I: _____ cm   U: _____ cm   J: _____ cm

5. Find something at home that is covered with square tiles or a square pattern. It might be a floor, wall, ceiling, gameboard, or piece of fabric. If you can't find anything, draw your own picture. Count the squares.

I counted squares on _____.

(name of the thing)

Number of squares: _____

Copyright © SRA/McGraw-Hill

Capacity

Family Note

Today children discussed units of capacity. Capacity is a measure of how much liquid (or other pourable substance, such as sand or rice) a container can hold. Your child recorded equivalent U.S. customary units of capacity (cup, pint, quart, half-gallon, gallon) and equivalent metric units of capacity (milliliter, liter). Please help your child pick out a recipe and identify the units of capacity in the list of ingredients.

Please return this Home Link to school tomorrow.

Ask someone at home to help you find a recipe that uses units of capacity. Copy those ingredients and the amounts called for by the recipe. Bring your list to school.

Example: $\frac{3}{4}$ *cup of milk*

_____

_____

"What's My Rule?"

Rule	
1 gal = 4 qt	

gal	qt
2	
	16
6	
10	

Rule	
1 pt = 2 c	

pt	c
2	
3	
	10
	14

Rule	
1 qt = 2 pt	

qt	pt
2	
4	
	12
8	

Copyright © SRA/McGraw-Hill

Weight

Family Note

In today's lesson, children discussed U.S. customary units of weight (pounds, ounces) and metric units of weight (grams, kilograms). Your child weighed different objects using a variety of scales. Help your child weigh items using scales in your home, or find items with weights written on them.

Please this return this Home Link to school tomorrow.

Find out what kinds of scales you have at home—for example, a bath scale, a letter scale, or a package scale. Weigh a variety of things on the scales, such as a person, a letter, or a book. Record your results below.

If you don't have any scales, look for cans and packages of food with weights written on them. Record those weights below. Remember that ounces (oz) measure weight and that fluid ounces (fl oz) measure capacity.

Object	**Weight** (include unit)
_____	_____
_____	_____
_____	_____
_____	_____
_____	_____
_____	_____

Copyright © SRA/McGraw-Hill

Family Letter

Unit 10: Decimals and Place Value

In this unit, children will review money concepts, such as names of coins and bills, money exchanges, and equivalent amounts. They will pretend to pay for items and to make change.

The unit also focuses on extending work with fractions and money by using decimal notation. Children will use calculators for money problems and estimation.

Later in this unit, children will work with place-value notation for 5-digit numbers. Here, as previously, the focus remains on strategies that help children automatically think of any digit in a numeral in terms of its value as determined by its place. For example, children will learn that in a number like 7,843, the 8 stands for 800, not 8, and the 4 for 40, not 4.

50¢

50 cents

$\frac{1}{2}$ of a dollar

$0.50

fifty cents

Please keep this Family Letter for reference as your child works through Unit 10.

Copyright © SRA/McGraw-Hill

Use with Lesson 9.11.

Vocabulary

Important terms in Unit 10:

decimal point The period that separates the whole number from the fraction in decimal notation. In money amounts, it separates the dollars from the fractions of a dollar (the cents).

flat A base-10 block that represents 100.

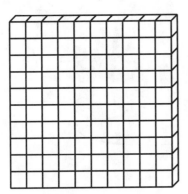

long A base-10 block that represents 10.

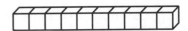

cube A base-10 block that represents 1.

place value The relative worth of each digit in a number, as determined by the digit's position. Each place has a value ten times that of the place to its right and one-tenth that of the place to its left. The chart below illustrates the place value of each digit in 7,843.

7	8	4	3
↑	↑	↑	↑
thousands	hundreds	tens	ones

Building Skills through Games

In Unit 10, your child will build his or her understanding of fractions and money by playing the following games:

Fraction Top-It

Players turn over two fraction cards and compare the shaded parts of the cards. The player with the larger fraction keeps both of the cards. The player with more cards at the end wins!

Money Exchange Game

Players roll a die and put that number of $1 bills on their Place-Value Mats. Whenever possible, they exchange ten $1 bills for one $10 bill. The first player to make an exchange for one $100 bill wins!

Pick-a-Coin

Players create coin collections based on rolls of a die. Players try to get the largest possible values for their collections.

Copyright © SRA/McGraw-Hill

Use with Lesson 9.11.

Do-Anytime Activities

To work with your child on the concepts taught in this unit and in previous units, try these interesting and rewarding activities:

1 Collect a variety of coins and help your child count them. Discuss what other coin combinations would equal the same amount. For example, each group of coins shown on this page equals $1.00.

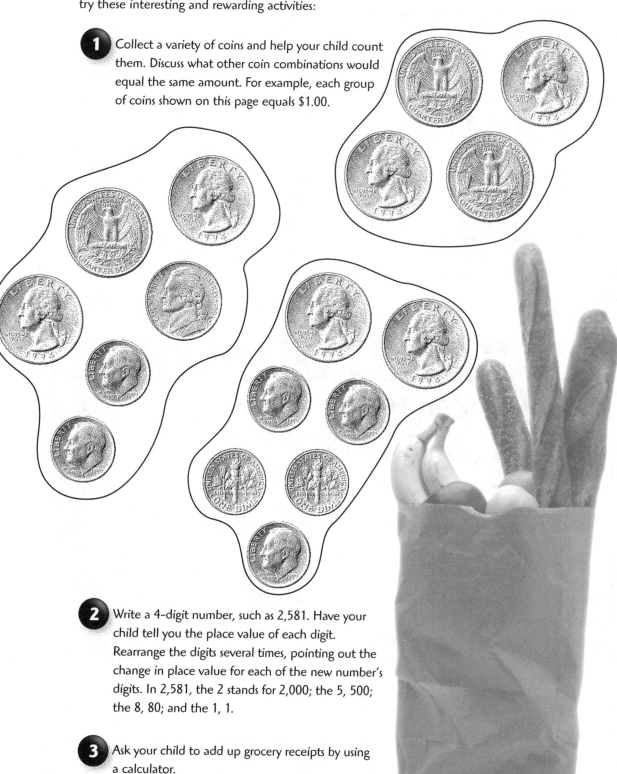

2 Write a 4–digit number, such as 2,581. Have your child tell you the place value of each digit. Rearrange the digits several times, pointing out the change in place value for each of the new number's digits. In 2,581, the 2 stands for 2,000; the 5, 500; the 8, 80; and the 1, 1.

3 Ask your child to add up grocery receipts by using a calculator.

Copyright © SRA/McGraw-Hill

Use with Lesson 9.11.

As You Help Your Child with Homework

As your child brings home assignments, you may want to go over the instructions together, clarifying them as necessary. The answers listed below will guide you through this unit's Home Links.

Home Link 10.1

1. 10 pennies = 10¢, or $0.10

 10 nickels = 50¢, or $0.50

 10 dimes = $1.00

 10 quarters = $2.50

 10 half-dollars = $5.00

 Total = $9.10

Home Link 10.2

1. $3.57 2. $3.55 3. $0.52 4. $0.08

5. Sample answers: $1 $1 Q Q D P P P P or
 $1 Q Q Q Q D D D D N N N P P P P

Home Link 10.3

1. $0.06; $0.50; $1.30; $1.50; $3.36

Home Link 10.4

1. 1.09; 2.5; 0.98; 3.18; 0.06

Home Link 10.5

1. $0.70 2. $2.60 3. $1.00

4. $1.30 5. $4.00 6. $1.20

7. $2.30 8. $1.30 + $0.50 = $1.80

9. $0.80 + $0.40 = $1.20

10. $0.70 + $0.90 = $1.60

11. $1.40 + $0.80 = $2.20

Home Link 10.7

1. 17 square cm 2. 17 sq cm

3. 23 cm² 4. 11 square cm

5. 9 sq cm 6. 9 cm²

Home Link 10.8

1. ④6 2 2. 1,③26 3. 5,⓪06

4. ⑧69 5. 2,③04 6. 4,⑤67

9. 1,183 10. 1,204 11. 1,050

Home Link 10.9

1. 0; 100; 200; 300; 400; 500; 600; 700; 800; 900; 1,000

2. 0; 1,000; 2,000; 3,000; 4,000; 5,000; 6,000; 7,000; 8,000; 9,000; 10,000

3.

Number	10 More	100 More	1,000 More
32	42	132	1,032
146	156	246	1,146
309	319	409	1,309
1,468	1,478	1,568	2,468
10,037	10,047	10,137	11,037

Home Link 10.10

3. 72,469 4. 72,569; 75,469; 72,369; 69,469

Home Link 10.11

1. 9 2. 15 3. 13 4. 6

5. 13 − (9 + 2) = 2

6. (28 − 8) − 4 = 16

7. (150 − 70) − 40 = 40

8. 800 − (200 + 300) = 300

9. [15]

 25 = (15 + 5)
 (25 − 15) + 5
 (17 − 9) + 7
 17 = (9 + 7)
 (3 + 6) + 6
 3 + (6 + 6)

10. [100]

 (50 + 150) − 100
 50 + (150 − 100)
 400 = (300 − 200)
 (400 − 300) + 200

Copyright © SRA/McGraw-Hill

Coin Combinations

Family Note

In today's lesson, your child practiced writing amounts of money. For example, in Problem 1, 10 pennies can be written as 10¢ or $0.10. Your child also showed different groups of coins that have the same monetary value. For example, your child could show 62¢ with 2 quarters, 1 dime, and 2 pennies; or 4 dimes, 4 nickels, and 2 pennies. For Problem 2, help your child find items in newspaper or magazine ads and think of different combinations of coins and bills to pay for the items.

Please return this Home Link to school tomorrow.

1. Pretend that you have 10 of each kind of coin.
   How much is that in all?

   10 pennies   = _____

   10 nickels   = _____

   10 dimes   = _____

   10 quarters   = _____

   10 half-dollars = _____

   Total   = _____

2. Find two ads in a newspaper or magazine for items that cost less than $3.00 each.

   • Ask for permission to cut out the ads.

   • Cut them out and glue them onto the back of this page.

   • Draw coins to show the cost of each item.

   (If you can't find ads, draw pictures of items and prices on the back of this page.)

Copyright © SRA/McGraw-Hill

How Much?

Family Note

In today's lesson, your child practiced reading and writing money amounts using dollars and cents. Ask your child to read each amount aloud. Remind your child that the digits before the decimal point stand for whole dollars; the digits after the decimal point stand for cents. When reading amounts, such as "3 dollars and fifty-seven cents," the word "and" is used to denote the decimal point.

Please return this Home Link to school tomorrow.

How much money? Write your answer in dollars-and-cents notation.

1. $1 $1 $1 Q Q N P P $___.___

2. $1 $1 Q Q Q Q D D D N N N N $___.___

3. Q D D P P P P P P P $___.___

4. N P P P $___.___

5. Use $1, Q, D, N, and P to draw $2.64 in two different ways.

Copyright © SRA/McGraw-Hill

Coin Values

Family Note

In today's lesson, your child used a calculator to enter amounts of money and find totals. For Problem 2, help your child collect and find the total value of each type of coin. Then find the grand total. If you wish to use a calculator, help your child enter the amounts. Remind your child that amounts like $1.00 and $0.50 will be displayed on the calculator as "1." and "0.5" because the calculator doesn't display ending zeros.

Please return this Home Link to school tomorrow.

1. Complete the table.

Coins	Number of Coins	Total Value
(P)	6	$____.____
(N)	10	$____.____
(D)	13	$____.____
(Q)	6	$____.____
Grand total		$____.____

2. Ask someone at home to help you collect pennies, nickels, dimes, quarters, and, if possible, half-dollars. Use the coins in your collection to complete the table below.

Coins	Number of Coins	Total Value
(P)		
(N)		
(D)		
(Q)		
Half-dollar		
Grand total		

Copyright © SRA/McGraw-Hill

Use with Lesson 10.3.

Calculators and Money

Family Note

In today's lesson, your child used a calculator to solve problems with money. In Problem 2, your child will ask you or another adult to compare the cost of an item when you were a child to its current cost. There are two ways to make this type of comparison. You might describe a *difference comparison*. For example: "A bicycle costs about $90.00 more now than it did then." You might also use a *ratio comparison*. For example, "A bicycle costs about 4 times as much now as it did then." You do not need to share the terms "difference comparison" and "ratio comparison" with your child, but it is important that your child be exposed to both types of comparisons.

Please return this Home Link to school tomorrow.

1. Enter the following amounts into your calculator.
What does your calculator show?

Enter	Calculator Shows
$1.09	_____
$2.50	_____
98¢	_____
$3.18	_____
6¢	_____

2. Ask an adult to think about an item that he or she remembers from when he or she was a child. Ask the adult to compare how much the item cost then and now. Make a record below of what you find out.

_____

_____

_____

Copyright © SRA/McGraw-Hill

Estimation to the Nearest 10¢

Home Link 10.5

Family Note

In today's lesson, your child estimated sums by first finding the nearest ten cents for each amount of money being added and then adding the amounts for the nearest ten cents together. For Problems 1–7, ask your child how she or he arrived at each answer. If needed, use coins to show which amount is actually closer. For Problems 8–11, help your child find the totals by thinking of a problem like $1.20 + $0.60 as 12 + 6 or as 120 cents + 60 cents.

Please return this Home Link to school tomorrow.

Write the correct answer to each question.
Talk with someone at home about your answers.

1. Is $0.69 closer to $0.60 or $0.70? _____

2. Is $2.59 closer to $2.50 or $2.60? _____

3. Is $0.99 closer to $0.90 or $1.00? _____

4. Is $1.31 closer to $1.30 or $1.40? _____

5. Is $3.99 closer to $3.90 or $4.00? _____

6. Is $1.17 closer to $1.10 or $1.20? _____

7. Is $2.34 closer to $2.30 or $2.40? _____

Fill in the blanks and estimate the total cost in each problem.

Example

$1.19 + $0.59 is about __*$1.20*__ + __*$0.60*__ = __*$1.80*__ .

8. $1.29 + $0.48 is about _____ + _____ = _____ .

9. $0.79 + $0.39 is about _____ + _____ = _____ .

10. $0.69 + $0.89 is about _____ + _____ = _____ .

11. $1.41 + $0.77 is about _____ + _____ = _____ .

Copyright © SRA/McGraw-Hill

Use with Lesson 10.5.

Making Change

Family Note

In today's lesson, your child made change by counting up. When counting out change, encourage your child to begin with the cost of the item and count up to the amount of money that the customer has given to the clerk. For the example listed in the table below, your child could do the following:

1. Say, "89 cents"—the price of the item.

2. Put a penny on the table and say, "90 cents."

3. Put a dime on the table and say, "$1.00."

4. Count the coins on the table. 1¢ + 10¢ = 11¢. The change is 11¢.

Please return this Home Link to school tomorrow.

Materials
☐ coins and bills (You can make bills out of paper.)
☐ items with prices marked

Practice making change with someone at home. Pretend you are the Clerk at a store and the other person is a Customer. The Customer buys one of the items and pays with a bill. You count out the change.

Record some purchases here.

Item	Price	Amount Used to Pay	Change
can of black beans	$0.89	$1.00	$0.11

If possible, go to the store with someone. Buy something and get change. Count the change. Is it correct?

Copyright © SRA/McGraw-Hill

Area

Family Note

In today's lesson, your child found the area of shapes by counting square centimeters. As you observe your child finding the areas below, check that he or she is counting squares that are more than $\frac{1}{2}$ shaded as 1 square centimeter and not counting squares that are less than $\frac{1}{2}$ shaded. For Problem 6, see if your child has a suggestion for what to do if exactly $\frac{1}{2}$ of a square is shaded. Remind your child that area is reported in square units. Other ways to write square centimeters are **sq cm** and **cm²**.

Please return this Home Link to school tomorrow.

Count squares to find the area of each shaded figure.

1.

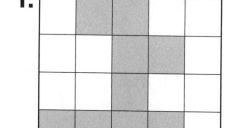

_____ square cm

2.

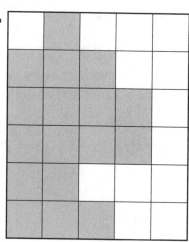

_____ sq cm

3.

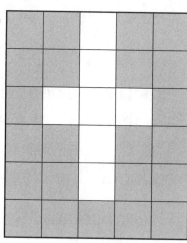

_____ cm²

4.

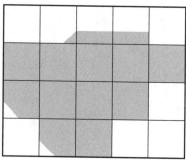

_____ square cm

5.

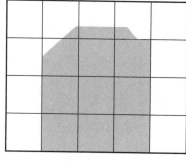

_____ sq cm

6.

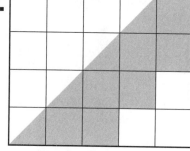

_____ cm²

Copyright © SRA/McGraw-Hill

Use with Lesson 10.7.

Place Value

Family Note

In this lesson, your child has been studying place value, or the value of digits in numbers. Listen as your child reads the numbers in Problems 1–6. You might ask your child to pick a few of the numbers and tell you the place value of each of the digits. For example, in 462, the value of 4 is 400, the value of 6 is 60, and the value of 2 is 2.

Please return this Home Link to school tomorrow.

In each number: • Circle the digit in the hundreds place.

                    • Underline the digit in the thousands place.

Example: 9 , ③ 4 2

1. 4 6 2

2. 1 , 3 2 6

3. 5 , 0 0 6

4. 8 6 9

5. 2 , 3 0 4

6. 4 , 5 6 7

7. Read the numbers in Problems 1–6 to someone at home.

Write the numbers represented by the base-10 blocks.

8. 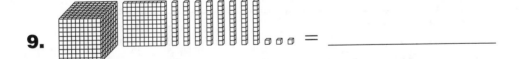 = _____ 247 _____

9. _____ = _____

10. _____ = _____

11. _____ = _____

Copyright © SRA/McGraw-Hill

Counting by 10s, 100s, and 1,000s

Family Note

In this lesson, your child used place value to count by 10s, 100s, and 1,000s. For Problems 1 and 2, listen carefully to find out if your child counts quickly and accurately. Help your child complete the table in Problem 3. If necessary, have your child use a calculator to find the answers. Ask your child to describe any patterns he or she sees in the completed table.

Please return this Home Link to school tomorrow.

1. Show someone at home how to count by 100s from 0 to 1,000. Record your counts.

_____

_____

2. Now count by 1,000s from 0 to 10,000. Record your counts.

_____

_____

3. Complete the table.

Number	10 More	100 More	1,000 More
32	42	132	1,032
146			
309			
1,468			
10,037			

Copyright © SRA/McGraw-Hill

4-Digit and 5-Digit Numbers

Family Note

In this lesson, your child read and displayed 4- and 5-digit numbers. Listen to your child read numbers to you. Remind your child not to say "and" when reading numbers, such as the ones below. (In reading numbers, "and" indicates a decimal point. For example, 7.9 is read as "seven and nine tenths.") However, don't go out of your way to correct your child if he or she inserts "and" occasionally. For Problem 2, write some 4- and 5-digit numbers as your child is writing numbers. Exchange your sets of numbers and read each other's numbers aloud.

Please return this Home Link to school tomorrow.

1. Read these numbers to someone at home.

   3,426; 6,001; 9,864; 13,400; 29,368; 99,999

2. Write other 4- and 5-digit numbers. Read your numbers to someone at home.

   _____

3. Write a number that has:

   4 in the hundreds place.

   6 in the tens place.

   2 in the thousands place.

   7 in the ten-thousands place.

   9 in the ones place.

   ____ ____ , ____ ____ ____

4. Use the number in Problem 3. What number is

   100 more? _____

   3,000 more? _____

   100 less? _____

   3,000 less? _____

Copyright © SRA/McGraw-Hill

Use with Lesson 10.10.

Grouping with Parentheses

Family Note

In this lesson, your child has solved problems and puzzles involving parentheses. For Problems 1–4, 9, and 10, remind your child that the calculations inside of the parentheses need to be done first. In Problem 1, for example, your child should first find $7 - 2$ and then add that answer (5) to 4. For Problems 5–8, observe as your child adds parentheses. Ask your child to explain what to do first in order to obtain the number on the right side of the equals sign.

Please return this Home Link to school tomorrow.

Solve problems containing parentheses.

1. $4 + (7 - 2) =$ _____

2. $(9 + 21) - 15 =$ _____

3. $6 + (12 - 5) =$ _____

4. $(15 + 5) - 14 =$ _____

Put in parentheses to solve the puzzles.

5. $13 - 9 + 2 = 2$

6. $28 - 8 - 4 = 16$

7. $150 - 70 - 40 = 40$

8. $800 - 200 + 300 = 300$

Cross out the names that don't belong in the name-collection boxes.

9.

15
$25 - (15 + 5)$
$(25 - 15) + 5$
$(17 - 9) + 7$
$17 - (9 + 7)$
$(3 + 6) + 6$
$3 + (6 + 6)$

10.

100
$(50 + 150) - 100$
$50 + (150 - 100)$
$400 - (300 - 200)$
$(400 - 300) + 200$

Copyright © SRA/McGraw-Hill

Use with Lesson 10.11.

Unit 11:
Whole-Number Operations Revisited

In the beginning of Unit 11, children will solve addition and subtraction stories with dollars and cents. Children will use estimation to examine their answers and determine whether the answers make sense.

Children will also review the uses of multiplication and division and begin to develop multiplication and division fact power, or the ability to automatically recall the basic multiplication and division facts.

Children will work with shortcuts, which will help them extend known facts to related facts. For example, the **turn-around rule for multiplication** shows that the order of the numbers being multiplied (the factors) does not affect the product; 3×4 is the same as 4×3. Children will also learn what it means to multiply a number by 0 and by 1. Patterns in a Facts Table and in fact families will also help children explore ways of learning multiplication and division facts.

×,÷	1	2	3	4	5	6	7	8	9	10
1	1	2	3	4	5	6	7	8	9	10
2	2	4	6	8	10	12	14	16	18	20
3	3	6	9	12	15	18	21	24	27	30
4	4	8	12	16	20	24	28	32	36	40
5	5	10	15	20	25	30	35	40	45	50
6	6	12	18	24	30	36	42	48	54	60
7	7	14	21	28	35	42	49	56	63	70
8	8	16	24	32	40	48	56	64	72	80
9	9	18	27	36	45	54	63	72	81	90
10	10	20	30	40	50	60	70	80	90	100

Multiplication/Division Facts Table

Finally, children will apply and extend their knowledge as they analyze and compare precipitation data obtained from a map.

Please keep this Family Letter for reference as your child works through Unit 11.

Copyright © SRA/McGraw-Hill

Vocabulary

Important terms in Unit 11:

multiplication diagram A diagram used to represent numbers in which several equal groups are being considered together. The diagram has three parts: a number of groups, a number in each group, and a total number.

Multiplication Diagram

rows	_____ per row	_____ in all

Number model: _____ × _____ = _____

factor One of the numbers being multiplied in a multiplication number model.

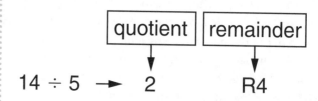

product The result of doing multiplication.

quotient The whole-number result when one number is divided by another number; the number of equal shares.

remainder The amount left over (if any) when a number is divided into equal shares.

$$\text{quotient} \quad \text{remainder}$$
$$14 \div 5 \rightarrow \quad 2 \qquad R4$$

fact power The ability to automatically recall basic multiplication and division facts.

turn-around rule for multiplication The order of numbers being multiplied does not affect the outcome. For example, $3 \times 4 = 12$ and $4 \times 3 = 12$.

fact family A collection of related addition and subtraction facts, or multiplication and division facts, made from the same numbers. For the numbers 3, 5, and 15, for example, the fact family consists of $3 \times 5 = 15$, $5 \times 3 = 15$, $15 \div 3 = 5$, and $15 \div 5 = 3$.

middle value The number in the middle when a set of data is organized in sequential order; also called the median. For example, in the set of data below, 35 is the middle value.

32 32 34 35 35 37 38

range The difference between the greatest and least numbers in a set of data. For example, in the set of data above, 6 is the range ($38 - 32 = 6$).

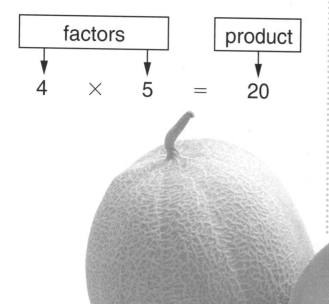

Copyright © SRA/McGraw-Hill

Use with Lesson 10.12.

Do-Anytime Activities

To work with your child on the concepts taught in this unit and in previous units, try these interesting and rewarding activities:

1 Review common multiplication shortcuts. Ask, for example: *What happens when you multiply a number by 1? By 0? By 10?* Use pennies to show that 2×3 pennies is the same as 3×2 pennies.

2 At a restaurant or while grocery shopping, work together to estimate the bill.

3 Take turns making up multiplication and division number stories to solve.

Building Skills through Games

In Unit 11, your child will practice multiplication skills and mental arithmetic by playing the following games:

Beat the Calculator

A "Calculator" (a player who uses a calculator to solve the problem) and a "Brain" (a player who solves the problem without a calculator) race to see who will be first to solve multiplication problems.

Hit the Target

Players choose a 2-digit multiple of ten as a "target number." One player enters a "starting number" into a calculator and tries to change the starting number to the target number by adding a number to it on the calculator. Children practice finding differences between 2-digit numbers and higher multiples of tens.

Copyright © SRA/McGraw-Hill

Use with Lesson 10.12.

As You Help Your Child with Homework

As your child brings home assignments, you may want to go over the instructions together, clarifying them as necessary. The answers listed below will guide you through this unit's Home Links.

Home Link 11.1

1. $2.22 **2.** $4.06 **3.** $3.34 **4.** $1.64

Home Link 11.2

1. glue stick; $0.14 **2.** glitter; $0.58
3. coloring pencils; $1.12 **4.** coloring pencils; $1.84
5. $0.11 **6.** $2.41

Home Link 11.3

1. 18 tennis balls; 6 × 3 = 18
2. 32 buns; 4 × 8 = 32

Home Link 11.4

1. 6 packages; 18 ÷ 3 → 6 R0
2. 6 cards; 25 ÷ 4 → 6 R1

Home Link 11.5

1. 12 **2.** 12 **3.** 10
4. 9
5. 14
6. 12

7. 2 nickels = 10 cents; 2 × 5 = 10
6 nickels = 30 cents; 6 × 5 = 30
8. 4 dimes = 40 cents; 4 × 10 = 40
7 dimes = 70 cents; 7 × 10 = 70
9. double 6 = 12; 2 × 6 = 12
double 9 = 18; 2 × 9 = 18

Home Link 11.6

2. a. 99 **b.** 502 **c.** 0 **d.** 0

Home Link 11.8

1. 5 × 7 = 35 **2.** 3 × 6 = 18
7 × 5 = 35 6 × 3 = 18
35 ÷ 5 = 7 18 ÷ 3 = 6
35 ÷ 7 = 5 18 ÷ 6 = 3
3. 4 × 6 = 24 **4.** 5 × 6 = 30
6 × 4 = 24 6 × 5 = 30
24 ÷ 4 = 6 30 ÷ 5 = 6
24 ÷ 6 = 4 30 ÷ 6 = 5

Home Link 11.9

1. Dave; 40 years **2.** Lily; 8 years
3. 32 years **4.** 12 years
5. Lily **6.** Diane
7. Jillian **8.** Dave

Copyright © SRA/McGraw-Hill

Use with Lesson 10.12.

Buying Art Supplies

Family Note

In today's lesson, your child solved number stories involving money amounts. Ask your child to explain to you how he or she solved each of the addition problems below. Challenge your child to find the total cost of 3 or 4 items. Encourage your child to use estimation before solving each problem. Ask such questions as: *Is the total cost of the crayons and glitter more or less than $3.00?* (less)

Please return this Home Link to school tomorrow.

$0.75

Crayons

$1.47

Glitter

$2.59

Coloring Pencils

$0.89

Glue Stick

Find the total cost of each pair of items.

1. crayons and glitter Total cost: _____	**2.** glitter and coloring pencils Total cost: _____
3. crayons and coloring pencils Total cost: _____	**4.** glue stick and crayons Total cost: _____

Copyright © SRA/McGraw-Hill

Use with Lesson 11.1.

Comparing Costs

Family Note

In today's lesson, your child solved subtraction number stories involving money amounts. Ask your child to explain how he or she solved each of the subtraction problems below. Encourage your child to use estimation before solving each problem. Ask such questions as: *Is the difference in cost between the crayons and glitter more or less than $1.00?* (less)

Please return this Home Link to school tomorrow.

$0.75

Crayons

Gold Glitter

$1.47

Glitter

COLORED PENCILS

8 Beautiful Colors

$2.59

Coloring Pencils

GLUE STICK

$0.89

Glue Stick

In Problems 1–4, circle the item that costs more.
Then find how much more.

1. glue stick or crayons

How much more? _____

2. glue stick or glitter

How much more? _____

3. glitter or coloring pencils

How much more? _____

4. coloring pencils or crayons

How much more? _____

5. Jenna bought a glue stick. She paid with a $1 bill. How much change should she get?

_____

6. Denisha bought a set of coloring pencils. She paid with a $5 bill. How much change should she get?

_____

Copyright © SRA/McGraw-Hill

Use with Lesson 11.2.

Multiplication Number Stories

Family Note

In today's lesson, your child solved multiplication number stories in which he or she found the total number of things in several equal groups. Observe the strategies your child uses to solve the problems below. The "multiplication diagram" is a device used to keep track of the information in a problem.

To solve Problem 1, your child would identify the known information by writing a 6 under *cans* and a 3 under *tennis balls per can*. To identify the unknown information, your child would write a ? under *tennis balls in all*.

Please return this Home Link to school tomorrow.

Show someone at home how to solve these multiplication stories.
Fill in each multiplication diagram.
Use counters or draw pictures or arrays to help you.

1. The store has 6 cans of tennis balls.
There are 3 balls in each can.
How many tennis balls are there in all?

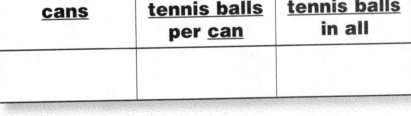

cans	tennis balls per can	tennis balls in all

Answer: _____ tennis balls

Number model: _____ × _____ = _____

Copyright © SRA/McGraw-Hill

Multiplication Stories (cont.)

Home Link 11.3

2. Hamburger buns come in packages of 8.
You buy 4 packages.
How many buns are there in all?

packages	buns per package	buns in all

Answer: _____ buns

Number model: _____ × _____ = _____

3. Make up and solve a multiplication number story below.

_____

_____

_____

_____	_____ per _____	_____ in all

Answer: _____

Number model: _____ × _____ = _____

Copyright © SRA/McGraw-Hill

Use with Lesson 11.3.

Division Number Stories

Family Note

Today your child solved division number stories about equal sharing and equal groups. The diagram used for multiplication can also be used for division number stories to identify known and unknown information. Your child will write a number model for each problem below. A number model is the symbolic representation of a number story. For example, in Problem 1, the number model is $18 \div 3 \rightarrow 6$ R0. This model is read as *18 divided by 3 gives 6, remainder 0.* An arrow is used instead of an equals ($=$) sign because the result of a division problem can be two whole numbers: the quotient and remainder.

Please return this Home Link to school tomorrow.

Show someone at home how to solve these division stories. Use counters or draw pictures or diagrams to help you.

1. Our group needs 18 pens. There are 3 pens in each package. How many packages must we buy?

packages	pens per package	pens in all

Answer: _____ packages

Number model: _____ ÷ _____ → __ R__

2. Four children are playing a game with 25 cards. How many cards can the dealer give each player?

children	cards per child	cards in all

Answer: _____ cards

Number model: _____ ÷ _____ → __ R__

3. Make up and solve a division story on the back of this sheet.

Copyright © SRA/McGraw–Hill

Multiplication Facts

Family Note

In this lesson, your child has been learning multiplication facts and has used arrays to represent those facts. The first factor in a multiplication fact tells the number of rows in the array, and the second factor tells the number of columns in the array. In Problem 1, for example, an array with 2 rows of 6 dots is used for the multiplication fact $2 \times 6 = 12$.

Please return this Home Link to school tomorrow.

Show someone at home how you can use arrays to find products. Use •s.

1. $2 \times 6 =$ _____ • • • • • • • • • • • •	**2.** $6 \times 2 =$ _____	**3.** $1 \times 10 =$ _____
4. $1 \times 9 =$ _____	**5.** $2 \times 7 =$ _____	**6.** $3 \times 4 =$ _____

7. 2 nickels = _____ cents $2 \times 5 =$ _____

6 nickels = _____ cents $6 \times 5 =$ _____

8. 4 dimes = _____ cents $4 \times 10 =$ _____

7 dimes = _____ cents $7 \times 10 =$ _____

9. double 6 = _____ $2 \times 6 =$ _____

double 9 = _____ $2 \times 9 =$ _____

Copyright © SRA/McGraw-Hill

Use with Lesson 11.5.

Multiplication Facts

Family Note

In today's lesson, your child practiced multiplication facts by using a table and discussed patterns in multiplication facts. For example, any number multiplied by 1 is that number; any number multiplied by 0 is 0; and if the order of the factors in a multiplication fact is reversed, the product remains the same.

Observe the strategies your child uses to find the answers below. By the end of second grade, your child should be proficient with 0s and 1s facts and developing proficiency with the 2s, 5s, and 10s facts.

Please return this Home Link to school tomorrow.

1. Show someone at home what you know about multiplication facts. You can use arrays or pictures to help solve the problems.

$0 \times 9 =$ ____	$8 \times 0 =$ ____	$4 \times 0 =$ ____	$0 \times 7 =$ ____
$1 \times 3 =$ ____	$3 \times 1 =$ ____	$1 \times 8 =$ ____	$10 \times 1 =$ ____
$2 \times 8 =$ ____	$3 \times 2 =$ ____	$2 \times 7 =$ ____	$4 \times 2 =$ ____
$5 \times 3 =$ ____	$2 \times 5 =$ ____	$6 \times 5 =$ ____	$5 \times 8 =$ ____
$10 \times 4 =$ ____	$3 \times 10 =$ ____	$9 \times 10 =$ ____	$10 \times 6 =$ ____

2. Explain to someone at home why it is easy to solve the following multiplication problems.

a.	99	**b.**	502	**c.**	37	**d.**	15,461
	$\times \quad 1$		$\times \quad 1$		$\times \quad 0$		$\times \qquad 0$

3. Make up and solve some multiplication problems of your own on the back of this page.

Copyright © SRA/McGraw-Hill

×, ÷ Fact Triangles

Family Note

Fact Triangles are tools for building mental arithmetic skills. You might think of them as the *Everyday Mathematics* version of the flash cards that you may remember from grade school. Fact Triangles, however, are more effective for helping children memorize facts because they emphasize fact families.

A **fact family** is a collection of related facts made from the same three numbers. For the numbers 4, 6, and 24, the multiplication/division fact family consists of $4 \times 6 = 24$, $6 \times 4 = 24$, $24 \div 6 = 4$, and $24 \div 4 = 6$.

Please help your child cut out the Fact Triangles attached to this letter.

To use Fact Triangles to practice multiplication with your child, cover the number next to the dot with your thumb. The number you have covered is the product.

Your child uses the numbers that are showing to tell you one or two multiplication facts: $3 \times 5 = 15$ or $5 \times 3 = 15$.

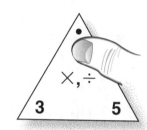

Multiplication

To practice division, use your thumb to cover a number without a dot.

Your child uses the numbers that are showing to tell you the division fact $15 \div 5 = 3$.

Now cover the other number without a dot. Your child now tells you the other division fact $15 \div 3 = 5$.

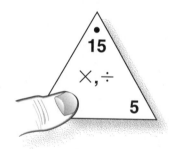

Division

If your child misses a fact, flash the other two fact problems on the card and then return to the fact that was missed.

Example: Sue can't answer $15 \div 3$. Flash 3×5, then $15 \div 5$, and finally $15 \div 3$ a second time.

Make this activity brief and fun. Spend about 10 minutes each night for the next few weeks, or until your child masters all of the facts. The work you do at home will support the work your child is doing at school.

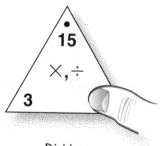

Division

Copyright © SRA/McGraw-Hill

Use with Lesson 11.7.

×, ÷ Fact Triangles (cont.)

Cut out the Fact Triangles. Show someone at home how you can use them to practice multiplication and division facts.

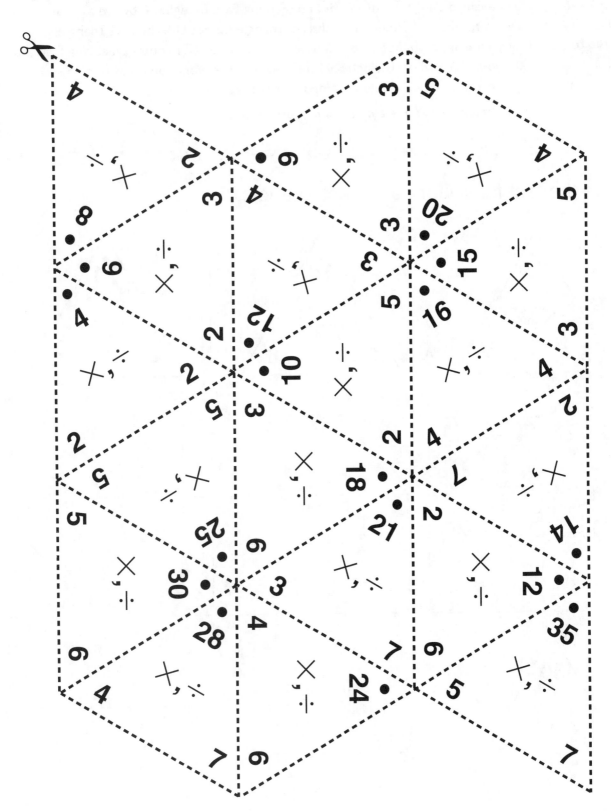

Copyright © SRA/McGraw-Hill

Fact Families

Family Note

Today your child continued to practice multiplication and division facts by playing a game called *Beat the Calculator* and by using Fact Triangles. Observe as your child writes the fact family for each Fact Triangle below. Use the Fact Triangles that your child brought home yesterday. Spend about 10 minutes practicing facts with your child. Make the activity brief and fun. The work you do at home will support the work your child is doing at school.

Please return this Home Link to school tomorrow.

Write the fact family for each Fact Triangle.

1.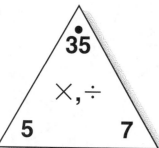

$$\underline{5} \times \underline{7} = \underline{35}$$

$$\underline{} \times \underline{} = \underline{}$$

$$\underline{35} \div \underline{5} = \underline{7}$$

$$\underline{} \div \underline{} = \underline{}$$

2.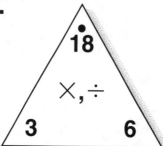

$$\underline{} \times \underline{} = \underline{}$$

$$\underline{} \times \underline{} = \underline{}$$

$$\underline{} \div \underline{} = \underline{}$$

$$\underline{} \div \underline{} = \underline{}$$

3.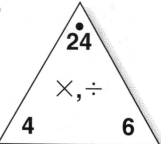

$$\underline{} \times \underline{} = \underline{}$$

$$\underline{} \times \underline{} = \underline{}$$

$$\underline{} \div \underline{} = \underline{}$$

$$\underline{} \div \underline{} = \underline{}$$

4.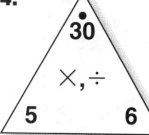

$$\underline{} \times \underline{} = \underline{} \qquad \underline{} \div \underline{} = \underline{}$$

$$\underline{} \times \underline{} = \underline{} \qquad \underline{} \div \underline{} = \underline{}$$

Copyright © SRA/McGraw-Hill

Data Analysis

Family Note

In this lesson, your child used multiplication and division to compare data. The **range** of a set of data is the difference between the greatest and the least values. In the table below, the range of the age data is 40 − 8, or 32 years. The **middle value** of a set of data is the number in the middle when the data are arranged in ascending or descending order. In the table below, the middle value of the age data is 12 years.

Please return this Home Link to school tomorrow.

Lily collected information about the ages of people in her family.

Complete.

Name	Age (Years)
Dave	40
Diane	36
Jillian	12
Lara	10
Lily	8

1. The oldest person is _____.

    Age: _____ years

2. The youngest person is _____.

    Age: _____ years

3. Range of the ages: _____ years

4. Middle value of the ages: _____ years

Fill in the blanks with the name of the correct person.

5. Jillian is about 4 years older than _____.

6. Lara is about 26 years younger than _____.

7. Diane is about 3 times as old as _____.

8. Lara is about $\frac{1}{4}$ as old as _____.

Copyright © SRA/McGraw-Hill

Unit 12: Year-End Reviews and Extensions

Rather than focusing on a single topic, Unit 12 reinforces some of the main topics covered in second grade.

Children will begin the unit by reviewing time measurements—telling time on clocks with hour and minute hands; using alternate names for time; using larger units of time, such as centuries and decades; and keeping track of longer periods of time in years, months, weeks, and days.

Children will also work with computation dealing with multiplication facts and the relationship between multiplication and division.

Finally, children will display and interpret measurement data, with special emphasis on the range, median, and mode of sets of data.

Please keep this Family Letter for reference as your child works through Unit 12.

Copyright © SRA/McGraw-Hill

Vocabulary

Important terms in Unit 12:

timeline A device for showing in sequence when certain events took place. For example, the timeline below shows when the telephone, radio, and television were invented.

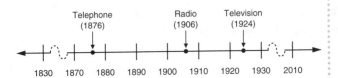

factors The numbers being multiplied.

product The result of doing multiplication.

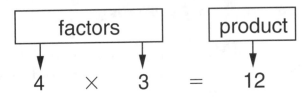

$$4 \times 3 = 12$$

turn-around rule The rule that states that the order of factors does not affect the product.

$$5 \times 6 = 30 \quad 6 \times 5 = 30$$

median The number in the middle when a set of data is organized in sequential order.

range The difference between the greatest and least numbers in a set of data.

mode The value that occurs most often in a set of data.

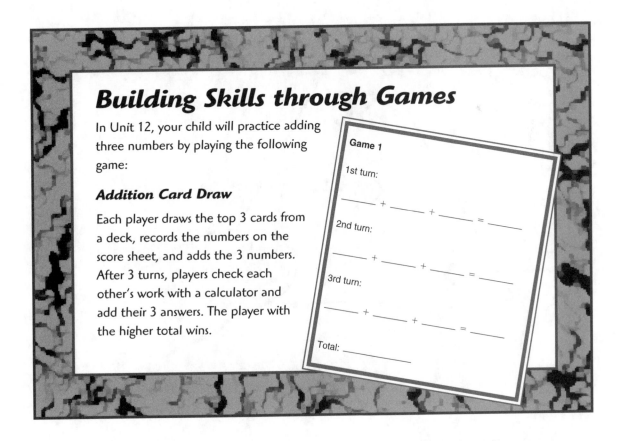

Building Skills through Games

In Unit 12, your child will practice adding three numbers by playing the following game:

Addition Card Draw

Each player draws the top 3 cards from a deck, records the numbers on the score sheet, and adds the 3 numbers. After 3 turns, players check each other's work with a calculator and add their 3 answers. The player with the higher total wins.

Game 1

1st turn:

——— + ——— + ——— = ———

2nd turn:

——— + ——— + ——— = ———

3rd turn:

——— + ——— + ——— = ———

Total: ———

Copyright © SRA/McGraw-Hill

Use with Lesson 11.10.

Do-Anytime Activities

To work with your child on the concepts taught in this unit and in previous units, try these interesting and rewarding activities:

1 Together, make up multidigit addition and subtraction number stories to solve. Share solution strategies.

2 Make timelines of your lives. In addition to personal historical information, mark various dates of things that interest you, such as musical, sports, historical, and political events.

3 Continue to ask the time. Encourage alternate ways of naming time, such as *twenty to nine* for 8:40 and *half-past two* for 2:30.

4 Continue to review and practice basic facts for all operations, emphasizing the multiplication facts.

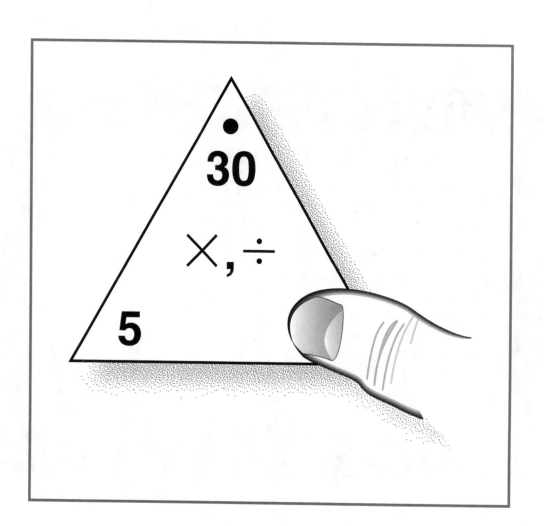

Copyright © SRA/McGraw-Hill

Use with Lesson 11.10.

As You Help Your Child with Homework

As your child brings home assignments, you may want to go over the instructions together, clarifying them as necessary. The answers listed below will guide you through this unit's Home Links.

Home Link 12.1

1. $9 \times 2 = 18$

$2 \times 9 = 18$

$18 \div 2 = 9$

$18 \div 9 = 2$

2. $1 \times 8 = 8$

$8 \times 1 = 8$

$8 \div 1 = 8$

$8 \div 8 = 1$

3. $5 \times 8 = 40$

$8 \times 5 = 40$

$40 \div 8 = 5$

$40 \div 5 = 8$

4. Sample answer:

$4 \times 5 = 20$

$5 \times 4 = 20$

$20 \div 5 = 4$

$20 \div 4 = 5$

Home Link 12.2

1. 4:10   **2.** 8:15   **3.** 10:45

4.    **5.**

6.    **7.**

8.    **9.**

Home Link 12.3

2. 1 hour   **3.** $1\frac{1}{2}$ hours

4. 7 hours   **5.** swimming

Home Link 12.5

1. 7   **2.** 6   **3.** 7   **4.** 3

5. 4   **6.** 4   **7.** 4   **8.** 5

9. 7   **10.** 8   **11.** 7   **12.** 9

13. 6   **14.** 9

Home Link 12.6

1. 30 years   **2.** dolphins and humans

3. 10 years   **4.** ostrich

5. squirrel, cat, lion, horse, ostrich, dolphin, human

6. 30 years

Home Link 12.7

1. a. 1,450   **b.** 1,750

2. a. 2,000   **b.** 1,300   **c.** 700

3. 1,450

4. 1,450

Copyright © SRA/McGraw-Hill

Use with Lesson 11.10.

Fact Triangles

Family Note

In class today, your child reviewed the calendar and continued to practice multiplication/division facts. Please spend a few minutes with your child as often as possible practicing facts. You can use Fact Triangles, or you can play a game like *Multiplication Top-It* or *Beat the Calculator.*

Please return this Home Link to school tomorrow.

Fill in the missing number in each Fact Triangle. Then write the fact family for the triangle.

1.

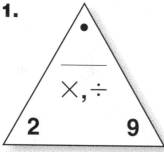

____ × ____ = ____

____ × ____ = ____

____ ÷ ____ = ____

____ ÷ ____ = ____

2.

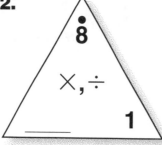

____ × ____ = ____

____ × ____ = ____

____ ÷ ____ = ____

____ ÷ ____ = ____

3.

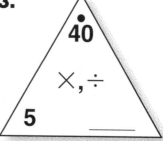

____ × ____ = ____

____ × ____ = ____

____ ÷ ____ = ____

____ ÷ ____ = ____

Challenge

4.

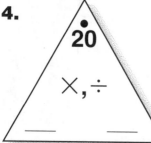

____ × ____ = ____   ____ ÷ ____ = ____

____ × ____ = ____   ____ ÷ ____ = ____

Copyright © SRA/McGraw-Hill

Use with Lesson 12.1.

Many Names for Times

Family Note

Because clocks with clock faces were used for centuries before the invention of digital clocks, people often name the time by describing the positions of the hour and minute hands. Observe as your child solves the time problems below.

Please return this Home Link to school tomorrow.

What time is it? Write the time shown on the clocks.

1.

_____:_____

2.

_____:_____

3.

_____:_____

Draw the hour hand and the minute hand to show the time.

4.

half-past nine

5.

six fifty

6.

a quarter-to two

7.

quarter-after ten

8.

two thirty

9.

four fifty-five

Copyright © SRA/McGraw-Hill

Timelines

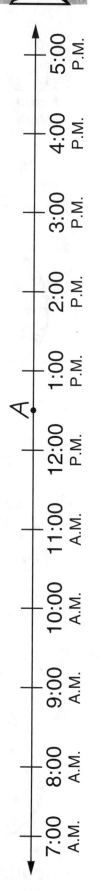

Family Note

A timeline is a way to display events in sequential order. Timelines may be divided into intervals, such as centuries, years, months, days, and hours. Observe your child as he or she fills in the timeline at the right.

Please return this Home Link to school tomorrow.

Emily's Day at the Beach

1. For each event below, make a dot on the timeline and write the letter for the event above the dot.

    A   Ate lunch (12:30 P.M.)

    B   Went fishing in a boat (10:00 A.M.)

    C   Arrived at the beach (9:00 A.M.)

    D   Returned from fishing trip (11:30 A.M.)

    E   Played volleyball (1:30 P.M.)

    F   Went swimming (2:00 P.M.)

    G   Drove home (4:00 P.M.)

    H   Built sandcastles (3:00 P.M.)

2. How long did Emily spend at the beach before she went on the fishing trip? _____ hour(s)

3. How long was the fishing trip? _____ hour(s)

4. How long was Emily's day at the beach? _____ hour(s)

5. Did Emily spend more time playing volleyball or swimming? _____

Copyright © SRA/McGraw-Hill

×, ÷ Fact Triangles

Family Note

Your child has been practicing multiplication facts. Today children reviewed shortcuts for solving multiplication problems with the numbers 2, 5, and 10. Encourage your child to practice with the Fact Triangles over the summer in preparation for third grade.

Cut out the Fact Triangles on these pages. Show someone at home how you can use them to practice multiplication facts.

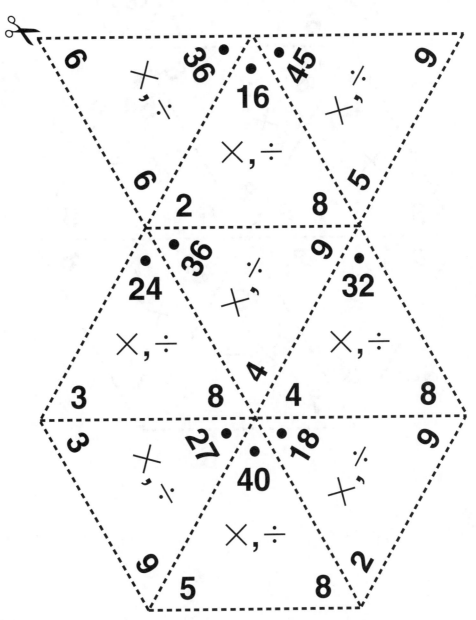

Copyright © SRA/McGraw-Hill

×, ÷ Fact Triangles (cont.)

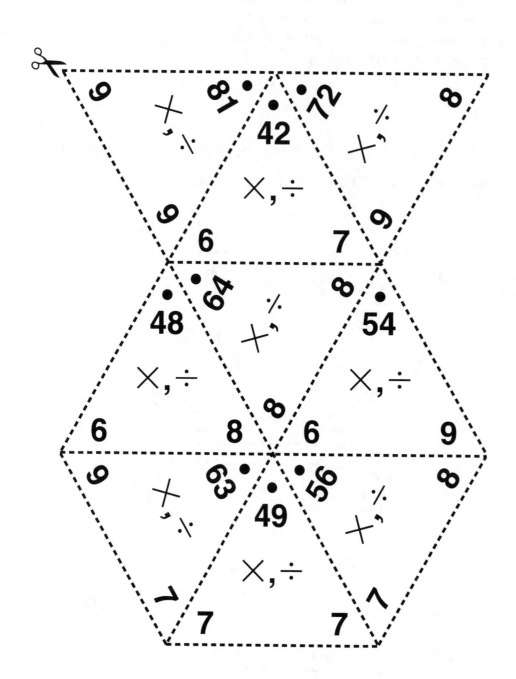

Copyright © SRA/McGraw–Hill

Use with Lesson 12.4.

×, ÷ Facts Practice

Family Note

In this lesson, your child has connected multiplication and division facts by using Fact Triangles and completing fact families. A good way to solve division problems is to think in terms of multiplication. For example, to divide 20 by 5, ask yourself: *5 times what number equals 20?* Since 5 × 4 = 20, 20 ÷ 5 = 4.

Please return this Home Link to school tomorrow.

Solve these division facts. Think multiplication.
Use the Fact Triangles to help you.

1. 14 ÷ 2 = _____

Think:
2 × ? = 14

14
×, ÷
2   7

2. 24 ÷ 4 = _____

Think:
4 × ? = 24

24
×, ÷
4   6

3. 21 ÷ 3 = _____

Think:
3 × ? = 21

21
×, ÷
3   7

4. 18 ÷ 6 = _____

Think:
6 × ? = 18

18
×, ÷
6   3

5. 28 ÷ 7 = _____

Think:
7 × ? = 28

28
×, ÷
7   4

6. 16 ÷ 4 = _____

Think:
4 × ? = 16

16
×, ÷
4   4

Copyright © SRA/McGraw-Hill

×, ÷ Facts Practice (cont.)

7. 20 ÷ 5 = _____

Think:
5 × ? = 20

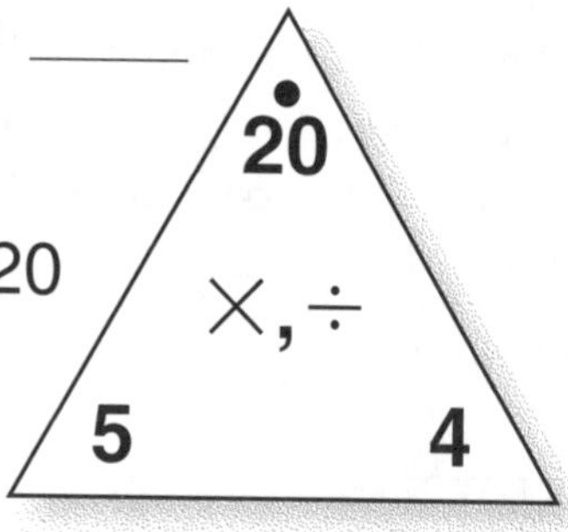

20
×, ÷
5   4

8. 30 ÷ 6 = _____

Think:
6 × ? = 30

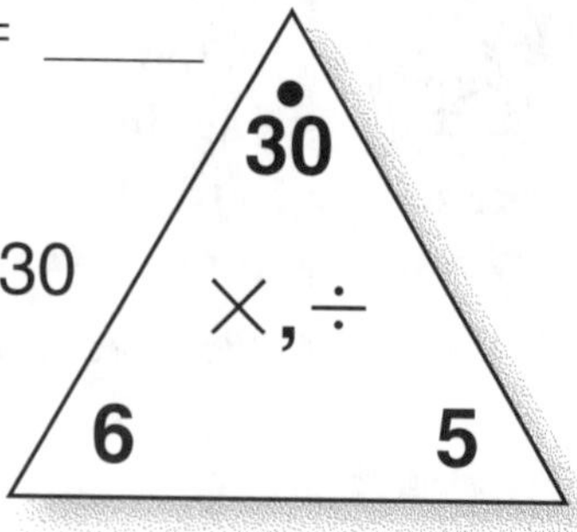

30
×, ÷
6   5

9. 35 ÷ 5 = _____

Think:
5 × ? = 35

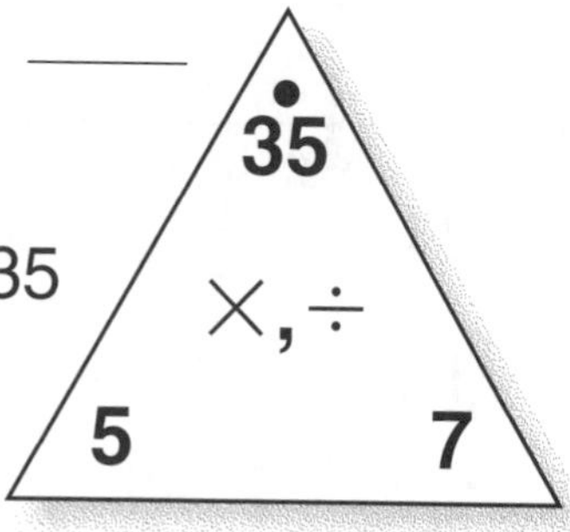

35
×, ÷
5   7

10. 32 ÷ 4 = _____

Think:
4 × ? = 32

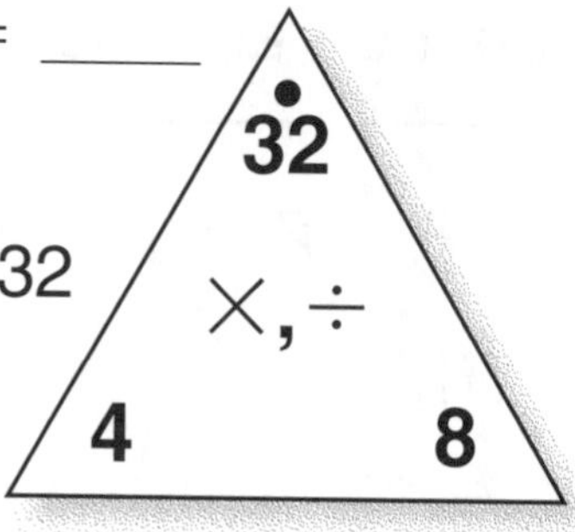

32
×, ÷
4   8

11. 42 ÷ 6 = _____

Think:
6 × ? = 42

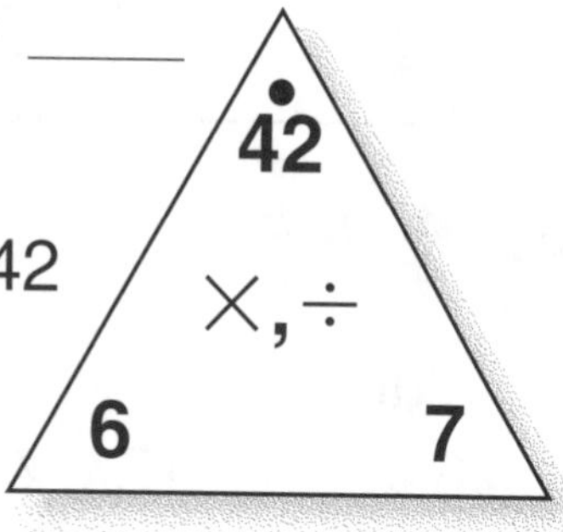

42
×, ÷
6   7

12. 63 ÷ 7 = _____

Think:
7 × ? = 63

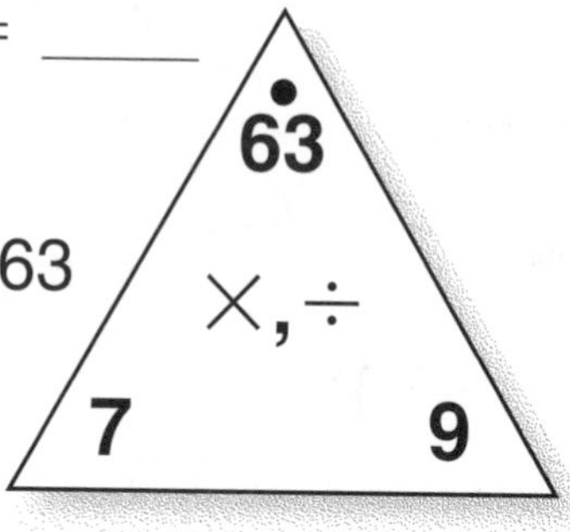

63
×, ÷
7   9

13. 54 ÷ 9 = _____

Think:
9 × ? = 54

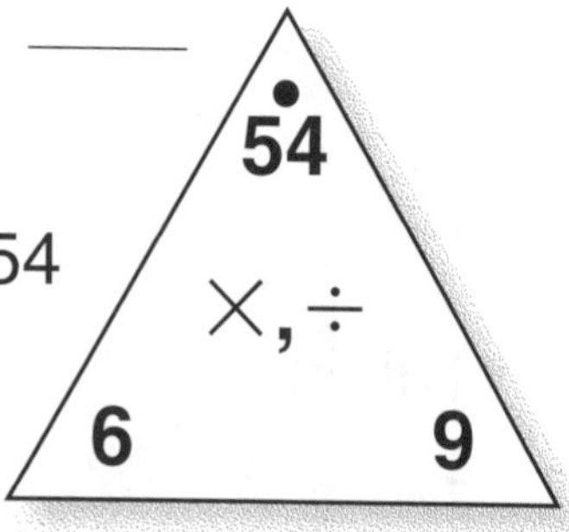

54
×, ÷
6   9

14. 81 ÷ 9 = _____

Think:
9 × ? = 81

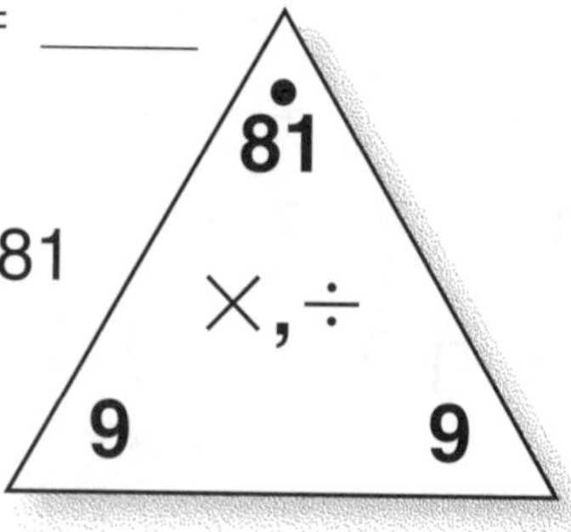

81
×, ÷
9   9

Copyright © SRA/McGraw–Hill

Family Note

In this lesson, your child has been reading, drawing, and interpreting bar graphs. Bar graphs are often useful when one wants to make rough comparisons quickly and easily. Provide your child with additional practice in interpreting a bar graph by asking questions like Problems 1–4.

Please return this Home Link to school tomorrow.

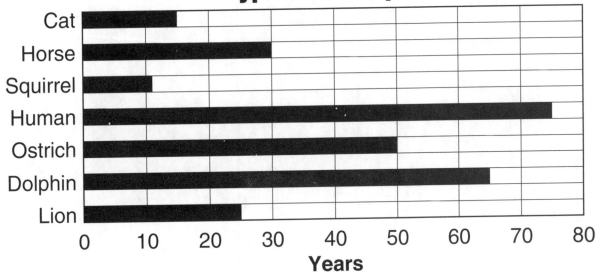

Typical Life Spans

1. About how long do horses live? _____ years

2. Which animals live longer than an ostrich?

   _____

3. About how much longer do lions live than cats? _____ years

4. Which animal lives about twice as long as lions? _____

Copyright © SRA/McGraw-Hill

Typical Life Spans (cont.)

5. List the animals in order from the shortest life span to the longest life span.

Life Spans

Animal	Years
shortest:	
longest:	

6. What is the middle value? _____ years
This is the **median.**

Copyright © SRA/McGraw-Hill

Interpret a Bar Graph

Family Note

In class today, your child interpreted graphs and identified the greatest value, the least value, the range, the middle value or the median, and the mode. The mode is the value or category that occurs most often in a set of data. For example, in the bar graph below, the river length of 1,450 miles is the mode.

Please return this Home Link to school tomorrow.

Approximate Lengths of Rivers

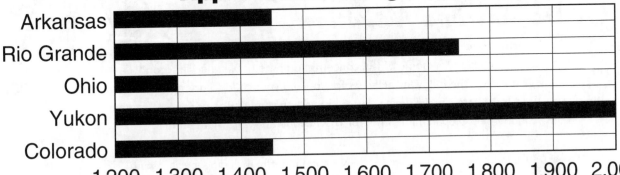

Miles

1. **a.** What is the length of the Colorado River? About _____ miles

   b. Of the Rio Grande? About _____ miles

2. **a.** What is the length of the longest river? About _____ miles

   b. What is the length of the shortest river? About _____ miles

   c. What is the difference in length between the longest and the shortest rivers? About _____ miles. This is the **range**.

3. Which river length occurs most often? About _____ miles This is the **mode**.

4. What is the middle length of the rivers? About _____ miles This is the **median**.

Copyright © SRA/McGraw-Hill

Family Letter

Congratulations!

By completing *Second Grade Everyday Mathematics*, your child has accomplished a great deal. Thank you for all of your support!

This Family Letter is provided as a resource for you to use throughout your child's vacation. It includes an extended list of Do-Anytime Activities, directions for games that can be played at home, an Addition/Subtraction Facts Table, and a sneak preview of what your child will be learning in *Third Grade Everyday Mathematics*. Enjoy your vacation!

Do-Anytime Activities

Mathematics concepts are more meaningful when rooted in real-life situations. To help your child review some of the concepts he or she has learned in second grade, we suggest the following activities for you and your child to do together over vacation. These activities will help your child build on the skills he or she has learned this year and help prepare him or her for *Third Grade Everyday Mathematics*.

1 Fill in blank calendar pages for the vacation months, including special events and dates. Discuss the number of weeks of vacation, days before school starts, and so on.

2 Continue to ask the time. Encourage alternate ways of naming time, such as *twenty to nine* for 8:40 and *a quarter-past five* for 5:15.

3 Continue to review and practice basic facts for all operations, especially those for addition and subtraction.

4 Use Fact Triangle cards to practice basic multiplication and division facts, such as the following:

$2 \times 2 = 4$	$4 \div 2 = 2$
$2 \times 3 = 6$	$6 \div 2 = 3$
$2 \times 4 = 8$	$8 \div 2 = 4$
$2 \times 5 = 10$	$10 \div 2 = 5$
$3 \times 4 = 12$	$12 \div 3 = 4$
$3 \times 3 = 9$	$9 \div 3 = 3$
$4 \times 4 = 16$	$16 \div 4 = 4$
$3 \times 5 = 15$	$15 \div 3 = 5$
$4 \times 5 = 20$	$20 \div 4 = 5$

Copyright © SRA/McGraw-Hill

Building Skills through Games

The following section describes games that can be played at home. The number cards used in some games can be made from 3" by 5" index cards or from a regular playing-card deck.

Addition Top-It

Materials ❑ 4 cards for each of the numbers 0–10 (1 set for each player)

Players 2 or more

Directions

Players combine and shuffle their cards and place them in a deck, facedown. Each player turns up a pair of cards from the deck and says the sum of the numbers. The player with the greater sum takes all of the cards then in play. The player with the most cards at the end of play is the winner. Ties are broken by drawing again—winner takes all.

Variation: *Subtraction Top-It*

Partners pool and shuffle their 0–20 number cards. Each player turns up a pair of cards from the facedown deck and says the difference between them. The player with the greater difference gets all four cards. The player with more cards at the end of play is the winner.

Variation: *Multiplication Top-It*

Players find the product of the numbers instead of the sum or difference. Use the 0–10 number cards.

Pick-a-Coin

Materials ❑ regular die

❑ record sheet (see example)

❑ calculator

Players 2 or 3

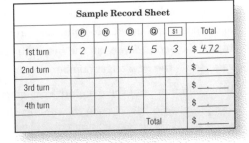

Sample Record Sheet						
	Ⓟ	Ⓝ	Ⓓ	Ⓠ	$1	Total
1st turn	2	1	4	5	3	$ 4.72
2nd turn						$ _____
3rd turn						$ _____
4th turn						$ _____
					Total	$ _____

Directions

Players take turns. At each turn, a player rolls a die five times. After each roll, the player records the number that comes up on the die in any one of the empty cells for that turn on his or her own Record Sheet. Then the player finds the total amount and records it in the table.

After four turns, each player uses a calculator to find his or her grand total. The player with the highest grand total wins.

Copyright © SRA/McGraw-Hill

Use with Lesson 12.8.

Multiplication Draw

Materials
- ❏ number cards 1, 2, 3, 4, 5, 10 (4 of each)
- ❏ record sheet (1 for each player)
- ❏ calculator

Players 2–4

Multiplication Draw Record Sheet

1st draw: _____ × _____ = _____

2nd draw: _____ × _____ = _____

3rd draw: _____ × _____ = _____

4th draw: _____ × _____ = _____

5th draw: _____ × _____ = _____

Sum of products: _____

Directions

Shuffle the cards and place the deck facedown on the playing surface. At each turn, players draw two cards from the deck to make up a multiplication problem. They record the problem on a record sheet and write the answer. If the answer is incorrect, it will not be counted. After five turns, players use a calculator to find the total of their correct answers. The player with the highest total wins.

Name That Number

Materials
- ❏ number cards 0–10 (4 of each)
- ❏ number cards 11–20 (1 of each)

Players 2 or 3

Directions

Shuffle the deck of cards and place facedown on the table. Turn the top five cards face up and place them in a row. Turn over the next card. This is the target number for the round.

In turn, players try to name the target number by adding, subtracting, multiplying, or dividing any two of the other faceup cards. Players write their solutions on a sheet of paper. Then they set aside the cards they used to name the target number and replace them with new cards from the top of the deck. Players put the target number on the bottom of the deck and turn over the top card. This is the new target number.

Play continues until there are not enough cards left in the deck to replace the players' cards. The player who has set aside the most cards at the end wins. Sample turns:

Mae's turn:

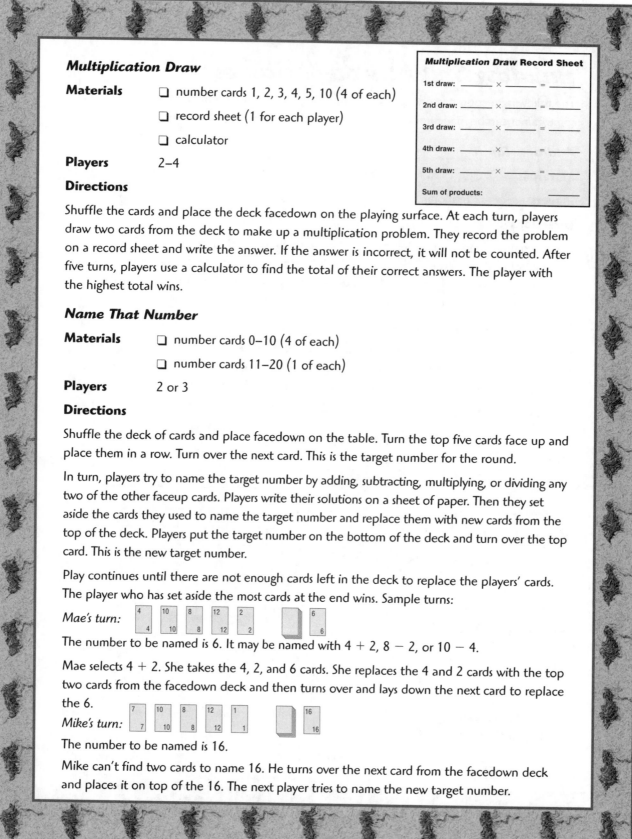

The number to be named is 6. It may be named with 4 + 2, 8 − 2, or 10 − 4.

Mae selects 4 + 2. She takes the 4, 2, and 6 cards. She replaces the 4 and 2 cards with the top two cards from the facedown deck and then turns over and lays down the next card to replace the 6.

Mike's turn:

The number to be named is 16.

Mike can't find two cards to name 16. He turns over the next card from the facedown deck and places it on top of the 16. The next player tries to name the new target number.

Copyright © SRA/McGraw-Hill

Use with Lesson 12.8.

Fact Power

Addition/subtraction fact families can also be practiced by using the Addition/Subtraction Facts Table. This table can be used to keep a record of facts that have been learned as well.

+,−	0	1	2	3	4	5	6	7	8	9
0	0	1	2	3	4	5	6	7	8	9
1	1	2	3	4	5	6	7	8	9	10
2	2	3	4	5	6	7	8	9	10	11
3	3	4	5	6	7	8	9	10	11	12
4	4	5	6	7	8	9	10	11	12	13
5	5	6	7	8	9	10	11	12	13	14
6	6	7	8	9	10	11	12	13	14	15
7	7	8	9	10	11	12	13	14	15	16
8	8	9	10	11	12	13	14	15	16	17
9	9	10	11	12	13	14	15	16	17	18

Looking Ahead:
Third Grade Everyday Mathematics

Next year, your child will ...

· Explore the relationship between multiplication and division

· Extend multiplication and division facts to multiples of 10, 100, and 1,000

· Use parentheses in writing number models

· Record equivalent units of length

· Use number models to find the areas of rectangles

· Explore 2- and 3-dimensional shapes and other geometric concepts

· Read and write numbers through 1,000,000

· Work with fractions and decimals

· Collect data for yearlong sunrise/sunset and high/low temperature projects

· Use map scales to estimate distances

Again, thank you for all of your support this year. Have fun continuing your child's mathematics experiences throughout the vacation!

Copyright © SRA/McGraw-Hill

Use with Lesson 12.8.

Unit 1 Checking Progress

1. Show 17 with tally marks. _____

2. Write the amount.

Total: $_____

3. Write the largest number you can with the digits 6, 3, and 9.

Use each digit only once. _____

4. Find each missing number.

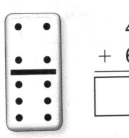 $\begin{array}{r} 4 \\ + \; 6 \\ \hline \square \end{array}$  $\begin{array}{r} 7 \\ + \; \square \\ \hline 12 \end{array}$  $\begin{array}{r} \square \\ + \; 5 \\ \hline 8 \end{array}$

5. Fill in the missing numbers.

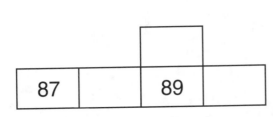   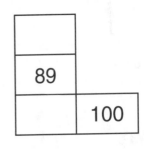

6. Draw coins to show 35¢ two different ways.
Use Ⓟ, Ⓝ, Ⓓ, and Ⓠ for coins.

7. Write three different names for 20.

_____   _____   _____

Copyright © SRA/McGraw-Hill

Unit 2 Checking Progress

1. Write the fact family for 2, 11, and 9.

_____   _____

_____   _____

2. Circle the names for 14.

9 + 5	7 − 3	12 + 2	5 + 6	8 + 6
1 + 11	7 + 7	3 + 9	18 − 4	

3. Fill in the empty frames.

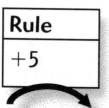

Rule			25				40	

+5

4. Find the rule and complete the table.

Rule

in	out
9	15
	12
4	10
7	
10	16
8	

Copyright © SRA/McGraw-Hill

Use with Lesson 2.14.

Unit 2 Checking Progress (cont.)

5. Add.

 a. $6 + 1 =$ _____ **b.** $0 + 9 =$ _____ **c.** _____ $= 2 + 6$

 d. $\begin{array}{r} 4 \\ +\ 4 \\ \hline \end{array}$ **e.** $\begin{array}{r} 3 \\ +\ 5 \\ \hline \end{array}$

6. Add.

 a. $7 + 7 =$ _____ **b.** $9 + 4 =$ _____ **c.** _____ $= 6 + 9$

 d. $\begin{array}{r} 8 \\ +\ 6 \\ \hline \end{array}$ **e.** $\begin{array}{r} 5 \\ +\ 7 \\ \hline \end{array}$

7. Subtract.

 a. $7 - 0 =$ _____ **b.** _____ $= 11 - 1$ **c.** $7 - 4 =$ _____

 d. $\begin{array}{r} 6 \\ -\ 2 \\ \hline \end{array}$ **e.** $\begin{array}{r} 9 \\ -\ 5 \\ \hline \end{array}$

8. Subtract.

 a. $16 - 9 =$ _____ **b.** $18 - 9 =$ _____ **c.** _____ $= 14 - 6$

 d. $\begin{array}{r} 15 \\ -\ 8 \\ \hline \end{array}$ **e.** $\begin{array}{r} 13 \\ -\ 5 \\ \hline \end{array}$

Copyright © SRA/McGraw-Hill

Use with Lesson 2.14.

Unit 3 Checking Progress

1. You buy a green pepper for 27¢. Write Ⓟ, Ⓝ, Ⓓ, or Ⓠ to show the coins you could use to pay the exact amount.

Show coins one way.

Show coins another way.

2. Fill in the frames.

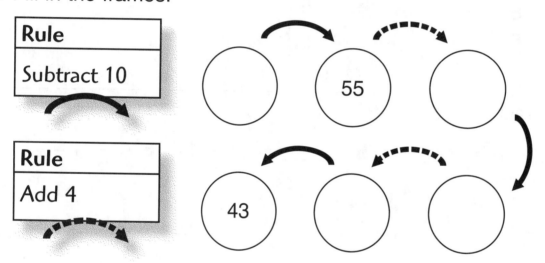

Rule
Subtract 10

Rule
Add 4

55

43

3. Find the second rule. Fill in the frames.

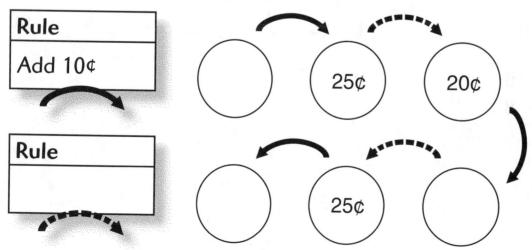

Rule
Add 10¢

Rule

25¢   20¢

25¢

Copyright © SRA/McGraw-Hill

Use with Lesson 3.9.

Unit 3 Checking Progress (cont.)

4. You buy carrot juice for 60¢. You put 3 quarters in the vending

machine. How much change should you receive? _____

5. You buy a head of lettuce for 68¢. You pay with a $1 bill.

How much change should you receive? _____

6. Draw the hands to show 5:15.

7. Draw the hands to show 9:05.

8. Write the time.

_____ : _____

9. Write the time.

_____ : _____

Copyright © SRA/McGraw-Hill

Use with Lesson 3.9.

Unit 4 Checking Progress

In the diagram for each number story:

- Write the numbers you know.

- Write ? for the number you want to find.

- Write the answer. Don't forget to include the unit.

- Write a number model.

1. Arlene has 20 dolls. Katie has 7 dolls. How many dolls do Arlene and Katie have in all?

Answer: _____
          (unit)

Number model: _____

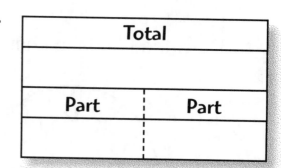

2. On Monday, Jen painted 30 beads for her necklace. On Tuesday, she painted 12 beads. How many beads did Jen paint in all?

Answer: _____
          (unit)

Number model: _____

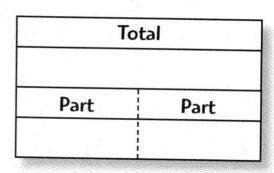

3. At 2:30 in the afternoon, the temperature was 68°F. During the night, it went down 20 degrees. What was the new temperature?

Answer: _____
          (unit)

Number model: _____

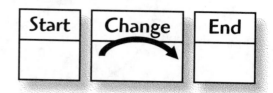

Copyright © SRA/McGraw-Hill

Use with Lesson 4.10.

Unit 4 Checking Progress (cont.)

4. Kevin brought 36 cupcakes to school for his birthday. He gave 10 away during lunch. How many cupcakes did he have then?

Start	Change	End

Answer: _____
                              (unit)

Number model: _____

Write the temperature shown on each thermometer.

5. °F

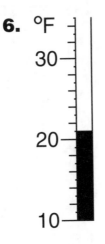

_____ °F

6. °F

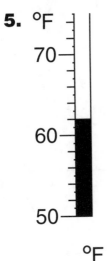

_____ °F

Mark each thermometer to show the temperature.

7. 30°F

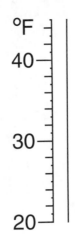

8. 49°F

Solve the addition problems.

9.   53
    + 66

10.   27
    + 48

11.   34
    + 37

12.   95
    + 63

Copyright © SRA/McGraw-Hill

Use with Lesson 4.10.

Unit 5 Checking Progress

1. Draw line segment *AB*.

2. Draw a line segment that is parallel to line segment *AB*. Label its endpoints *C* and *D*.

3. Draw a line segment that is not parallel to line segment *AB*. Label its endpoints *E* and *F*.

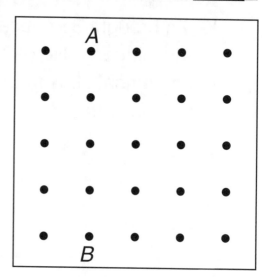

In Problems 4–9, fill in the oval next to the correct answer.

4. This shape is a
   - O hexagon.
   - O rhombus.
   - O square.

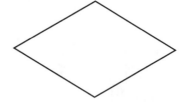

5. This shape is a
   - O rectangle.
   - O triangle.
   - O trapezoid.

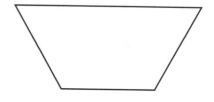

6. This is a picture of a
   - O rectangular prism.
   - O sphere.
   - O pyramid.

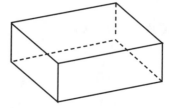

Copyright © SRA/McGraw-Hill

Unit 5 Checking Progress (cont.)

7. This is a picture of a   O cylinder.

                           O cone.

                           O sphere.

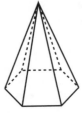

8. This is a picture of a   O cylinder.

                           O pyramid.

                           O rectangular prism.

9. Which things have a line of symmetry?

O 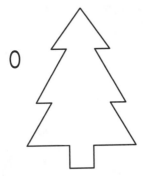   O    O

10. Which shape doesn't belong? Circle it.

Copyright © SRA/McGraw-Hill

Unit 6 Checking Progress

1. Choose a unit. Solve the problems.

Unit

$12 + 7 + 8 =$ _____   _____ $= 24 + 30 + 6$

_____ $= 13 + 9 + 11$ $17 + 12 + 33 =$ _____

Subtract.

2. 78
 − 52

3. 64
 − 29

4. 83
 − 59

5.
• • • • • • •
• • • • • • •
• • • • • • •
• • • • • • •

How many rows? _____

How many dots
in each row? _____

How many dots in all? _____

Number model:

_____ × _____ = _____

6. Draw an array with 3 rows
and 5 dots in each row.

How many dots in all? _____

Number model:

_____ × _____ = _____

7. Fish J weighs 24 pounds.
Fish H weighs 14 pounds.
How much more does
Fish J weigh?

_____ pounds more

8. Fish K weighs 35 pounds.
Fish G weighs 10 pounds.
How much do they weigh
together?

_____ pounds

Copyright © SRA/McGraw-Hill

Use with Lesson 6.12.

Unit 7 Checking Progress

1. Solve.

$$23 + \underline{\hphantom{00}} = 30 \qquad\qquad \underline{\hphantom{00}} + 51 = 60$$

$$40 = \underline{\hphantom{00}} + 32 \qquad\qquad 70 = 66 + \underline{\hphantom{00}}$$

2. Solve.

$$47 + \underline{\hphantom{00}} = 60 \qquad\qquad 90 = \underline{\hphantom{00}} + 54$$

$$\underline{\hphantom{00}} + 39 = 50 \qquad\qquad 40 = 28 + \underline{\hphantom{00}}$$

3. Find the median.

7, 3, 4 _____   27, 45, 63, 45, 50 _____

3, 9, 7, 14, 12 _____   3, 5, 9, 7 _____

4. Add.

$$15 + 13 + 17 = \underline{\hphantom{00}} \qquad\qquad \underline{\hphantom{00}} = 15 + 25 + 10$$

$$\underline{\hphantom{00}} = 26 + 24 + 25 \qquad\qquad 22 + 18 + 15 + 14 = \underline{\hphantom{00}}$$

5. Measure each line to the nearest inch.

_____

about _____ inches

_____

about _____ inches

Copyright © SRA/McGraw–Hill

Unit 7 Checking Progress (cont.)

6. Measure each line to the nearest centimeter.

_____

about _____ centimeters

_____

about _____ cm

7. Solve the number-grid puzzles.

43		

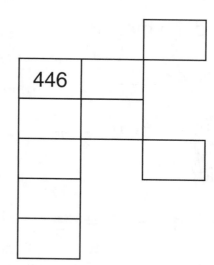

Copyright © SRA/McGraw-Hill

Unit 8 Checking Progress

1. Which shows $\frac{1}{4}$ shaded? Fill in the oval.

2. Which shows $\frac{2}{3}$ shaded? Fill in the oval.

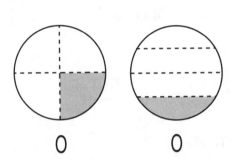

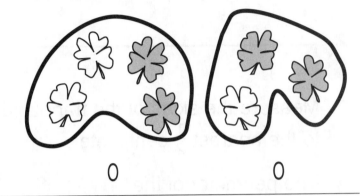

O   O   O   O

Which fraction shows how much is shaded? Fill in the oval.

3.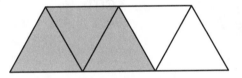

O   O   O

$\frac{3}{4}$ $\frac{3}{5}$ $\frac{3}{6}$

4.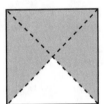

O   O   O

$\frac{3}{4}$ $\frac{3}{6}$ $\frac{3}{8}$

5.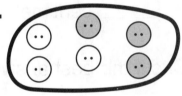

O   O   O

$\frac{3}{6}$ $\frac{1}{3}$ $\frac{3}{5}$

6. Color $\frac{5}{8}$.

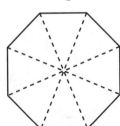

7. Color $\frac{1}{5}$.

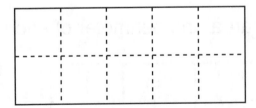

8. Color $\frac{7}{8}$.

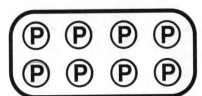

9. Color $\frac{1}{2}$.

Copyright © SRA/McGraw-Hill

Use with Lesson 8.8.

Unit 9 Checking Progress

Measure each line segment to the nearest $\frac{1}{2}$ inch.

1. _____ _____ inches

2. _____ _____ inches

3. Measure the sides of the trapezoid to the nearest $\frac{1}{2}$ centimeter.

4. The perimeter of the trapezoid is about

_____ centimeters.

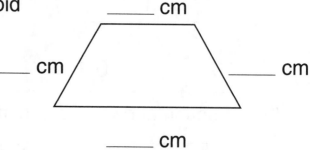

_____ cm

_____ cm   _____ cm

_____ cm

Circle the best answer.

5. The height of a man might be about

   6 inches   6 feet   6 yards   6 miles

6. A baby might weigh about

   7 meters   7 feet   7 pounds   7 cups

Find the area and perimeter of each shape.

7.

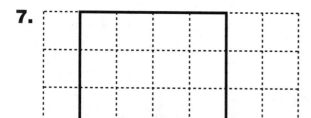

Area = _____ sq cm

Perimeter = _____ cm

8.

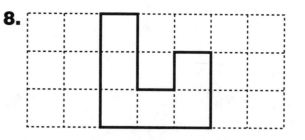

Area = _____ sq cm

Perimeter = _____ cm

Copyright © SRA/McGraw-Hill

Unit 10 Checking Progress

1. Write the amount.

$1 Ⓠ Ⓠ Ⓓ Ⓓ Ⓓ Ⓝ Ⓟ Ⓟ Ⓟ Ⓟ = $_____

2. Use $1 , Ⓠ , Ⓓ , Ⓝ , and Ⓟ . Show $1.83 in two different ways.

Complete.

3. 1 quarter = _____ nickels   **4.** 1 dollar = _____ dimes

5. 1 dime = _____ pennies   **6.** 1 dollar = _____ pennies

7. 1 dime = _____ nickels

8. You buy:

Oranges
1 lb at $1.49 lb

and Yogurt
6-pack at $2.09

a. Estimate the total cost.

Estimated cost: $_____ + $_____ = $_____

b. Find the exact cost, with or without a calculator.

Exact cost: $_____

Copyright © SRA/McGraw-Hill

Unit 10 Checking Progress (cont.)

9. You have $5.00. You buy:

Cheese
8 oz. for $1.49

and Bananas
1 lb at 59¢ lb

and Bread
16 oz for 99¢

  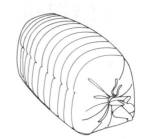

a. Estimate the total cost.

Estimated cost: $_____ + $_____ + $_____ = $_____

b. Find the exact cost, with or without a calculator.

Exact cost: $_____

c. Find the amount of change you will get back from $5.00. You may use your calculator.

Change: $_____

Fill in the blanks. Write ones, tens, hundreds, thousands, or ten-thousands.

10. The 7 in 3,745 stands for 7 _____.

11. The 3 in 36,051 stands for 3 _____.

12. The 6 in 465 stands for 6 _____.

13. The 8 in 21,938 stands for 8 _____.

14. The 2 in 92,645 stands for 2 _____.

Copyright © SRA/McGraw-Hill

Use with Lesson 10.12.

Unit 11 Checking Progress

Add or subtract.

1. $1.30
    − $0.64 | **Answer** |

2. $3.46
    + $1.78 | **Answer** |

3. $5.82
    − $2.47 | **Answer** |

Multiply. If you need help, make arrays with 0s or Xs.

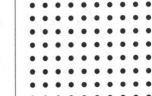

4. $3 \times 6 =$ _____

5. $5 \times 4 =$ _____

6. $8 \times 3 =$ _____

7. Write the fact family for the Fact Triangle.

_____ × _____ = _____

_____ × _____ = _____

_____ ÷ _____ = _____

_____ ÷ _____ = _____

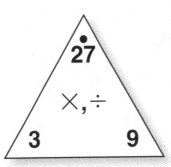

8. Write a multiplication story and a division story on the back of this page.

• Draw a picture or diagram.

• Write the answer.

• Write a number model.

Copyright © SRA/McGraw-Hill

Use with Lesson 11.10.

Unit 12 Checking Progress

Record the time shown on the clock.

1.  **2.**  **3.**

_____ : _____   _____ : _____   _____ : _____

Draw the hour and minute hands to match the time.

4.  **5.** 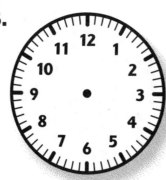 **6.**

4:10   10:50   2:05

7. Write the fact family for the Fact Triangle.

_____ × _____ = _____   _____ ÷ _____ = _____

_____ × _____ = _____   _____ ÷ _____ = _____

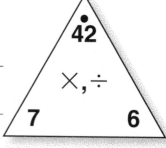

Solve.

8. $6 \times 10 =$ _____   **9.** $2 \times 7 =$ _____   **10.** _____ $= 3 \times 2$

11. _____ $= 4 \times 5$ **12.** _____ $= 3 \times 10$ **13.** $3 \times 5 =$ _____

14. $6 \times 2 =$ _____   **15.** $5 \times 6 =$ _____   **16.** _____ $= 7 \times 10$

Copyright © SRA/McGraw-Hill

Use with Lesson 12.8.

Unit 12 Checking Progress (cont.)

The bar graph below shows the number of miles each member of the track team ran during practice.

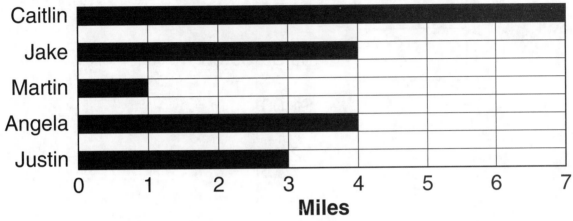

Miles Run by Track Team

17. What was the fewest number of miles? _____ mile

What was the greatest number of miles? _____ miles

18. What is the difference between the fewest
and the greatest numbers of miles (range)? _____ miles

19. What is the middle number of miles (median)? _____ miles

20. Who ran fewer miles than Justin? _____

Who ran more miles than Angela? _____

21. What is the number of miles that occurred most often (mode)?

_____ miles

Copyright © SRA/McGraw-Hill

Midyear Assessment

1. Find the rule and complete the table.

Rule

in	out
$1.25	$1.00
$0.30	$0.05
$1.00	
$2.40	

2. Complete the Fact Triangle. Write the fact family.

____ + ____ = ____

____ + ____ = ____

____ − ____ = ____

____ − ____ = ____

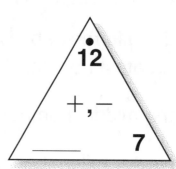

3. 524

Which digit is in the tens place? _____

Which digit is in the hundreds place? _____

Which digit is in the ones place? _____

What is the smallest number
you can make with these 3 digits? _____

Copyright © SRA/McGraw-Hill

Midyear Assessment (cont.)

4. Write at least 5 names in the 100-box.

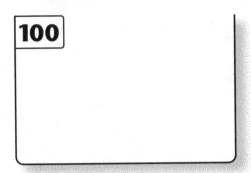

5. What is the total value of the coins?

$ _____

6. Carlos had 40 cents. His brother gave him 70 cents.

How much money does Carlos have now? _____

7. Jenna has 60 dolls in her collection. Tyshona has 20 dolls.

How many more dolls does Jenna have? _____ more dolls

Is the answer to the question an odd or even number? _____

8. Fill in the frames.

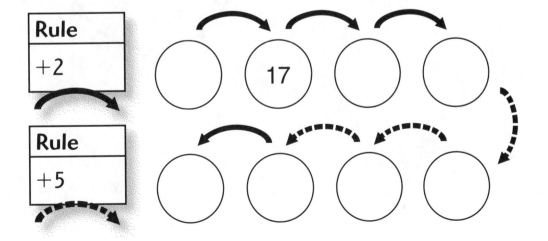

Copyright © SRA/McGraw–Hill

Midyear Assessment (cont.)

Solve.

9.   34   49
     + 21   + 18

10.   65   42
      − 43   − 26

11. This shape is a
    0 hexagon
    0 rhombus
    0 trapezoid

12. This is a picture of a
    0 pyramid
    0 cylinder
    0 rectangular prism

13. Draw the hour and minute hands to show 6:40.

How many minutes

until 7:00? _____ minutes

Copyright © SRA/McGraw-Hill

End-of-Year Assessment

1. Measure the line segment to the nearest inch and to the nearest centimeter.

   _____

   _____ inches   _____ centimeters

2. Circle the correct unit of measure.

   Allison weighs 50

   pounds   miles   gallons

   Jake ran 6

   inches   feet   miles

   Kenneth filled the car's tank with 10 _____ of gasoline.

   cups   gallons   quarts

3. The temperature is _____°F.

Copyright © SRA/McGraw-Hill

End-of-Year Assessment (cont.)

4. Complete the bar graph.

Tia read 6 books.
Ian read 3 books.
Theo read 5 books.

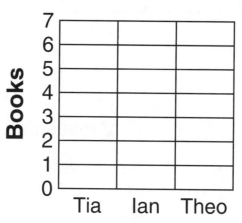

Number of Books Read

Maximum number of books: _____

Minimum number of books: _____

Median number of books: _____

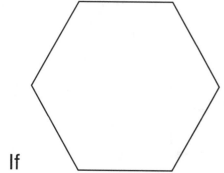

5. If   is the ONE, then  is _____.

6. What fraction of the circles is shaded? _____

Use with Lesson 12.8.

Copyright © SRA/McGraw-Hill

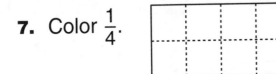

End-of-Year Assessment (cont.)

7. Color $\frac{1}{4}$.

Fill in the oval next to the best estimate.

8. 138 + 263 is about _____

    0 200

    0 300

    0 400

9. 92 − 59 is about _____

    0 20

    0 30

    0 40

10. The perimeter of the rectangle is

_____ centimeters.

The area of the rectangle is

_____ square centimeters.

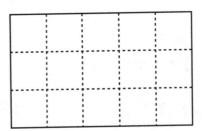

11.   56   124   **12.**   72   346

     + 67   + 208   − 46   − 183

Copyright © SRA/McGraw-Hill

End-of-Year Assessment (cont.)

13. This shape is a …

O hexagon

O rhombus

O trapezoid

14. This shape is a …

O pyramid

O cylinder

O rectangular prism

15. Complete the number grid.

	743	

Write the time.

16.

_____:_____

17.

_____:_____

18.

_____:_____

Copyright © SRA/McGraw-Hill

Use with Lesson 12.8.

End-of-Year Assessment (cont.)

19. In the number 3,761 ...

Which digit is in the tens place? _____

Which digit is in the hundreds place? _____

Which digit is in the ones place? _____

Which digit is in the thousands place? _____

What is the smallest number
you can make with these 4 digits? _____

20. Insert <, >, or =.

209 _____ 2,009

462 _____ 624

5,421 _____ 5,421

7,036 _____ 6,704

21. 4 rows of chairs. 5 chairs in each row.

How many chairs in all? _____ chairs

3 boxes of cookies. 10 cookies per box.

How many cookies in all? _____ cookies

Copyright © SRA/McGraw-Hill

22. 15 stickers. 3 children.

How many stickers per child? _____ stickers

40 candies. 4 candies per child.

How many children? _____ children

23. Find the rule and complete the table.

in	out
3	6
5	10
	14
	18

Rule

24. Complete.

1 week = _____ days

1 day = _____ hours

1 hour = _____ minutes

1 minute = _____ seconds

Copyright © SRA/McGraw-Hill

Use with Lesson 12.8.

End-of-Year Assessment (cont.)

25. Ian saved $4.35 for his mother's birthday present.
His sister saved $3.90.
How much money did they save altogether?
Write a number model.

Answer: _____

Number model: _____

26. Caitlin had $9.50 in her wallet.
She spent $6.75 at the movies.
How much money does she have now?
Write a number model.

Answer: _____

Number model: _____

Copyright © SRA/McGraw-Hill

Use with Lesson 12.8.

Class Checklist: Unit 1

Class _____

Dates _____

Children's Names	Learning Goals	1a Calculate the values of coin and bill combinations.	1b Know addition facts for sums to 10.	1c Identify place value for ones, tens, and hundreds.	1d Complete number sequences; identify and use number patterns to solve problems.	1e Find equivalent names for numbers.	1f Compare numbers; write the symbol <, >, or =.	1g Count by 2s, 5s, and 10s.	1h Make tallies and give the total.					
1.														
2.														
3.														
4.														
5.														
6.														
7.														
8.														
9.														
10.														
11.														
12.														
13.														
14.														
15.														
16.														
17.														
18.														
19.														
20.														
21.														
22.														
23.														
24.														
25.														
26.														
27.														
28.														
29.														
30.														

Copyright © SRA/McGraw-Hill

Use with Lesson 1.14.

Individual Profile of Progress: Unit 1

Check ✔			Learning Goals	Comments
B	D	S		
			1a Calculate the values of coin and bill combinations.	
			1b Know addition facts for sums to 10.	
			1c Identify place value for ones, tens, and hundreds.	
			1d Complete number sequences; identify and use number patterns to solve problems.	
			1e Find equivalent names for numbers.	
			1f Compare numbers; write the symbol $<$, $>$, or $=$.	
			1g Count by 2s, 5s, and 10s.	
			1h Make tallies and give the total.	

Notes to Parents

_____

_____

_____

_____

Copyright © SRA/McGraw-Hill

B = **B**eginning; **D** = **D**eveloping; **S** = **S**ecure

Use with Lesson 1.14.

Class Checklist: Unit 2

Class _____

Dates _____

Learning Goals

Children's Names	2a Know "harder" subtraction facts.	2b Know "harder" addition facts.	2c Know "easier" subtraction facts.	2d Complete "What's My Rule?" tables.	2e Solve subtraction number stories.	2f Know "easier" addition facts.	2g Construct fact families for addition and subtraction.	2h Complete Frames-and-Arrows diagrams.	2i Solve addition number stories.	2j Find equivalent names for numbers.		
1.												
2.												
3.												
4.												
5.												
6.												
7.												
8.												
9.												
10.												
11.												
12.												
13.												
14.												
15.												
16.												
17.												
18.												
19.												
20.												
21.												
22.												
23.												
24.												
25.												
26.												
27.												
28.												
29.												
30.												

Copyright © SRA/McGraw-Hill

Use with Lesson 2.14.

Individual Profile of Progress: Unit 2

Check ✔			Learning Goals	Comments
B	**D**	**S**		
			2a Know "harder" subtraction facts.	
			2b Know "harder" addition facts.	
			2c Know "easier" subtraction facts.	
			2d Complete "What's My Rule?" tables.	
			2e Solve subtraction number stories.	
			2f Know "easier" addition facts.	
			2g Construct fact families for addition and subtraction.	
			2h Complete Frames-and-Arrows diagrams.	
			2i Solve addition number stories.	
			2j Find equivalent names for numbers.	

Notes to Parents

_____

_____

_____

_____

B = **B**eginning; **D** = **D**eveloping; **S** = **S**ecure

Use with Lesson 2.14.

Copyright © SRA/McGraw-Hill

Class _____

Dates _____

Learning Goals

- 3a Solve Frames-and-Arrows problems having two rules.
- 3b Make change.
- 3c Know "harder" subtraction facts.
- 3d Tell time to 5-minute intervals.
- 3e Identify place value in 2-digit and 3-digit numbers.
- 3f Show Ⓟ, Ⓝ, Ⓓ, and Ⓠ for a given amount.
- 3g Know addition facts.
- 3h Know "easier" subtraction facts.

Children's Names

	3a	3b	3c	3d	3e	3f	3g	3h				
1.												
2.												
3.												
4.												
5.												
6.												
7.												
8.												
9.												
10.												
11.												
12.												
13.												
14.												
15.												
16.												
17.												
18.												
19.												
20.												
21.												
22.												
23.												
24.												
25.												
26.												
27.												
28.												
29.												
30.												

Copyright © SRA/McGraw-Hill

Use with Lesson 3.9.

Individual Profile of Progress: Unit 3

Check ✔			Learning Goals	Comments
B	**D**	**S**		
			3a Solve Frames-and-Arrows problems having two rules.	
			3b Make change.	
			3c Know "harder" subtraction facts.	
			3d Tell time to 5-minute intervals.	
			3e Identify place value in 2-digit and 3-digit numbers.	
			3f Show Ⓟ, Ⓝ, Ⓓ, and Ⓠ for a given amount.	
			3g Know addition facts.	
			3h Know "easier" subtraction facts.	

Notes to Parents

_____

_____

_____

_____

B = **B**eginning; **D** = **D**eveloping; **S** = **S**ecure

Copyright © SRA/McGraw-Hill

Class Checklist: Unit 4

Class _____

Dates _____

Learning Goals

- **4a** Devise and use strategies for finding sums of 2-digit numbers.
- **4b** Devise and use strategies for finding differences of 2-digit numbers.
- **4c** Estimate approximate costs and sums.
- **4d** Read °F on a thermometer.
- **4e** Add and subtract with multiples of 10.

Children's Names	4a	4b	4c	4d	4e						
1.											
2.											
3.											
4.											
5.											
6.											
7.											
8.											
9.											
10.											
11.											
12.											
13.											
14.											
15.											
16.											
17.											
18.											
19.											
20.											
21.											
22.											
23.											
24.											
25.											
26.											
27.											
28.											
29.											
30.											

Use with Lesson 4.10.

Copyright © SRA/McGraw-Hill

Individual Profile of Progress: Unit 4

Check ✔			Learning Goals	Comments
B	**D**	**S**		
			4a Devise and use strategies for finding sums of 2-digit numbers.	
			4b Devise and use strategies for finding differences of 2-digit numbers.	
			4c Estimate approximate costs and sums.	
			4d Read °F on a thermometer.	
			4e Add and subtract with multiples of 10.	

Notes to Parents

_____

_____

_____

_____

B = **B**eginning; **D** = **D**eveloping; **S** = **S**ecure

Use with Lesson 4.10.

Copyright © SRA/McGraw-Hill

Class Checklist: Unit 5

Class _____

Dates _____

Learning Goals

- **5a** Identify 3-dimensional shapes, such as rectangular prisms, cylinders, pyramids, cones, and spheres.
- **5b** Identify symmetrical figures.
- **5c** Find common attributes of shapes.
- **5d** Identify parallel and nonparallel line segments.
- **5e** Draw line segments.
- **5f** Identify 2-dimensional shapes.

Children's Names	5a	5b	5c	5d	5e	5f						
1.												
2.												
3.												
4.												
5.												
6.												
7.												
8.												
9.												
10.												
11.												
12.												
13.												
14.												
15.												
16.												
17.												
18.												
19.												
20.												
21.												
22.												
23.												
24.												
25.												
26.												
27.												
28.												
29.												
30.												

Copyright © SRA/McGraw-Hill

Use with Lesson 5.10.

Individual Profile of Progress: Unit 5

Check ✔			Learning Goals	Comments
B	**D**	**S**		
			5a Identify 3-dimensional shapes, such as rectangular prisms, cylinders, pyramids, cones, and spheres.	
			5b Identify symmetrical figures.	
			5c Find common attributes of shapes.	
			5d Identify parallel and nonparallel line segments.	
			5e Draw line segments.	
			5f Identify 2-dimensional shapes.	

Notes to Parents

_____

_____

_____

_____

B = **B**eginning; **D** = **D**eveloping; **S** = **S**ecure

Use with Lesson 5.10.

Copyright © SRA/McGraw-Hill

Class Checklist: Unit 6

Class _____

Dates _____

Learning Goals

- **6a** Solve stories about multiples of equal groups.
- **6b** Solve equal-grouping and equal-sharing division problems.
- **6c** Use the trade-first method to solve 2-digit subtraction problems.
- **6d** Make ballpark estimates of exact answers.
- **6e** Model multiplication problems with arrays.
- **6f** Add three 2-digit numbers mentally.
- **6g** Add and subtract with multiples of 10.
- **6h** Solve addition and subtraction number stories.
- **6i** Add three 1-digit numbers mentally.

Children's Names	6a	6b	6c	6d	6e	6f	6g	6h	6i			
1.												
2.												
3.												
4.												
5.												
6.												
7.												
8.												
9.												
10.												
11.												
12.												
13.												
14.												
15.												
16.												
17.												
18.												
19.												
20.												
21.												
22.												
23.												
24.												
25.												
26.												
27.												
28.												
29.												
30.												

Copyright © SRA/McGraw-Hill

Use with Lesson 6.12.

Individual Profile of Progress: Unit 6

Check ✔			Learning Goals	Comments
B	**D**	**S**		
			6a Solve stories about multiples of equal groups.	
			6b Solve equal-grouping and equal-sharing division problems.	
			6c Use the trade-first method to solve 2-digit subtraction problems.	
			6d Make ballpark estimates of exact answers.	
			6e Model multiplication problems with arrays.	
			6f Add three 2-digit numbers mentally.	
			6g Add and subtract with multiples of 10.	
			6h Solve addition and subtraction number stories.	
			6i Add three 1-digit numbers mentally.	

Notes to Parents

_____

_____

_____

_____

B = **B**eginning; **D** = **D**eveloping; **S** = **S**ecure

Use with Lesson 6.12.

Copyright © SRA/McGraw-Hill

Class Checklist: Unit 7

Class _____

Dates _____

Learning Goals

Children's Names	7a Find missing addends for any multiple of 10.	7b Find the median (middle value) of a data set.	7c Add three 2-digit numbers mentally.	7d Measure to the nearest inch.	7e Measure to the nearest centimeter.	7f Know complements of 10.	7g Count by 2s, 5s, and 10s and describe the patterns.	7h Find missing addends for the next multiple of 10.	7i Solve number-grid puzzles.	7j Plot data on a bar graph.				
1.														
2.														
3.														
4.														
5.														
6.														
7.														
8.														
9.														
10.														
11.														
12.														
13.														
14.														
15.														
16.														
17.														
18.														
19.														
20.														
21.														
22.														
23.														
24.														
25.														
26.														
27.														
28.														
29.														
30.														

Copyright © SRA/McGraw-Hill

Use with Lesson 7.10.

Individual Profile of Progress: Unit 7

Check ✔			Learning Goals	Comments
B	**D**	**S**		
			7a Find missing addends for any multiple of 10.	
			7b Find the median (middle value) of a data set.	
			7c Add three 2-digit numbers mentally.	
			7d Measure to the nearest inch.	
			7e Measure to the nearest centimeter.	
			7f Know complements of 10.	
			7g Count by 2s, 5s, and 10s and describe the patterns.	
			7h Find missing addends for the next multiple of 10.	
			7i Solve number-grid puzzles.	
			7j Plot data on a bar graph.	

Notes to Parents

_____

_____

_____

_____

Copyright © SRA/McGraw-Hill

B = **B**eginning; **D** = **D**eveloping; **S** = **S**ecure

Use with Lesson 7.10.

Class _____

Dates _____

Learning Goals

- **8a** Compare fractions less than one.
- **8b** Understand fractions as names for equal parts of a region or set.
- **8c** Understand that the amount represented by a fraction depends on the size of the whole (ONE).
- **8d** Shade a specified fractional part of a set.
- **8e** Give the fraction name for the shaded part of a set.
- **8f** Find equivalent fractions for given fractions.
- **8g** Shade a specified fractional part of a region.
- **8h** Give the fraction name for the shaded part of a region.

Children's Names

	8a	8b	8c	8d	8e	8f	8g	8h				
1.												
2.												
3.												
4.												
5.												
6.												
7.												
8.												
9.												
10.												
11.												
12.												
13.												
14.												
15.												
16.												
17.												
18.												
19.												
20.												
21.												
22.												
23.												
24.												
25.												
26.												
27.												
28.												
29.												
30.												

Copyright © SRA/McGraw-Hill

Use with Lesson 8.8.

Individual Profile of Progress: Unit 8

Check ✔			Learning Goals	Comments
B	**D**	**S**		
			8a Compare fractions less than one.	
			8b Understand fractions as names for equal parts of a region or set.	
			8c Understand that the amount represented by a fraction depends on the size of the whole (ONE).	
			8d Shade a specified fractional part of a set.	
			8e Give the fraction name for the shaded part of a set.	
			8f Find equivalent fractions for given fractions.	
			8g Shade a specified fractional part of a region.	
			8h Give the fraction name for the shaded part of a region.	

Notes to Parents

_____

_____

_____

_____

B = **B**eginning; **D** = **D**eveloping; **S** = **S**ecure

Copyright © SRA/McGraw-Hill

Use with Lesson 8.8.

Class Checklist: Unit 9

Class _____

Dates _____

Learning Goals

- **9a** Identify equivalencies for mm, cm, dm, and m.
- **9b** Measure to the nearest $\frac{1}{2}$ inch.
- **9c** Measure to the nearest $\frac{1}{2}$ cm.
- **9d** Use appropriate units for measurement and recognize sensible measurements.
- **9e** Find area concretely.
- **9f** Find perimeter concretely.
- **9g** Identify equivalencies for inches, feet, and yards.
- **9h** Use a ruler, tape measure, and meter/yardstick correctly.

Children's Names	9a	9b	9c	9d	9e	9f	9g	9h					
1.													
2.													
3.													
4.													
5.													
6.													
7.													
8.													
9.													
10.													
11.													
12.													
13.													
14.													
15.													
16.													
17.													
18.													
19.													
20.													
21.													
22.													
23.													
24.													
25.													
26.													
27.													
28.													
29.													
30.													

Copyright © SRA/McGraw-Hill

Use with Lesson 9.11.

Individual Profile of Progress: Unit 9

Check ✔ B	D	S	Learning Goals	Comments
			9a Identify equivalencies for mm, cm, dm, and m.	
			9b Measure to the nearest $\frac{1}{2}$ inch.	
			9c Measure to the nearest $\frac{1}{2}$ cm.	
			9d Use appropriate units for measurement and recognize sensible measurements.	
			9e Find area concretely.	
			9f Find perimeter concretely.	
			9g Identify equivalencies for inches, feet, and yards.	
			9h Use a ruler, tape measure, and meter/yardstick correctly.	

Notes to Parents

_____

_____

_____

_____

Copyright © SRA/McGraw-Hill

B = **B**eginning; **D** = **D**eveloping; **S** = **S**ecure

Use with Lesson 9.11.

Class Checklist: Unit 10

Class _____

Dates _____

Learning Goals

Children's Names	10a Use parentheses in number models.	10b Solve money stories involving change.	10c Estimate totals for "ballpark" check of exact answers.	10d Know and express automatically the values of digits in 5-digit numbers.	10e Read and write money amounts in decimal notation.	10f Use equivalent coins to show money amounts in different ways.	10g Use a calculator to compute money amounts.	10h Exchange pennies, nickels, dimes, and quarters.	10i Know and express automatically the values of digits in 2-, 3-, and 4-digit numbers.			
1.												
2.												
3.												
4.												
5.												
6.												
7.												
8.												
9.												
10.												
11.												
12.												
13.												
14.												
15.												
16.												
17.												
18.												
19.												
20.												
21.												
22.												
23.												
24.												
25.												
26.												
27.												
28.												
29.												
30.												

Copyright © SRA/McGraw–Hill

Use with Lesson 10.12.

Individual Profile of Progress: Unit 10

Check ✔			Learning Goals	Comments
B	**D**	**S**		
			10a Use parentheses in number models.	
			10b Solve money stories involving change.	
			10c Estimate totals for "ballpark" check of exact answers.	
			10d Know and express automatically the values of digits in 5-digit numbers.	
			10e Read and write money amounts in decimal notation.	
			10f Use equivalent coins to show money amounts in different ways.	
			10g Use a calculator to compute money amounts.	
			10h Exchange pennies, nickels, dimes, and quarters.	
			10i Know and express automatically the values of digits in 2-, 3-, and 4-digit numbers.	

Notes to Parents

_____

_____

_____

_____

B = **B**eginning; **D** = **D**eveloping; **S** = **S**ecure

Copyright © SRA/McGraw-Hill

Use with Lesson 10.12.

Class Checklist: Unit 11

Class _____

Dates _____

Children's Names	**Learning Goals**	11a Estimate and solve addition and subtraction number stories with dollars and cents.	11b Solve 1-digit multiplication stories (multiples of equal groups).	11c Solve equal grouping and equal sharing division stories.	11d Multiply numbers with 2, 5, or 10 as a factor.	11e Complete multiplication/division fact families.	11f Make difference and ratio comparisons.	11g Multiply numbers with 0 or 1 as a factor.					
1.													
2.													
3.													
4.													
5.													
6.													
7.													
8.													
9.													
10.													
11.													
12.													
13.													
14.													
15.													
16.													
17.													
18.													
19.													
20.													
21.													
22.													
23.													
24.													
25.													
26.													
27.													
28.													
29.													
30.													

Copyright © SRA/McGraw–Hill

Use with Lesson 11.10.

Individual Profile of Progress: Unit 11

Check ✔			Learning Goals	Comments
B	**D**	**S**		
			11a Estimate and solve addition and subtraction number stories with dollars and cents.	
			11b Solve 1-digit multiplication stories (multiples of equal groups).	
			11c Solve equal grouping and equal sharing division stories.	
			11d Multiply numbers with 2, 5, or 10 as a factor.	
			11e Complete multiplication/division fact families.	
			11f Make difference and ratio comparisons.	
			11g Multiply numbers with 0 or 1 as a factor.	

Notes to Parents

_____

_____

_____

_____

B = **B**eginning; **D** = **D**eveloping; **S** = **S**ecure

Use with Lesson 11.10.

Copyright © SRA/McGraw-Hill

Class Checklist: Unit 12

Class _____

Dates _____

Learning Goals

Children's Names	12a Use alternate names for times.	12b Know multiplication facts.	12c Determine the mode of a data set.	12d Determine the median, maximum, minimum, and range of a data set.	12e Complete multiplication/division fact families.	12f Multiply numbers with 2, 5, and 10 as a factor.	12g Tell time to 5-minute intervals.	12h Demonstrate calendar concepts and skills.	12i Compare quantities from a bar graph.			
1.												
2.												
3.												
4.												
5.												
6.												
7.												
8.												
9.												
10.												
11.												
12.												
13.												
14.												
15.												
16.												
17.												
18.												
19.												
20.												
21.												
22.												
23.												
24.												
25.												
26.												
27.												
28.												
29.												
30.												

Copyright © SRA/McGraw-Hill

Use with Lesson 12.8.

Individual Profile of Progress: Unit 12

Check ✔			Learning Goals	Comments
B	**D**	**S**		
			12a Use alternate names for times.	
			12b Know multiplication facts.	
			12c Determine the mode of a data set.	
			12d Determine the median, maximum, minimum, and range of a data set.	
			12e Complete multiplication/division fact families.	
			12f Multiply numbers with 2, 5, and 10 as a factor.	
			12g Tell time to 5-minute intervals.	
			12h Demonstrate calendar concepts and skills.	
			12i Compare quantities from a bar graph.	

Notes to Parents

_____

_____

_____

_____

Copyright © SRA/McGraw-Hill

B = **B**eginning; **D** = **D**eveloping; **S** = **S**ecure

Use with Lesson 12.8.

Class Checklist: 1st Quarter

Class _____

Dates _____

Learning Goals

1. Calculate the values of coin and bill combinations. **(1a)**
2. Show Ⓟ, Ⓝ, Ⓓ, and Ⓠ for a given amount. **(3f)**
3. Make change. **(3b)**
4. Complete number sequences; identify and use number patterns to solve problems. **(1d)**
5. Compare numbers; write the symbol <, >, or =. **(1i)**
6. Count by 2s, 5s, and 10s. **(1g)**
7. Make tallies and give the total. **(1h)**
8. Find equivalent names for numbers. **(1e, 2j)**
9. Construct fact families for addition and subtraction. **(2g)**
10. Solve subtraction number stories. **(2e)**
11. Solve addition number stories. **(2i)**

Children's Names

	1.	2.	3.	4.	5.	6.	7.	8.	9.	10.	11.		
1.													
2.													
3.													
4.													
5.													
6.													
7.													
8.													
9.													
10.													
11.													
12.													
13.													
14.													
15.													
16.													
17.													
18.													
19.													
20.													
21.													
22.													
23.													
24.													
25.													
26.													
27.													
28.													
29.													
30.													

Copyright © SRA/McGraw-Hill

Use with Lesson 3.9.

Class _____

Dates _____

Learning Goals

12. Know "harder" subtraction facts. (2a, 3c)
13. Identify place value in 2-digit and 3-digit numbers. (1c, 3e)
14. Know addition facts. (1b, 2b, 2f, 3g)
15. Know "easier" subtraction facts. (2c, 3h)
16. Complete "What's My Rule?" tables. (2d)
17. Complete Frames-and-Arrows diagrams. (2h)
18. Solve Frames-and-Arrows problems having two rules. (3a)
19. Tell time to 5-minute intervals. (3d)

Children's Names

	12	13	14	15	16	17	18	19				
1.												
2.												
3.												
4.												
5.												
6.												
7.												
8.												
9.												
10.												
11.												
12.												
13.												
14.												
15.												
16.												
17.												
18.												
19.												
20.												
21.												
22.												
23.												
24.												
25.												
26.												
27.												
28.												
29.												
30.												

Copyright © SRA/McGraw-Hill

Use with Lesson 3.9.

Individual Profile of Progress: 1st Quarter

Check ✔			Learning Goals	Comments
B	**D**	**S**		
			1. Calculate the values of coin and bill combinations. **(1a)**	
			2. Show Ⓟ, Ⓝ, Ⓓ, and Ⓠ for a given amount. **(3f)**	
			3. Make change. **(3b)**	
			4. Complete number sequences; identify and use number patterns to solve problems. **(1d)**	
			5. Compare numbers; write the symbol $<$, $>$, or $=$. **(1f)**	
			6. Count by 2s, 5s, and 10s. **(1g)**	
			7. Make tallies and give the total. **(1h)**	
			8. Find equivalent names for numbers. **(1e, 2j)**	
			9. Construct fact families for addition and subtraction. **(2g)**	
			10. Solve subtraction number stories. **(2e)**	
			11. Solve addition number stories. **(2i)**	
			12. Know "harder" subtraction facts. **(2a, 3c)**	
			13. Identify place value in 2-digit and 3-digit numbers. **(1c, 3e)**	
			14. Know addition facts. **(1b, 2b, 2f, 3g)**	
			15. Know "easier" subtraction facts. **(2c, 3h)**	
			16. Complete "What's My Rule?" tables. **(2d)**	
			17. Complete Frames-and-Arrows diagrams. **(2h)**	
			18. Solve Frames-and-Arrows problems having two rules. **(3a)**	
			19. Tell time to 5-minute intervals. **(3d)**	

B = **B**eginning; **D** = **D**eveloping; **S** = **S**ecure

Copyright © SRA/McGraw-Hill

Use with Lesson 3.9.

Class Checklist: 2nd Quarter

Class _____

Dates _____

Learning Goals

1. Devise and use strategies for finding sums of 2-digit numbers. **(4a)**
2. Devise and use strategies for finding differences of 2-digit numbers. **(4b)**
3. Estimate approximate costs and sums. **(4c)**
4. Solve stories about multiples of equal groups. **(6a)**
5. Use the trade-first method to solve 2-digit subtraction problems. **(6c)**
6. Make ballpark estimates of exact answers. **(6d)**
7. Add three 2-digit numbers mentally. **(6f)**
8. Add and subtract with multiples of 10. **(4e, 6g)**
9. Solve addition and subtraction number stories. **(6h)**
10. Add three 1-digit numbers mentally. **(6i)**
11. Solve equal-grouping and equal-sharing division problems. **(6b)**
12. Model multiplication problems with arrays. **(6e)**

Children's Names

	1.	2.	3.	4.	5.	6.	7.	8.	9.	10.	11.	12.
1.												
2.												
3.												
4.												
5.												
6.												
7.												
8.												
9.												
10.												
11.												
12.												
13.												
14.												
15.												
16.												
17.												
18.												
19.												
20.												
21.												
22.												
23.												
24.												
25.												
26.												
27.												
28.												
29.												
30.												

Copyright © SRA/McGraw–Hill

Use with Lesson 6.12.

Class _____

Dates _____

Learning Goals

13. Identify 3-dimensional shapes, such as rectangular prisms, cylinders, pyramids, cones, and spheres. **(5a)**

14. Identify symmetrical figures. **(5b)**

15. Find common attributes of shapes. **(5c)**

16. Identify parallel and nonparallel line segments. **(5d)**

17. Draw line segments. **(5e)**

18. Identify 2-dimensional shapes. **(5f)**

19. Read °F on a thermometer. **(4d)**

Children's Names

1.											
2.											
3.											
4.											
5.											
6.											
7.											
8.											
9.											
10.											
11.											
12.											
13.											
14.											
15.											
16.											
17.											
18.											
19.											
20.											
21.											
22.											
23.											
24.											
25.											
26.											
27.											
28.											
29.											
30.											

Copyright © SRA/McGraw-Hill

Use with Lesson 6.12.

Individual Profile of Progress: 2nd Quarter ✔

Check ✔			Learning Goals	Comments
B	**D**	**S**		
			1. Devise and use strategies for finding sums of 2-digit numbers. **(4a)**	
			2. Devise and use strategies for finding differences of 2-digit numbers. **(4b)**	
			3. Estimate approximate costs and sums. **(4c)**	
			4. Solve stories about multiples of equal groups. **(6a)**	
			5. Use the trade-first method to solve 2-digit subtraction problems. **(6c)**	
			6. Make ballpark estimates of exact answers. **(6d)**	
			7. Add three 2-digit numbers mentally. **(6f)**	
			8. Add and subtract with multiples of 10. **(4e, 6g)**	
			9. Solve addition and subtraction number stories. **(6h)**	
			10. Add three 1-digit numbers mentally. **(6i)**	
			11. Solve equal-grouping and equal-sharing division problems. **(6b)**	
			12. Model multiplication problems with arrays. **(6e)**	
			13. Identify 3-dimensional shapes, such as rectangular prisms, cylinders, pyramids, cones, and spheres. **(5a)**	
			14. Identify symmetrical figures. **(5b)**	
			15. Find common attributes of shapes. **(5c)**	
			16. Identify parallel and nonparallel line segments. **(5d)**	
			17. Draw line segments. **(5e)**	
			18. Identify 2-dimensional shapes. **(5f)**	
			19. Read °F on a thermometer. **(4d)**	

B = **B**eginning; **D** = **D**eveloping; **S** = **S**ecure

Copyright © SRA/McGraw-Hill

Use with Lesson 6.12.

Class Checklist: 3rd Quarter

Class _____

Dates _____

Learning Goals

1. Find missing addends for any multiple of 10. **(7a)**
2. Add three 2-digit numbers mentally. **(7c)**
3. Know complements of 10. **(7l)**
4. Count by 2s, 5s, and 10s and describe the patterns. **(7g)**
5. Find missing addends for the next multiple of 10. **(7h)**
6. Solve number-grid puzzles. **(7i)**
7. Find the median (middle value) of a data set. **(7b)**
8. Plot data on a bar graph. **(7j)**
9. Measure to the nearest inch. **(7d)**
10. Measure to the nearest centimeter. **(7e)**
11. Identify equivalencies for mm, cm, dm, and m. **(9a)**
12. Measure to the nearest $\frac{1}{2}$ inch. **(9b)**
13. Measure to the nearest $\frac{1}{2}$ cm. **(9c)**

Children's Names	1	2	3	4	5	6	7	8	9	10	11	12	13	
1.														
2.														
3.														
4.														
5.														
6.														
7.														
8.														
9.														
10.														
11.														
12.														
13.														
14.														
15.														
16.														
17.														
18.														
19.														
20.														
21.														
22.														
23.														
24.														
25.														
26.														
27.														
28.														
29.														
30.														

Copyright © SRA/McGraw-Hill

Use with Lesson 9.11.

Class _____

Dates _____

Learning Goals

14. Use appropriate units for measurement and recognize sensible measurements. **(9d)**
15. Identify equivalencies for inches, feet, and yards. **(9g)**
16. Use a ruler, tape measure, and meter/yardstick correctly. **(9h)**
17. Find area concretely. **(9e)**
18. Find perimeter concretely. **(9f)**
19. Compare fractions less than one. **(8a)**
20. Understand fractions as names for equal parts of a region or set. **(8b)**
21. Understand that the amount represented by a fraction depends on the size of the whole (ONE). **(8c)**
22. Shade a specified fractional part of a set. **(8d)**
23. Give the fraction name for the shaded part of a set. **(8e)**
24. Find equivalent fractions for given fractions. **(8f)**
25. Shade a specified fractional part of a region. **(8g)**
26. Give the fraction name for the shaded part of a region. **(8h)**

Children's Names	14	15	16	17	18	19	20	21	22	23	24	25	26
1.													
2.													
3.													
4.													
5.													
6.													
7.													
8.													
9.													
10.													
11.													
12.													
13.													
14.													
15.													
16.													
17.													
18.													
19.													
20.													
21.													
22.													
23.													
24.													
25.													
26.													
27.													
28.													
29.													
30.													

Copyright © SRA/McGraw–Hill

Use with Lesson 9.11.

Individual Profile of Progress: 3rd Quarter

Check ✔				
B	**D**	**S**	**Learning Goals**	**Comments**
			1. Find missing addends for any multiple of 10. **(7a)**	
			2. Add three 2-digit numbers mentally. **(7c)**	
			3. Know complements of 10. **(7f)**	
			4. Count by 2s, 5s, and 10s and describe the patterns. **(7g)**	
			5. Find missing addends for the next multiple of 10. **(7h)**	
			6. Solve number-grid puzzles. **(7i)**	
			7. Find the median (middle value) of a data set. **(7b)**	
			8. Plot data on a bar graph. **(7j)**	
			9. Measure to the nearest inch. **(7d)**	
			10. Measure to the nearest centimeter. **(7e)**	
			11. Identify equivalencies for mm, cm, dm, and m. **(9a)**	
			12. Measure to the nearest $\frac{1}{2}$ inch. **(9b)**	
			13. Measure to the nearest $\frac{1}{2}$ cm. **(9c)**	
			14. Use appropriate units for measurement and recognize sensible measurements. **(9d)**	
			15. Identify equivalencies for inches, feet, and yards. **(9g)**	
			16. Use a ruler, tape measure, and meter/yardstick correctly. **(9h)**	
			17. Find area concretely. **(9e)**	
			18. Find perimeter concretely. **(9f)**	
			19. Compare fractions less than one. **(8a)**	
			20. Understand fractions as names for equal parts of a region or set. **(8b)**	
			21. Understand that the amount represented by a fraction depends on the size of the whole (ONE). **(8c)**	
			22. Shade a specified fractional part of a set. **(8d)**	
			23. Give the fraction name for the shaded part of a set. **(8e)**	
			24. Find equivalent fractions for given fractions. **(8f)**	
			25. Shade a specified fractional part of a region. **(8g)**	
			26. Give the fraction name for the shaded part of a region. **(8h)**	

B = **B**eginning; **D** = **D**eveloping; **S** = **S**ecure

Use with Lesson 9.11.

Copyright © SRA/McGraw-Hill

Class _____

Dates _____

Learning Goals

1. Use parentheses in number models. **(10a)**
2. Estimate totals for "ballpark" check of exact answers. **(10c)**
3. Know and express automatically the values of digits in 5-digit numbers. **(10d)**
4. Know and express automatically the values of digits in 2-, 3-, and 4-digit numbers. **(10i)**
5. Solve money stories involving change. **(10b)**
6. Read and write money amounts in decimal notation. **(10e)**
7. Use equivalent coins to show money amounts in different ways. **(10f)**
8. Use a calculator to compute money amounts in **(10g)**
9. Exchange pennies, nickels, dimes, and quarters. **(10h)**
10. Estimate and solve addition and subtraction number stories with dollars and cents. **(11a)**
11. Solve 1-digit multiplication stories (multiples of equal groups). **(11b)**

Children's Names	1	2	3	4	5	6	7	8	9	10	11		
1.													
2.													
3.													
4.													
5.													
6.													
7.													
8.													
9.													
10.													
11.													
12.													
13.													
14.													
15.													
16.													
17.													
18.													
19.													
20.													
21.													
22.													
23.													
24.													
25.													
26.													
27.													
28.													
29.													
30.													

Copyright © SRA/McGraw–Hill

Use with Lesson 12.8.

Class _____

Dates _____

Learning Goals

12. Solve equal grouping and equal sharing division stories. **(11c)**
13. Make difference and ratio comparisons. **(11f)**
14. Multiply numbers with 0 or 1 as a factor. **(11g)**
15. Know multiplication facts. **(12b)**
16. Complete multiplication/division fact families. **(11e, 12e)**
17. Multiply numbers with 2, 5, and 10 as a factor. **(11d, 12f)**
18. Use alternate names for times. **(12a)**
19. Tell time to 5-minute intervals. **(12g)**
20. Demonstrate calendar concepts and skills. **(12h)**
21. Determine the mode of a data set. **(12c)**
22. Determine the median, maximum, minimum, and range of a data set. **(12d)**
23. Compare quantities from a bar graph. **(12i)**

Children's Names	12.	13.	14.	15.	16.	17.	18.	19.	20.	21.	22.	23.
1.												
2.												
3.												
4.												
5.												
6.												
7.												
8.												
9.												
10.												
11.												
12.												
13.												
14.												
15.												
16.												
17.												
18.												
19.												
20.												
21.												
22.												
23.												
24.												
25.												
26.												
27.												
28.												
29.												
30.												

Copyright © SRA/McGraw–Hill

Use with Lesson 12.8.

Individual Profile of Progress: 4th Quarter

Check ✔			Learning Goals	Comments
B	**D**	**S**		
			1. Use parentheses in number models. **(10a)**	
			2. Estimate totals for "ballpark" check of exact answers. **(10c)**	
			3. Know and express automatically the values of digits in 5-digit numbers. **(10d)**	
			4. Know and express automatically the values of digits in 2-, 3-, and 4-digit numbers. **(10i)**	
			5. Solve money stories involving change. **(10b)**	
			6. Read and write money amounts in decimal notation. **(10e)**	
			7. Use equivalent coins to show money amounts in different ways. **(10f)**	
			8. Use a calculator to compute money amounts. **(10g)**	
			9. Exchange pennies, nickels, dimes, and quarters. **(10h)**	
			10. Estimate and solve addition and subtraction number stories with dollars and cents. **(11a)**	
			11. Solve 1-digit multiplication stories (multiples of equal groups). **(11b)**	
			12. Solve equal grouping and equal sharing division stories. **(11c)**	
			13. Make difference and ratio comparisons. **(11f)**	
			14. Multiply numbers with 0 or 1 as a factor. **(11g)**	
			15. Know multiplication facts. **(12b)**	
			16. Complete multiplication/division fact families. **(11e, 12e)**	
			17. Multiply numbers with 2, 5, and 10 as a factor. **(11d, 12f)**	
			18. Use alternate names for times. **(12a)**	
			19. Tell time to 5-minute intervals. **(12g)**	
			20. Demonstrate calendar concepts and skills. **(12h)**	
			21. Determine the mode of a data set. **(12c)**	
			22. Determine the median, maximum, minimum, and range of a data set. **(12d)**	
			23. Compare quantities from a bar graph. **(12i)**	

B = **B**eginning; **D** = **D**eveloping; **S** = **S**ecure

Use with Lesson 12.8.

Copyright © SRA/McGraw-Hill

List of Assessment Sources

Ongoing Assessment

_____

_____

_____

_____

Product Assessment

_____

_____

_____

_____

Periodic Assessment

_____

_____

_____

_____

Outside Tests

_____

_____

_____

_____

Other

_____

_____

_____

_____

Copyright © SRA/McGraw-Hill

Use as needed.

Child's Name _____   Date _____

Individual Profile of Progress

Check ✔				
B	**D**	**S**	**Learning Goals**	**Comments**
			1.	
			2.	
			3.	
			4.	
			5.	
			6.	
			7.	
			8.	
			9.	
			10.	

Notes to Parents

_____

_____

_____

_____

_____

_____

_____

B = **B**eginning; **D** = **D**eveloping; **S** = **S**ecure

Use as needed.

Copyright © SRA/McGraw-Hill

Class Checklist

Class _____

Dates _____

Learning Goals

Children's Names

1.																
2.																
3.																
4.																
5.																
6.																
7.																
8.																
9.																
10.																
11.																
12.																
13.																
14.																
15.																
16.																
17.																
18.																
19.																
20.																
21.																
22.																
23.																
24.																
25.																
26.																
27.																
28.																
29.																
30.																

Copyright © SRA/McGraw–Hill

Use as needed.

Names

Names

1.
2.
3.
4.
5.
6.
7.
8.
9.
10.
11.
12.
13.
14.
15.
16.
17.
18.
19.
20.
21.
22.
23.
24.
25.
26.
27.
28.
29.
30.

Names

1.
2.
3.
4.
5.
6.
7.
8.
9.
10.
11.
12.
13.
14.
15.
16.
17.
18.
19.
20.
21.
22.
23.
24.
25.
26.
27.
28.
29.
30.

Names

1.
2.
3.
4.
5.
6.
7.
8.
9.
10.
11.
12.
13.
14.
15.
16.
17.
18.
19.
20.
21.
22.
23.
24.
25.
26.
27.
28.
29.
30.

Copyright © SRA/McGraw-Hill

Use as needed.

Class Progress Indicator

Mathematical Topic Being Assessed: _____

	BEGINNING	DEVELOPING OR DEVELOPING+	SECURE OR SECURE+
First Assessment After Lesson: _____ Dates included: _____ to _____			
Second Assessment After Lesson: _____ Dates included: _____ to _____			
Third Assessment After Lesson: _____ Dates included: _____ to _____			

Notes

_____

_____

_____

_____

Copyright © SRA/McGraw-Hill

Use as needed.

Child's Name   Date

Parent Reflections

Use some of the following questions (or your own) and tell us how you see your child progressing in mathematics.

Do you see evidence of your child using mathematics at home?

What do you think are your child's strengths and challenges in mathematics?

Does your child demonstrate responsibility for completing Home Links?

What thoughts do you have about your child's progress in mathematics?

Copyright © SRA/McGraw-Hill

Use as needed.

Rubric

Beginning (B)

Developing (D)

Secure (S)

Copyright © SRA/McGraw-Hill

Use as needed.

About My Math Class

Draw a face or write the words
that show how you feel.

Good   OK   Not so good

1. This is how I feel about math:	**2.** This is how I feel about working with a partner or in a group:	**3.** This is how I feel about working by myself:
4. This is how I feel about solving number stories:	**5.** This is how I feel about doing Home Links with my family:	**6.** This is how I feel about finding new ways to solve problems:

Circle **yes, sometimes,** or **no.**

7. I like to figure things out. I am curious.

yes   sometimes   no

8. I keep trying even when I don't understand something right away.

yes   sometimes   no

Copyright © SRA/McGraw-Hill

Use as needed.

About My Math Class

Circle the word that best describes how you feel.

1. I enjoy mathematics class.   **yes**   **sometimes**   **no**

2. I like to work with a partner
or in a group.   **yes**   **sometimes**   **no**

3. I like to work by myself.   **yes**   **sometimes**   **no**

4. I like to solve problems
in mathematics.   **yes**   **sometimes**   **no**

5. I enjoy doing Home Links
with my family.   **yes**   **sometimes**   **no**

6. In mathematics, I am good at _____

_____

_____ .

7. One thing I like about mathematics is _____

_____

_____ .

8. One thing I find difficult in mathematics is _____

_____

_____ .

Copyright © SRA/McGraw-Hill

Use as needed.

Math Log A

What did you learn in mathematics this week?

Copyright © SRA/McGraw-Hill

Use as needed.

Math Log B

Question:

Copyright © SRA/McGraw-Hill

Use as needed.

Copyright © SRA/McGraw-Hill

Name   Date   Time

Math Log C

Work Box

Tell how you solved
this problem.

_____

_____

_____

_____

_____

Use as needed.

495

Copyright © SRA/McGraw-Hill

Name   Date   Time

Math Log C

Work Box

Tell how you solved
this problem.

_____

_____

_____

_____

_____

Use as needed.

495

Name _____ Date _____ Time _____

Good Work!

I like this work because

_____

- -

_____

- -

_____

- -

_____

- -

_____

- -

_____

- -

_____

- -

_____

Copyright © SRA/McGraw–Hill

Use as needed.

Name   Date   Time

My Work

This work shows that I can _____

_____

_____

_____.

I am still learning to _____

_____

_____.

Use as needed.

Copyright © SRA/McGraw-Hill

✂ -

Name   Date   Time

My Work

This is what I know about _____

_____

_____

_____

_____

_____

Use as needed.

Copyright © SRA/McGraw-Hill

My Exit Slip

Copyright © SRA/McGraw-Hill

Use as needed.

✂

My Exit Slip

Copyright © SRA/McGraw-Hill

Use as needed.

Linear Measurement and Perimeter

Use your Pattern-Block Template. Trace these shapes: square, large hexagon, trapezoid, and one of the rhombuses. Measure and label each side of each shape. Then find the perimeters.

Square

Perimeter = _____ cm

Large Hexagon

Perimeter = _____ in.

Trapezoid

Perimeter = _____ in.

Rhombus

Perimeter = _____ cm

Copyright © SRA/McGraw–Hill

Use as needed.

Geometry

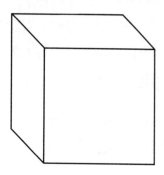

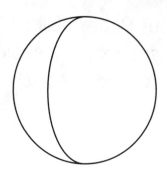

1. Name 3 things in the classroom that look like a cube.

_____

_____

_____

2. Name 3 things in the classroom that look like a sphere.

_____

_____

_____

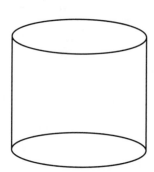

3. Name 3 things in the classroom that look like a cylinder.

_____

_____

_____

4. Name a shape found in the classroom. Draw it and tell what it is.

_____

_____

_____

Copyright © SRA/McGraw-Hill

Use as needed.

DISCARD

DISCARD

DISCARD

Lourdes Library
Gwynedd-Mercy College
P.O. Box 901
Gwynedd Valley, PA 19437-0901

DISCARD

DISCARD

LOURDES LIBRARY
CURRICULUM COLLECTION